Tom Lemke/La Escuela Fratney

"Let us put
our heads
together
and see
what life we
will make
for our
children."

Tatanka Iotanka
(Sitting Bull, Lakota)

Rethinking Columbus
The Next 500 Years

edited by
Bill Bigelow
and
Bob Peterson

Rethinking Schools
Milwaukee, Wisconsin

Rethinking Schools, Ltd. is a nonprofit educational publisher of books, booklets, and a quarterly journal on school reform, with a focus on issues of equity and social justice.

Rethinking Columbus: The Next 500 Years
© 1998, Rethinking Schools, Ltd.

Cover photo © David F. Clobes. The image is of a young shawl dancer at the Mankato (Minnesota) Pow-Wow, 1996.

cover design: Maclean & Tuminelly
page design: C.C. Krohne
page layout: Jeff Hansen

ISBN-10: 0-942961-20-X
ISBN-13: 978-0-942961-20-1

To request a catalog or subscribe to the *Rethinking Schools* journal, contact:

Rethinking Schools
1001 East Keefe Ave.
Milwaukee, Wisconsin 53212
800-669-4192
www.rethinkingschools.org

Acknowledgments

It is with deep respect and gratitude that we acknowledge the contributions of the diverse authors, poets, photographers, and graphic artists whose work appears within these pages.

In particular, we would like to thank the following individual photographers:

David F. Clobes (cover and p. 21); Andrew Connors and the Indian Community Scool of Milwaukee (pp. 11, 33, and 37); Patricia Goudvis (p. 161); Jean-Claude Lejeune (pp. 17 and 35); Tom Lemke (frontispiece); Sofia Lee Moran (p. 158); Deborah Preusch (p. 171); Rick Reinhard (p. 147); Susan L. Ruggles (p. 130); Stephen Trimble (pp. 14 and 176), whose photos come from the book *The People: Indians of the American Southwest;* and James Watts (p. 143).

Special thanks to Impact Visual's photographers and to the Indian Law Resource Center for help in locating photographs.

The portion of a Thanksgiving prayer on p. 71 is from a translation by Chuck Larsen (Seneca).

Special thanks to Steve Kelley (Copley News Service) for the use of the cartoon on p. 13 and to Don Monet for his cartoon on p. 167.

Thanks to Geroge Russell for permission to reprint his map series showing the decline in Indian lands since 1492 (p. 155).

Graphics used throughout the book come from various sources, including *North American Indian Designs,* by Eva Wilson (Dover, 1984), and from the newsletter and annual reports of the Indian Law Resource Center.

Katrine Barber, Linda Christensen, and Deborah Menkart contributed teaching ideas used at the conclusion of several chapters.

For use of song lyrics, we would like to thank:
Buffy Sainte-Marie, for use of the lyrics to "My Country, 'Tis of Thy People You're Dying," copyright 1966, Almo Music Corp., as administrator for Gypsy Boy Music, Inc. (ASCAP). Used by permission. All rights reserved.

Nancy Schimmel, for use of the lyrics to "1492" (p. 41), copyright 1991, Nancy Schimmel. Used by permission. All rights reserved.

Special thanks to Barbara Miner who co-edited and worked tirelessly on the first edition of *Rethinking Columbus.*

And finally, with great respect, our thanks to the poets and authors whose work is the heart of this book, and to their publishers and sponsors who have encouraged this important work and allowed our use of portions of it in this anthology for educational, nonprofit purposes. Earlier publication credits are given with the articles. All of this material is copyright by the authors and their publishers, and all rights are reserved by them.

Dedicated
to the children
of the Americas

Table of Contents

INTRODUCTION
Why Rethink Columbus?... *the editors* 10
We Have No Reason to Celebrate.....................................*Suzan Shown Harjo* 12
America to Indians: Stay in the 19th Century!...............................*Jan Elliott* 14

BEGINNINGS
Indians Claim Italy by "Right of Discovery" ....*from* The New York Times 16
Discovering Columbus: Re-reading the Past ....*Bill Bigelow* 17
Sugar & Slavery...*Philip Martin* 22
African-American Resistance ....*Bill Fletcher* 24
My Country, 'Tis of Thy People You're Dying ....*Buffy Sainte-Marie* 28
Historic Tribal Locations ....*map* 30

ELEMENTARY SCHOOL ISSUES
What Not to Teach...*June Sark Heinrich* 32
A Friend of the Indians...*Joseph Bruchac* 34
Columbus & Native Issues in the Elementary Classroom ....*Bob Peterson* 35
1492 (song) ....*Nancy Schimmel* 41
The Untold Story..*Tina Thomas* 42
The Sacred Buffalo ....*Rosalie Little Thunder* 44
Once Upon a Genocide: Columbus in Children's Literature............*Bill Bigelow* 47
George Washington: An American Hero? ....*CIBC* 56
Scalping: Fact & Fantasy ....*Philip Martin* 58
Indian Lands for Sale ....*poster* 60
A Barbie-Doll Pocahontas ....*Cornel Pewewardy* 61
Good Intentions Are Not Enough: Recent Children's Books
    on the Columbus-Taíno Encounter...................................*Bill Bigelow* 62
Teaching Ideas 69

RETHINKING THANKSGIVING
The Delight Song of Tsoai-Talee.....................................*N. Scott Momaday* 72
Giving Thanks: The Story of Indian Summer ....*Joseph Bruchac* 73
Thanking the Birds...*Joseph Bruchac* 74
Alphabet of the Americas 75
Why I'm Not Thankful for Thanksgiving ....*Michael Dorris* 76
Plagues & Pilgrims:
    The Truth about the First Thanksgiving ....*James W. Loewen* 79
Teaching Ideas & Suggested Activities 83

THE TRIAL (The People vs. Columbus, et al.)
For the Sake of Gold ....*Hans Koning* 86
A Class Role Play...*Bill Bigelow* 87
The Trial in the Elementary Classroom................................*Bob Peterson* 94
Columbus's Diary: Reading Between the Lines ....*Bill Bigelow* 95
The First Few Days: The Journal of Christopher Columbus 96
Timeline: Spain, Columbus, and Taínos 99
"Open Your Hearts".......................................*adapt. from Bartolomé de las Casas* 103

THE TAÍNOS
The Taínos: "Men of the Good" ....*José Barreiro* 106
Imagining the Taínos ....*Bill Bigelow* 108
The Gold People ....*Anna Hereford* 110

Taíno Resistance: Enrique's Uprising ....Alvin Josephy, Jr.   111
Rethinking Terms .... Philip Tajitsu Nash and Emilienne Ireland   112

SECONDARY SCHOOL ISSUES
Ceremony .... Leslie Marmon Silko   114
Talking Back to Columbus: Teaching for Justice and Hope ....Bill Bigelow   115
Columbus Day.. Jimmie Durham   123
Broken Spears Lie in the Roads.. unknown Aztec Poet   124
Black Indians & Resistance ....William Loren Katz   125
Indian Singing in 20th Century America..Gail Tremblay   128
Cowboys and Indians: On the Playground .... Ray Gonzalez   129
Human Beings Are Not Mascots..Barbara Munson   131
Looney Tunes and Peter Pan: Unlearning Racist Stereotypes ....Linda Christensen   133
Bones of Contention..Tony Hillerman   134
Three Thousand Dollar Death Song ....Wendy Rose   135
Canada Apologizes to its Native People ....from the Associated Press   136
What's in an Apology? .... Bob Peterson   137
Elizabeth Peratrovich Day   138
Teaching Ideas   139

CONTEMPORARY STRUGGLES
Current Struggles around the Hemisphere..   142
Treaty Rights: An Overview ....Philip Martin   144
A Modern Hero: Rigoberta Menchú..Deborah Menkart   146
Resistance at Oka ....Peter Blue Cloud   148
The Unity of Native Peoples..Billy Redwing Tayac   150
Leonard Peltier: An American Political Prisoner..Philip Martin   151
Loo-Wit ....Wendy Rose   152
The Theft of the Black Hills ....Philip Martin   153
Shrinking Indian Lands..map series   155
The Earth Is a Satellite of the Moon..Leonel Rugama   156
Teaching Ideas   157

ENVIRONMENTAL ISSUES
To the Women of the World: Our Future, Our Responsibility....................... Winona LaDuke   160
People vs. Nature in 15th-century Europe ....Kirkpatrick Sale   162
Radioactive Mining: Good Economics or Genocide? .... Ward Churchill   163
All Pigs on Deck: The Columbus Myth & the Environment ....Bill Bigelow   165
The Land of the Spotted Eagle ....Luther Standing Bear   166
The Earth and the American Dream: Selected Quotes ....from the video   167
The Earth and the American Dream: Questions..   169
Red Ribbons for Emma ....Deb Preusch, et al.   170
Teaching Ideas   172

FINAL WORDS
Remember ....Joy Harjo   174
For Some, a Time of Mourning ....Wendy Rose   175
The Blue Tiger..Eduardo Galeano   177
Colibrí ....Martín Espada   179

RESOURCES
Books for young readers and adults, curriculum materials, videos,
    websites, organizations, and more   182

INTRODUCTION

We have no reason to celebrate
an invasion
that caused the demise
of so many of our people
and is still causing
destruction
today.

— Suzan Shown Harjo

WHY RETHINK COLUMBUS?

Students at Jefferson High School in Portland, Oregon, commemorated the 500th anniversary of Columbus's arrival in the Americas by launching a school-wide "discovery." They invaded other classrooms, stole teachers' purses, and claimed them as theirs. Adapting a lesson described in the first edition of *Rethinking Columbus* (p. 17 in this edition), students emptied a purse in front of a teacher and her class, then remarked on its contents: "This sure is good gum, think I'll have a piece ... or two; you all know this is my purse, 'cause this is just my shade of lipstick." Kids in the assaulted classrooms figured out what was going on only when the invaders compared their "discovery" to Columbus's "discovery." The high-school students, with advance permission from other teachers, led discussions and described Columbus's policies toward the Taíno Indians on Hispaniola. They concluded by offering black armbands to students as a way to demonstrate solidarity with Native Americans' 500 years of resistance.

Just two years before, in October of 1990, the *Chicago Tribune* had promised that the Columbus Quincentenary would be the "most stupendous international celebration in the history of notable celebrations." The Portland students' "Discovery Day" is not what the *Tribune* had in mind.

Prompted by widespread Native American activism leading up to the Quincentenary, educators throughout the Americas re-evaluated the social and ecological consequences of the Europeans' arrival in 1492. Teacher unions, community groups, social justice organizations, universities, and school districts initiated workshops and teach-ins. New curricula, videos and children's books appeared. In 1991, Rethinking Schools published the first edition of *Rethinking Columbus*, which subsequently went through seven printings and sold 225,000 copies. We were pleased to be a part of a movement to question a myth that dismissed the very humanity of entire peoples. We believe this critical work by so many has made a profound impact in schools.

But we have a long way to go. Too many children's books, textbooks, and curricula continue to tout the traditional Columbus myth. For many youngsters, the "discovery of America" is their first curricular exposure to the encounter between two cultures and to the encounter between two races.

The "Columbus-as-Discoverer" myth teaches children whose voices to listen for as they go out into the world — and whose to ignore. Pick up a typical children's book on Columbus: See Chris; see Chris talk; see Chris grow up, have ideas, have feelings; see Chris plant the flag... In these volumes, native peoples of the Caribbean, the "discovered," are portrayed without thoughts or feelings. And thus children begin a scholastic voyage that encourages them to disregard the perspectives, the lives, of people of color. Both the words and images of the Columbus myth implicitly tell children that it is acceptable for one group of heavily-armed, white people from a "civilized" country to claim and control the lands of distant non-white *others*.

During the Quincentenary, a more "balanced" approach to European/Native American conflict also emerged. According to a Library of Congress-produced curriculum that exemplified this seemingly neutral inquiry, "The story of the Americas, more than any other area of the world, is the story of peoples and cultures coming together," resulting in "a cultural mixture." This newer framework suggested that world history since 1492 has been a series of trades and trade-offs. "They" gave "us" the potato, corn, and a great deal of gold. "We" gave "them" the horse, sugar, and, regrettably, germs. This process planted "seeds of change," in the words of the Smithsonian Institution. While offering important insights, this approach failed to address questions of the origins of racism, economic exploitation, and resistance.

In this new edition of *Rethinking Columbus*, we try to offer an alternative narrative. Our goal is not to idealize native people, demonize Europeans, or present a depressing litany of victimization. We hope to encourage a deeper understanding of the European invasion's consequences, to honor the rich legacy of resistance to the injustices it created, to convey some appreciation for the diverse indigenous cultures of the hemisphere, and to reflect on what this all means for us today.

We have tried to provide a forum for native people to tell some of their side of the encounter — through interviews, poetry, analysis, and stories. The point is not to present "two sides," but to tell parts of the story that have been mostly neglected.

It would be nice to think that the biases in the curriculum disappear after Columbus. But the Columbus myth is only the beginning of a winners' history that profoundly neglects the lives and perspectives of many "others": people of color, women, working-class people, the poor.

Columbus's Legacy

Columbus is dead but his legacy is not. In 1492, Columbus predicted, "Considering the beauty of the land, it could not be but that there was gain to be got." From the poisonous chemical dumps and mining projects that threaten groundwater, to oil spills on the coastal shorelines to the massive clearcutting of old-growth forests, Columbus's exploitative spirit lives on. Likewise, the slave system Columbus introduced to this hemisphere was ultimately overthrown, but not the calculus that weighs human lives in terms of private profit — of the "gain to be got."

We've featured essays and interviews that underscore contemporary resistance to the spirit of Columbus. We believe that children need to know that while injustice persists, so does the struggle for humanity and the environment.

In a very real sense, most of us are living on stolen land. However, this knowledge must not be used to make white children feel guilty. There is nothing students can do to change history. And they should not feel responsible for what others did before

they were born. However, we hope the materials in *Rethinking Columbus* will help you teach that people of all backgrounds do have a responsibility to learn from history. We can choose whether to reverse the legacy of injustice or continue it. This is one reason that we've made special efforts in this edition to highlight people who have chosen to stand for justice.

We hope that these materials will also help students to discover new ways of understanding relationships between society and nature. Even the very words used by different cultures to describe the natural world are suggestive: compare the West's "environment" — something which surrounds us — to native peoples' "Mother Earth" — she who gives us life. Native views of the earth challenge students to locate new worlds of ecological hope.

Through critiquing traditional history and imagining alternatives, students can begin to discover the excitement that comes from asserting oneself morally and intellectually — refusing to be passive consumers of official stories. This is as true for 4th graders as it is for juniors in high school. Students can continue to renew and deepen this personal awakening as they seek out other curricular silences and sources of knowledge.

As the scholar Edward Said noted, "Nations are narratives." For too many, this country has been a narrative that started with the myth of Columbus. It's time to hear other voices. We offer this second edition of *Rethinking Columbus* as our contribution to a many-sided and ongoing discussion about the future.

—*the editors*

WE HAVE NO REASON TO CELEBRATE AN INVASION

AN INTERVIEW WITH SUZAN SHOWN HARJO

Suzan Shown Harjo, who is Cheyenne and Creek, is president and director of the Morning Star Foundation in Washington, DC, an indigenous peoples' rights organization. She was interviewed by Barbara Miner of Rethinking Schools *about her views on the long-term impact of the legacy of Columbus.*

Columbus was just "a man of his times." Why are you so critical of him? Why not look at the positive aspects of his legacy?

As Native American peoples in this red quarter of Mother Earth, we have no reason to celebrate an invasion that caused the demise of so many of our people and is still causing destruction today. The Europeans stole our land and killed our people.

For people who are in survival mode, it's very difficult to look at the positive aspects of death and destruction, especially when it is carried through to our present. There is a reason we are the poorest people in America. There is a reason we have the highest teen suicide rate. There is a reason why our people are ill-housed and in poor health, and we do not live as long as the majority population.

That reason has to do with the fact that we were in the way of Western Civilization and we were in the way of westward expansion. We suffered the excesses of "civilization" such as murder, pillage, rape, destruction of the major waterways, destruction of land, the destruction and pollution of the air.

What are those "positive" aspects of the Columbus legacy? If we're talking about the horse, that's good. We like the horse. Indians raised the use of the horse to high military art, especially among the Cheyenne people and the tribes of the plains states.

Was that a good result of that invasion? Yes. Is it something we would have traded for the many Indian peoples who are no longer here because of that invasion? No.

> It's difficult to take seriously an apology that is not coupled with atonement. It's as if they're saying, "I'm sorry, oops, and we'll be better in the next hemisphere."

We also like the beads that came from Europe, and again we raised their use to a high art. Would we have traded those beads for the massacres of our people, such as the Sand Creek Massacre [in which U.S. soldiers killed hundreds of Native American men, women, and children at Sand Creek, Colorado in 1864]? No.

Isn't criticism of Columbus a form of picking on the Spaniards? Were they any worse than other Europeans who came to America?

In my estimation, the Spaniards were no worse than any number of other Europeans. The economy of slavery and serfdom that existed in northern Europe — how do you measure that in cruelty and in long-term effects against the Spanish Inquisition?

I view the issue more as the oppressive nature and arrogance of the Christian religions. And that continues today.

Our Indian religions are not missionary religions. We are taught to respect other religions. It was a shock when we were met with proselytizing zealots, especially those who thought that if your soul can't be saved, you're better off dead — or if your soul can be saved, you should be dead so you can go to heaven. And that's the history of that original encounter.

How does that arrogance and ignorance manifest itself today?

How? Well, for example, the Catholic Church said that 1992 [the year of the Columbus Quincentenary commemoration] was a time to enter into a period of grace and healing and to celebrate the evangelization of the Americas. My word, how can you be graceful and healing about the tens of thousands of native people who were killed because they would not convert to a religion they didn't understand, or because they didn't understand the language of those making the request?

It's difficult to take seriously an apology that is not coupled with atonement. It's as if they're saying, "I'm sorry, oops, and we'll be better in the next hemisphere." That doesn't cut it. We've had empty platitudes before.

Aren't some of the criticisms of Columbus just substituting Native-centrism for Euro-centrism?

Oppressed people need to be centered within themselves. Racism and centrism become a problem if you are in the dominant society and are subjugating other people as a result of your centrism. I don't accept the question. I think it's an empty argument.

What should be the goal and perspective of teachers when telling their elementary and high school students about Columbus?

First, that no one knows the truth about Columbus. His story is a very complex history in and of itself. Too often, this history is posed as romantic myth, and the uncomfortable facts about Columbus are eliminated.

Explaining the unpleasant truths about Columbus does not take away from the fact that he was able to lurch over to these shores in three little boats. In fact, it gives the story of Columbus more dimension. It also makes it easier for kids in school to accept not only Columbus but other things.

Teachers need to respect the truth. What happens if I'm sitting in a classroom and teachers are telling me that Thomas Jefferson was one of the greatest men in the world, and I also know that he owned slaves, but they don't tell me that? What am I going to do when I'm told "don't use or abuse drugs or alcohol"? Will I think there may be another side to that too? What else am I being told that isn't true?

Kids are smart. And they have not experienced enough setbacks to know that they have to be sheep. But that's what they're taught in the public schools — how to exercise not personal discipline, but top-down discipline. It's the "do as you're told" approach to the world, rather than trying to help kids understand their place in the world.

We have to inject more truth in the classroom generally. And that only comes from discussion.

What are the key struggles that native people face today?

We need, in the first instance, basic human rights such as religious freedom. Or how about life, liberty and the pursuit of happiness, and other things that many people in the United States view as standard fare but are out of reach for Indian people?

There is also the issue of land and treaty rights. We have property that we don't own and we should, and we have property that we own that we don't control and we should.

We have treaties with the United States that are characterized in the U.S. Constitution as the supreme law of the land. Yet every one, without exception, of nearly 400 treaties signed between native peoples and the U.S. government has been broken. Every one of them.

A good place to start would be for the United States to live up to every treaty agreement. It's also the way you get at resolving some of the problems of poverty, alcoholism, unemployment, and poor health.

If we don't handle the big things, we can't get to the manifestations of the problem. We have to go to the basic human rights issues, the basic treaty rights issues.

If we don't resolve these issues, then all people in this country are going to be complicit in the continuing effort to wipe out our Indian people. It's as simple as that.

Steve Kelley/Copley News Service

AMERICA TO INDIANS: "Stay in the 19th Century!"

BY JAN ELLIOTT

As I was leaving the theater after my first viewing of the movie, *Dances With Wolves*, I happened to be walking between two white couples. All of them were raving about how wonderful the movie was and how "accurately" it had portrayed the Indians. One of the men said, "I'm so ashamed of this culture that we live in and how it treated (past tense) the Indians. If I had been around back then, I would have fought on the side of the Indians."

I couldn't resist asking, "Where were you guys this summer when 4,000 heavily-armed Canadian soldiers were sent into Oka to take 250 Mohawk Indians, most of whom were women and children? And where have you been since 1986 when the U.S. government started its forced removal of the Hopi/Navajo people from their lands at Big Mountain?" His reply was, "Oh, I don't mean those kind of Indians, I meant the real Indians."

Ignoring Modern-Day Indians

I started to wonder why a movie such as *Dances With Wolves* became a major event, and why a movie such as *Powwow Highway*, which became a cult classic in Indian country, was virtually ignored by white America. The answer is that white America doesn't want to know about or even recognize modern-day Indians; it doesn't want to deal with the problems that the reservation system has created in the way of extreme poverty, hopelessness, created dependency, and alcohol and drug addiction that for many are the only way out of the concentration camp horror of their reserves or homelands (called reservations in America).

As Vine Deloria says in Chapter 3 of *God Is Red*:

"The tragedy of America's Indians — that is, the Indians that America loves, and loves to read about — is that they no longer exist, except in the pages of books. Rather, the modern Indians dress much the same as any other person, attend pretty much the same schools, work at many of the same jobs, and suffer racial discrimination in the same manner as do other racial minorities."

Except that Indians are the only minority group that the Indian lovers won't let out of the 19th cen-

Satellite dish painted with Navajo design.

tury. They love Indians as long as they can picture them riding around on ponies wearing their beads and feathers, living in picturesque tipi villages and making long profound speeches.

I am frequently invited by elementary school teachers here in Gainesville, Florida, to come and talk to the children about Indians and "tell them what they are like." Always, without fail, they ask if I can wear my "Indian clothes." By Indian clothes, they mean beads and feathers and Indian jewelry. I explain that as a graduate student at the University of Florida, I have very few occasions to wear Indian clothes. But the children, they say, will be so disappointed if I don't look like a real Indian.

These teachers are asking me to collaborate with them in perpetuating the stereotype of what America wants its Indians to look like. They want us to look like we never moved past 1890. This is almost always the cut-off year for "Real Indians." America still won't let Indians into the 21st century.

Jan Elliott is a Cherokee activist and scholar of Native American philosophy. A version of this article appeared first in the journal Indigenous Thought.

BEGINNINGS

"Discovery"
represents the point of view
of the
supposed
discoverers.

It's the invaders
masking their theft.

And when the word
gets repeated in
textbooks,
those textbooks become
the propaganda
of the
winners.

INDIANS CLAIM ITALY by "Right of Discovery"

From the New York Times
Rome, Sept. 24, 1973

Italy, cradle of Western civilization, woke up today to the fact that it has never actually been discovered. The situation, however, was remedied at 11 o'clock in the morning when the chief of the Indian Chippewa tribe, Adam Nordwall, stepped off an Alitalia jumbo jet and claimed it for the Indian people.

The intrepid explorer, in full Indian dress, accompanied by his wife — in ordinary clothes because her suitcase had been lost in New York — stood on the tarmac of Fiumicino airport here and took possession of Italy "by right of discovery."

The fact that Italy has long been inhabited by people who consider themselves to be in full possession of the place was exactly the point that Mr. Nordwall was trying to make. "What right had Columbus to discover America when it was already inhabited for thousands of years? The same right that I have to come now to Italy and claim to have discovered your country," he said.

The difference, however, was that Columbus "came to conquer a country by force where a peaceful people were living, while I am on a mission of peace and goodwill."

Mr. Nordwall led a party of Indians which occupied the prison on Alcatraz in San Francisco Bay in 1969 to call attention to the conditions in which Indians were compelled to live in America.

from the New York Times

Adam Nordwall, Chippewa activist, steps off the airplane and claims Italy.

DISCOVERING COLUMBUS
Re-reading the Past

BY BILL BIGELOW

Jean-Claude Lejeune

Most of my students have trouble with the idea that a book — especially a textbook — can lie. That's why I start my U.S. history class by stealing a student's purse.

As the year opens, my students may not know when the Civil War was fought or what James Madison or Frederick Douglass did; but they know that a brave fellow named Christopher Columbus discovered America. Indeed, this bit of historical lore may be the only knowledge class members share in common.

What students don't know is that their textbooks have, by omission or otherwise, lied to them.

Finders, Keepers

So I begin class by stealing a student's purse. I announce that the purse is mine, obviously, because look who has it. Most students are fair-minded. They saw me take the purse off the desk so they protest: "That's not yours, it's Nikki's. You took it. We saw you." I brush these objections aside and reiterate that it is, too, mine and to prove it, I'll show all the things I have inside.

I unzip the bag and remove a brush or a comb, maybe a pair of dark glasses. A tube of lipstick works best: "This is my lipstick," I say. "There, that proves it is my purse." They don't buy it and, in fact, are mildly outraged that I would pry into someone's possessions with such utter disregard for her privacy. (I've alerted the student to the demonstration before the class, but no one else knows that.)

"OK, if it's Nikki's purse, how do you know? Why are you all so positive it's not my purse?" Different answers: "We saw you take it; that's her lipstick, we know you don't wear lipstick; there is stuff in there with her name on it." To get the point across,

I even offer to help in their effort to prove Nikki's possession: "If we had a test on the contents of the purse, who would do better, Nikki or I?" "Whose labor earned the money that bought the things in the purse, mine or Nikki's?" Obvious questions, obvious answers.

I make one last try to keep Nikki's purse: "What if I said I *discovered* this purse, then would it be mine?" A little laughter is my reward, but I don't get any takers; they still think the purse is rightfully Nikki's.

"So," I ask, "Why do we say that Columbus discovered America?"

Was It Discovery?

Now they begin to see what I've been leading up to. I ask a series of questions which implicitly link Nikki's purse and the Indians' land: Were there people on the land before Columbus arrived? Who had been on the land longer, Columbus or the Indians? Who knew the land better? The students see where I'm going — it would be hard not to. "And yet," I continue, "What is the first thing that Columbus did when he arrived in the New World?" Right: he took possession of it. After all, he had discovered the place.

We talk about phrases other than "discovery" that textbooks could use to describe what Columbus did. Students start with phrases they used to describe what I did to Nikki's purse: He stole it; he took it; he ripped it off. And others: He invaded it; he conquered it.

I want students to see that the word "discovery" is loaded. The word itself carries a perspective, a bias. "Discovery" represents the point of view of the supposed discoverers. It's the invaders masking their theft. And when the word gets repeated in textbooks, those textbooks become, in the phrase of one historian, "the propaganda of the winners."

To prepare students to examine textbooks critically, we begin with alternative, and rather unsentimental, explorations of Columbus's "enterprise," as he called it. The Admiral-to-be was not sailing for mere adventure and to prove the world was round, as I learned in 4th grade, but to secure the tremendous profits that were to be made by reaching the Indies.

Mostly I want the class to think about the human beings Columbus was to "discover" — and then destroy. I read from a letter Columbus wrote to Lord Raphael Sanchez, treasurer of Aragón, and one of his patrons, dated March 14, 1493, following his return from the first voyage. He reports being enormously impressed by the indigenous people:

"As soon ... as they see that they are safe and have laid aside all fear, they are very simple and honest and exceedingly liberal with all they have; none of them refusing anything he [sic] may possess when he is asked for it, but, on the contrary, inviting us to ask them. They exhibit great love toward all others in preference to themselves. They also give objects of great value for trifles, and content themselves with very little or nothing in return .... I did not find, as some of us had expected, any cannibals among them, but, on the contrary, men of great deference and kindness."

But, on an ominous note, Columbus writes in his log, "... should your Majesties command it, all the inhabitants could be taken away to Castile [Spain], or made slaves on the island. With 50 men we could subjugate them all and make them do whatever we want."

I ask students if they remember from elementary school days what Columbus brought back from the Americas. Students recall that he returned with parrots, plants, some gold, and a few of the people Columbus had taken to calling "Indians." This was Columbus's first expedition and it is also where most school textbook accounts of Columbus end — conveniently.

But what about his second voyage?

I read to them a passage from Hans

Spanish colonists use dogs to hunt Native Americans in this detailed engraving by Theodore de Bry (1528-1598).

Koning's book, *Columbus: His Enterprise*:

We are now in February 1495. Time was short for sending back a good "dividend" on the supply ships getting ready for the return to Spain. Columbus therefore turned to a massive slave raid as a means for filling up these ships. The [Columbus] brothers rounded up 1,500 Arawaks [Taínos] — men, women, and children — and imprisoned them in pens in Isabela, guarded by men and dogs. The ships had room for no more than five hundred, and thus only the best specimens were loaded aboard. The Admiral then told the Spaniards they could help themselves from the remainder to as many slaves as they wanted. Those whom no one chose were simply kicked out of their pens. Such had been the terror of these prisoners that (in the description by Michele de Cuneo, one of the colonists) "they rushed in all directions like lunatics, women dropping and abandoning infants in the rush, running for miles without stopping, fleeing across mountains and rivers."

Of the 500 slaves, 300 arrived alive in Spain, where they were put up for sale in Seville by Don Juan de Fonseca, the archdeacon of the town. "As naked as the day they were born," the report of this excellent churchman says, "but with no more embarrassment than animals ..."

The slave trade immediately turned out to be "unprofitable, for the slaves mostly died." Columbus decided to concentrate on gold, although he writes, "Let us in the name of the Holy Trinity go on sending all the slaves that can be sold."

Looking Through Different Eyes

Students and I role-play a scene from Columbus's second voyage. Slavery is not producing the profits Columbus is seeking. He believes there is gold and the Indians are selfishly holding out on him.

Students play Columbus; I play the Indians: "Chris, we don't have any gold, honest. Can we go back to living our lives now and you can go back to wherever you came from?"

I call on several students to respond to the Indians' plea. Columbus thinks the Indians are lying. Student responses range from sympathetic to ruthless: OK, we'll go home; please bring us your gold; we'll lock you up in prison if you don't bring us your gold; we'll torture you if you don't fork it over, etc.

After I've pleaded for awhile and the students-as-Columbus have threatened, I read aloud another passage from Koning's book, describing Columbus's system for extracting gold from the Indians:

Every man and woman, every boy or girl of fourteen or older, in the province of Cibao ... had to collect gold for the Spaniards. As their measure, the Spaniards used ... hawks' bells .... Every three months, every Indian had to bring to one of the forts a hawks' bell filled with gold dust. The chiefs had to bring in about ten times that amount.

> *If you dis•cov•er that some among them steal, you must punish them by cutting off nose and ears, for those are parts of the Body which cannot be concealed.*
>
> Christopher Columbus, 1494

Deborah Small/1492

In the other provinces of Hispaniola, twenty five pounds of spun cotton took the place of gold.

Copper tokens were manufactured, and when an Indian had brought his or her tribute to an armed post, he or she received such a token, stamped with the month, to be hung around the neck. With that they were safe for another three months while collecting more gold.

Whoever was caught without a token was killed by having his or her hands cut off ....

There were no gold fields, and thus, once the Indians had handed in whatever they still had in gold ornaments, their only hope was to work all day in the streams, washing out gold dust from the pebbles. It was an impossible task, but those Indians who tried to flee into the mountains were systematically hunted down with dogs and killed, to set an example for the others to keep trying....

During those two years of the administration of the brothers Columbus, an estimated one half of the entire population of Hispaniola was killed or killed themselves. The estimates run from one hundred and twenty-five thousand to one-half million.

The goal is not to titillate or stun, but to force the question: Why wasn't I told this before?

Re-examining Basic Truths

I ask students to find a textbook, preferably one they used in elementary school, and critique the book's treatment of Columbus and the Indians. I distribute the following handout and review the questions aloud. I don't want them to merely answer the questions, but to consider them as guidelines.

• How factually accurate was the account?

• What was omitted — left out — that in your judgment would be important for a full understanding of Columbus? (for example, his treatment of the Taínos; slave taking; his method of getting gold; the overall effect on the Indians.)

• What motives does the book give to Columbus? Compare those with his real motives.

• Who does the book get you to root for, and how is that accomplished? (For example, are the books horrified at the treatment of Indians or thrilled that

A classic depiction of Columbus's triumphant act of claiming land for the King and Queen, in the name of God.

Columbus makes it to the New World?)

• How do the publishers use illustrations? What do these communicate about Columbus and his "enterprise"?

• In your opinion, why does the book portray the Columbus/Indian encounter the way it does?

• Can you think of any groups in our society who might have an interest in people having an inaccurate view of history?

I tell students that this last question is tough but crucial. Is the continual distortion of Columbus simply an accident, or are there social groups who benefit from children developing a false or limited understanding of the past?

The assignment's subtext is to teach students that text material, indeed all written material, should be read skeptically. I want students to explore the politics of print — that perspectives on history and social reality underlie the written word, and that to read is both to comprehend what is written, but also to question why it is written. My intention is not to encourage an 'I-don't-believe-anything' cynicism, but rather to equip students to analyze a writer's assumptions and determine what is and isn't useful in any particular work.

For practice, we look at excerpts from a textbook, *The Story of American Freedom* (Macmillan, 1964). We read aloud and analyze several paragraphs. The arrival of Columbus and crew is especially revealing — and obnoxious. The reader watches the events from the Spaniards' point of view. We are told how Columbus and his men "fell upon their knees and gave thanks to God," a passage included in virtually all elementary school accounts of Columbus. "He then took possession of it [the island] in the name of

King Ferdinand and Queen Isabella of Spain." No question is raised of Columbus's right to assume control over a land which was already occupied. The account is so respectful of the Admiral that students can't help but sense it approves of what is, quite simply, an act of naked imperialism.

The book keeps us close to God and the Church throughout its narrative. Upon returning from the New World, Columbus shows off his parrots and Indians. Immediately following the show, "the king and queen lead the way to a near-by church. There a song of praise and thanksgiving is sung." Intended or not, linking church and Columbus removes him still further from criticism.

Students' Conclusions

I give students a week before I ask them to bring in their written critiques. Students share their papers with one another in small groups. They note themes that recur in the papers and any differences that emerge. Here are excerpts from some students' papers in a class that Linda Christensen and I co-taught:

Matthew wrote: "As people read their evaluations the same situations in these textbooks came out. Things were conveniently left out so that you sided with Columbus's quest to 'boldly go where no man has gone before'.... None of the harsh violent reality is confronted in these so-called true accounts."

Gina tried to explain why the books were so consistently rosy:

It seemed to me as if the publishers had just printed up some "glory story" that was supposed to make us feel more patriotic about our country. In our group, we talked about the possibility of the government trying to protect young students from such violence. We soon decided that that was probably one of the farthest things from their minds. They want us to look at our country as great, and powerful, and forever right. They want us to believe Columbus was a real hero. We're being fed lies. We don't question the facts, we just absorb information that is handed to us because we trust the role models that are handing it out.

Rebecca's reflected the general tone of disillusion with the textbooks: "Of course, the writers of the books probably think it's harmless enough — what does it matter who discovered America, really; and besides, it makes them feel good about America. But the thought that I have been lied to all my life about this, and who knows what else, really makes me angry."

Why Do We Do This?

The students' written reflections became the basis for a class discussion. Repeatedly, students blasted their textbooks for giving readers inadequate, and ultimately untruthful, understandings. While we didn't press to arrive at definitive explanations for the omissions and distortions, we tried to underscore the contemporary abuses of historical ignorance. If the books wax romantic about Columbus planting the flag on island beaches and taking possession of land occupied by naked red-skinned Indians, what do young readers learn from this about today's world? That might — or wealth — makes right? That it's justified to take people's land if you are more "civilized" or have a "better" religion?

Whatever the answers, the textbooks condition students to accept inequality; nowhere do they suggest that the Indians were sovereign peoples with a right to control their own lands. And, if Columbus's motives are mystified or ignored, then students are less apt to question U.S. involvements in, say, Central America or the Middle East. As Bobby, approaching his registration day for the military draft, pointed out in class: "If people thought they were going off to war to fight for profits, maybe they wouldn't fight as well, or maybe they wouldn't go."

It's important to note that some students are troubled by these myth-popping discussions. One student wrote that she was "left not knowing who to believe." Josh was the most articulate in his skepticism. He had begun to "read" our class from the same critical distance from which we hoped students would approach textbooks:

I still wonder ... If we can't believe what our first grade teachers told us, why should we believe you? If they lied to us, why wouldn't you? If one book is wrong, why isn't another? What is your purpose in telling us about how awful Chris was? What interest do you have in telling us the truth? What is it you want from us?

They were wonderful questions. Linda and I responded by reading them (anonymously) to the entire class. We asked students to take a few minutes to write additional questions and comments on the Columbus activities or to imagine our response as teachers — what was the point of our lessons?

We hoped students would see that the intent was

to present a new way of reading, and ultimately, of experiencing the world. Textbooks fill students with information masquerading as final truth and then ask students to parrot back the information in end of the chapter "checkups." We wanted to tell students that they shouldn't necessarily trust the "authorities," but instead need to participate in their learning, probing for unstated assumptions and unasked questions.

Josh asked what our "interest" was in this approach. It's a vital question. Linda and I see teaching as

David F. Clobes

political action: we want to equip students to build a truly democratic society. As Brazilian educator Paulo Freire once wrote, to be an actor for social change one must "read the word and the world."

We hope that if a student maintains a critical distance from the written word, then it's possible to maintain that same distance from one's society: to stand back, look hard, and ask, "Why is it like this? Who benefits and who suffers?

"How can I make it better?"

Bill Bigelow (bbpdx@aol.com) teaches at Franklin High School in Portland, Oregon, and is an editor of the journal Rethinking Schools.

For additional resources on the arrival and impact of Columbus on the Americas, including Hans Koning's Columbus: His Enterprise, *quoted in this article, see page 182.*

SUGAR & SLAVERY

BY PHILIP MARTIN

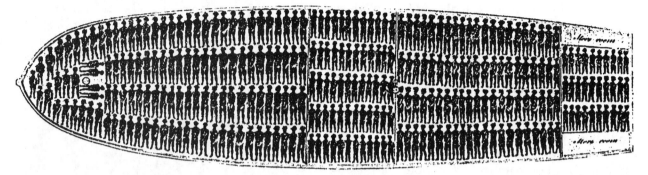

This grotesque and disturbing 1789 engraving is a diagram showing how ships' captains packed African slaves in their lower deck for transport to the Americas.

Carried in the hold of one of Columbus's ships on his second voyage were some small cuttings of a plant which would prove deadly to millions of people. Not so much by its consumption — although it produced a rather unhealthy food. And not because of its manner of cultivation, although it did require a lot of hard labor. But deadly because of the greed of those who wanted to grow it for profit, including Columbus and his sons.

The plant was sugarcane. This plant had first been introduced to Spain in the 10th century by Islamic Moors. During the Crusades to the Middle East around the year 1100, many Europeans discovered the pleasures of sugar, and their craving for the sweetness grew and grew.

As the demand grew, the Spaniards looked to increase production. But the Spanish had only a few areas where sugarcane grew well, including the Canary Islands in the Atlantic — Columbus's last stop before heading west. On that fateful voyage, Columbus loaded in some sugarcane plants. When he got to the islands of the Caribbean, he planted the tiny plants, and they thrived in the soil and the climate.

Sugarcane was most profitable when grown in a plantation. A plantation is a type of farm that focuses on a single crop (like sugarcane or coffee beans or cotton). The uniform crop all matures about the same time, so a plantation owner wanted lots of cheap labor — big crews of workers ready to pick, clean, and process the crop very quickly.

To the sugar-plantation owners, the concept of slaves was appealing. The owners cared less about the cost in human agony and more about the money they could make if they could buy lots of slaves, clear as much land as possible, and control the slaves so they could not escape.

The planting of the first sugarcane was overseen by Columbus. His son, Diego, really got the plantations going. At first, the Spaniards forced the Indians to work for them, but by 1505, the Indians around the settlements were nearly gone — driven away or killed by overwork, disease, murder, and suicide.

So the Europeans turned to Africa. Between 1505 and 1888, an estimated 9.5 million Africans were brought to the Americas as slaves. About 2.5 million worked in the Caribbean, mostly on sugar plantations. For over 300 years, slavery reigned, and millions of human beings suffered, labored in terrible conditions, and died harvesting sugarcane.

The sugar season started in August or September, as the slaves prepared the fields for planting. In the searing hot sun, they dug little holes and planted cuttings of sugarcane. The crop would mature about a year and three months later.

As soon as the cane was ripe, it had to be quickly cut, in as little as 24 hours, or it spoiled in the field. From daybreak to nightfall, the slaves cut the cane, stripped the leaves, bound together the stalks, and loaded heavy bundles into carts that were pulled to a grinding mill located right on the plantation. The work was frantic, and the overseers used their whips to keep everyone moving.

The slaves who ran the grinding mills had the dangerous job of feeding the cane stalks into rollers that crushed the cane. Fingers or hands if caught could pull a man into the machine — so one man's job was to stand by, with a hatchet, to chop off an arm if it was caught in the rollers, as occasionally happened.

Other slaves ran the boiling operation — hot, messy, and painstaking — as the juices of the crushed cane were boiled and re-boiled, until the solids suddenly crystallized into sugar, which was skimmed

Enslaved Africans cutting sugarcane on a Caribbean plantation. Sugarcane was introduced to the islands in 1493 by Christopher Columbus.

off the top. The liquid remaining was drained off as molasses. The boilermen's task required skill, but they suffered many serious burns from tending the bubbling hot syrup.

Why? So drinkers could sweeten their tea, or coffee, or chocolate. So people could put out plates of sweets for guests. So penny candy could be made. So molasses could be distilled into rum, a cheap form of alcohol sold to the working class.

What was the price of sweet cravings? What was the cost of the desire of Spanish plantation owners — soon joined by Portuguese, French, Dutch, English, Swedes, and Danes — to clear-cut ancient forests, to start sugarcane plantations, and to buy slaves, so they could make a profit? All it took was a willingness to use manacles, whips, guns, swords, and torture to keep their slaves under their thumbs.

What was the cost? Ask the ghosts of sugar-plantation slaves — backs broken, arms mangled, bodies bruised and bloodied and burned — that haunt the islands of the Caribbean, where Columbus had landed and triumphantly claimed the land to satisfy the cravings of himself, his crew, and his investors, for a new world of sweet, deadly wealth.

The Spaniards trained bloodhounds and organized hunting parties called **rancheadores** *to capture runaway slaves.*

AFRICAN-AMERICAN RESISTANCE

BY BILL FLETCHER, JR.

African-Americans have no reason to celebrate the arrival of Columbus in the Americas. Rather, we should mourn his arrival — and celebrate those who resisted him and the colonial powers he ushered in.

Columbus opened up the Western Hemisphere to European invasion and exploitation. This had devastating consequences not only for Africans, but for Hispanics, Native Americans, and other people of color.

Columbus also initiated the trans-Atlantic slave trade, sending 500 Taínos back to Spain during his second voyage. In later decades, millions of Africans were kidnapped and brought as slaves to the Western Hemisphere. The slave trade not only killed and dehumanized millions of people, it irrevocably distorted the development of African civilization. Families were torn apart, societies collapsed, and the way was opened for Europe's invasion and colonization of that continent as well.

Understanding this can help us understand current problems. African-Americans still suffer the effects of the racist ideology that justified slavery. Likewise, the European-American ruling class still uses racism to maintain its power. Just as in the previous 500 years, discrimination and division based on skin color is used to prevent unity between people of color and poor and working-class whites.

Columbus is integrally connected to these legacies. He initiated large-scale experiments in exploitation which would become trademarks of the European invasion of the Americas: the plundering of gold and silver, and the enslavement of native peoples. He brought sugarcane root from the Canary Islands and planted it on what is now the Dominican Republic. By the early 1500s, African slaves owned by his son Diego were harvesting sugarcane. Throughout the West Indies, hundreds of thousands of Africans suffered early deaths from overwork on sugar plantations.

It is also important to understand that Africans and native peoples resisted the European slave

> When asked to honor the legacy of Columbus, we should reply that we refuse to celebrate the kidnapping and enslavement of millions of Africans.

trade. Their resistance ranged from individual escapes to rebellions involving hundreds and, in some cases, tens of thousands of people.

Columbus Boasts of Slavery

From the first day Columbus arrived in the Western Hemisphere, he thought about enslaving native peoples. As he wrote the Spanish monarchs Ferdinand and Isabella, "Should your majesties command it, all the inhabitants could be taken away to Castile, or made slaves on the island. With 50 men we could subjugate them all and make them do whatever we want."

On his second voyage, Columbus tried to make good on this boast. Some 500 Taíno Indians were sent back to Spain to be sold as slaves, although most of them died enroute or shortly after arriving.

Only a few years later, the Spanish and Portuguese decided to bring African slaves to the Americas. The European colonizers realized that while Native Americans were able to flee into the forests, Africans would have a hard time escaping on an alien continent.

By 1501, the Spanish monarchs had issued their first laws governing the African slave trade. By 1510, hundreds of slaves had been transported to the Americas for sale. By the 1700s, slavery was flourishing in the middle and lower colonies of British America, in the West Indies, and on the mainland of South America.

The impact of the African slave trade was staggering. By the time it was over in the mid 1800s, Africa had lost millions of people. No one knows how many; estimates range from 5 million to as high as 40 million.

In his book, *Before the Mayflower: A History of Black America*, Lerone Bennett, Jr. points out that the slave trade's consequences cannot be captured by mere statistics:

The slave trade was a black man who stepped out

24

In this 16th-century engraving, European colonists employ violent means to keep their African slaves working in the mines.

Theodore de Bry

of his house for a breath of fresh air and ended up, ten months later, in Georgia with bruises on his back and a brand on his chest.

The slave trade was a black mother suffocating her newborn baby because she didn't want him to grow up a slave.

The slave trade was a "kind" captain forcing his suicide-minded passengers to eat by breaking their teeth, though, as he said, he was "naturally compassionate."

The slave trade was a bishop sitting on an ivory chair on a wharf in the Congo and extending his fat hand in wholesale baptism of slaves who were rowed beneath him, going in chains to the slave ships.

The Evolution Toward Slavery

Slavery did not immediately assume a leading position in the economic life of the Western Hemisphere.

In what is now the United States, the colonial upper classes initially relied upon European paupers [poor people thrown in jail for their inability to pay their debts] for much of their labor force. Many immigrants came as indentured servants who had to work seven years before they could gain their freedom. Others came as "redemptioners," obligated to pay their trans-Atlantic fare within two years of their arrival or be sold to the highest bidder. Much of this servant class was provided by Irish, English, and German tenant farmers seeking a better life.

The demand for a colonial workforce also encouraged unscrupulous practices: kidnappers snatched adults and children off the streets of London and Bristol, and magistrates transported religious dissenters and people convicted of petty thievery.

Together, the indentured servants, redemptioners, those kidnapped, and former "convicts" comprised about one-half of all English immigrants during the colonial period.

By the middle of the 1600s, the upper classes in Europe and the colonies saw drawbacks in this approach. In Britain, merchants worried that emigration was depriving them of inexpensive wage laborers. And in the British colonies in America along the Atlantic seaboard, poor whites remained scarce in relation to labor needs, and threatened to become an independent political force. Further, indentured servants often escaped, or demanded land at the end of their service.

Black slaves thus became an attractive source of labor. Racism conveniently justified slavery. And from the upper-class perspective, using African slaves made economic sense. The same amount of money it took to buy 10 years of a poor white person's labor would buy the entire lifetime of a black person's.

To make slavery work, laws and ideas in the colonies had to be changed. From 1619, when the first Africans appeared in English America, until about 1660, blacks shared many of the rights enjoyed by poor whites. Black indentured servants could gain their freedom after seven years, just as whites could. In many places, blacks were allowed to own land, vote, and testify in court.

With Virginia and Maryland in the lead, the colonies began to develop the prejudices, legal codes, and customs upon which a slave economy could flourish. Laws were passed which made blacks slaves for life and which outlawed intermarriage. Confronted with the embarrassment of Christian slaves, presumably possessing souls equal to those of whites in the eyes of God, Virginia legislators passed a 1667 law which stipulated, "The conferring of baptisme doth not alter the condition of the person as to his bondage or freedom."

Toussaint L'Ouverture defeated English, Spanish, and French armies in fighting for Haitian independence.

Once sanctioned by law and religion, slavery in the 13 colonies took off. In 1710, there were 50,000 slaves in what is now the United States. In 1776 there were 500,000. And on the eve of the Civil War, there were 4 million.

Slavery brought immense wealth to a tiny class of Europeans both in Europe and the Western Hemisphere. This wealth not only supported extravagant lifestyles, it provided the money needed to launch modern-day capitalism and the industrial revolution.

This wealth first came from the gold and silver taken from the Western Hemisphere — mined by slaves, both black and Native-American, and forced laborers. Other endeavors based on slavery, especially the production of sugar, cotton, and tobacco, also became a tremendous source of capital. In addition, slave products from the Western Hemisphere, such as cotton, provided raw materials for British factories.

Slave Resistance

From the beginning of the trans-Atlantic slave trade, Africans organized rebellions. Historian Herbert Aptheker has documented 250 conspiracies, revolts, and acts of resistance in the United States during the slave era. Insurrection leaders such as Gabriel Prosser, Denmark Vesey, and Nat Turner struck terror into the hearts of slave owners. In addition, at least 40,000 slaves in the U.S. escaped to states where slavery was illegal and to Canada, using the "Underground Railroad" organized by black and white abolitionists.

The largest slave revolts took place in South America and the West Indies. The longest rebellion took place in Northeast Brazil, where escaped slaves organized the kingdom of Palmares — which grew to one-third the size of Portugal. For most of the 18th century, until ultimate defeat, thousands of former slaves living there successfully resisted dozens of Dutch and Portuguese military expeditions.

The most famous slave revolt was led by the Haitian slave Toussaint L'Ouverture in the early 1800s. A brilliant general, L'Ouverture defeated English, Spanish, and French armies — laying the groundwork for Haitian independence from France in 1825. Haiti thus became the first free black republic in the Western Hemisphere.

Faced with a common oppressor, Native Americans and African slaves were often allies. One remarkable example in what is now the United States were the "Seminole Wars" in Florida from the early 1800s until 1842. The Seminoles were comprised of Creek Indians who settled in Florida, runaway slaves, and remnants of the original tribes in the area. Together, they resisted the U.S. Army during the Seminole Wars — the costliest wars ever fought by the United States against Native Americans, which never ended in clear victory for the U.S. Army.

According to historian Jan Carew, U.S. soldiers sent to fight these insurgents "brought back tales of extraordinary courage, of the Indians and Negroes fighting together, Indians under the leadership of Negroes, Negroes under the leadership of Indians, and of the great devotion between the two groups."

Columbus's African Legacy

While North Americans, both black and white, have had to confront the reverberations of slavery in the United States, we have scant knowledge of the slave trade's profound impact on Africa. To the extent most Americans think of Africa, it is as a homogeneous place — rather than a massive continent filled with many different ethnic groups which defy easy generalizations.

Perhaps one safe generalization is that most of Africa's peoples were eventually affected by Columbus's voyages. His pioneering ventures in thievery and enslavement helped set in motion events which left Africa vulnerable to over 400 years of invasion and colonization.

The slave trade had the same effect on various societies in Africa that the kidnapping of an individual family member would have on an individual family — multiplied several million times. To fuel the slave trade, European invaders pitted ethnic groups and empires against one another, supplying some groups with weapons and then buying the prisoners from any wars. As a result, many societies became fractured and demoralized, particularly in Western Africa. Class divisions and inequalities deepened as African rulers provided increasing numbers of people to the slave market.

As historian Hosea Jaffe notes, "Slaving became the major commerce inside Africa itself, involving more people and money than all other commerce put together."

While slavery existed among Africans before the European slave trade, slaves owned by Africans were not treated with the absolute brutality which characterized the European slave trade. And by encouraging the capture of slaves for export, the trans-Atlantic slave trade inalterably changed life in large regions of Africa.

West Indian historian Walter Rodney describes the impact of slavery in West Africa this way: "For the vast majority it [the slave trade] brought insecurity and fear, whether or not they were able to escape sale into slavery, because the slave trade meant violence in the form of skirmishes, ambushes and kidnappings — often carried out by professional man-hunters under the supervision of the ruling elites. This atmosphere of fear caused people to flee their villages into the bush or remove their homes to places which were difficult to get to and agriculturally inhospitable. Alternatively,

Abraham, a Florida slave who became an influential interpreter and counselor with the Seminoles.

as was noticeable on the waterside, many Africans walked in armed expectation of attack."

What Should We Celebrate?

While Columbus deserves condemnation for many of his actions, we should also remember to criticize the political and economic forces which he both represented and encouraged.

When asked to commemorate the legacy of Columbus, we should reply that we refuse to celebrate the European plunder of the Western Hemisphere's riches. We refuse to celebrate the European subjugation of the Western Hemisphere's native peoples. We refuse to celebrate the kidnapping and enslavement of millions of Africans.

There is only one thing we should celebrate: the 500 years of resistance to Columbus and the greed and cruelty that he represents.

Bill Fletcher, Jr. is the Belle Zeller Visiting Professor at Brooklyn College–City University of New York.

Additional Resources:

Aptheker, Herbert, ed. Documentary History of the Negro People in the United States. Vol. 1. *New York: Citadel Press, 1951.*

Bennett, Lerone, Jr. Before the Mayflower: A History of Black America. *New York: Penguin Books, 1984.*

Carew, Jan. Fulcrums of Change. *Trenton, NJ: Africa World Press, 1988.*

MY COUNTRY, 'TIS OF THY PEOPLE YOU'RE DYING

BY BUFFY SAINTE-MARIE

Now that your big eyes
have finally opened
Now that you're wondering
how must they feel
meaning them that you've chased
across America's movie screens.
Now that you're wondering
how can it be real
that the ones you've called
colorful, noble, and proud
in your school propaganda,
they starve in their splendor
You've asked for my comment
I simply will render:

My country, 'tis of thy people you're dying.

Now that the long houses
reap superstition
You've forced us to send
our toddlers away
to your schools where they're taught
to despise their traditions
forbid them their languages,
temper their say
that America's history
really began
when Columbus set sail
out of Europe and stressed
that the nation of leeches
that conquered this land
are the biggest and bravest
and boldest and best

And yet where in your history books
is the tale
of the genocide basic
to this country's birth
of the preachers who lied,
how the Bill of Rights failed,
how a nation of patriots
returned to their earth?
And where will it tell
of the Liberty Bell
as it rang with a thud,
over tinsel of mud
and a brave Uncle Sam
in Alaska this year?

My country, 'tis of thy people you're dying.

Hear how the bargain was made
for the West
with her shivering children
in zero degrees
"blankets for your land,"
so the treaties attest.
Oh, well, blankets for land
is a bargain indeed.
And the blankets were those
Uncle Sam had collected
from smallpox disease-dying
soldiers that day
and the tribes were wiped out,
and the history books censored,
a hundred years
of your statesmen have felt

it's better this way.
Yet a few of the conquered
have somehow survived.
Their blood runs the red earth
though genes have been paled
from the Grand Canyon's caverns,
to craven sad hills,
the wounded, the losers,
the robbed sing their tale.
From Los Angeles County
to Upstate New York,
the white nation fattens
while others grow lean.
Oh, the tricked and evicted
they know what I mean.

My country, 'tis of thy people you're dying.

The past, it just crumbled,
the future just threatens
Our life blood shut up
in your chemical tanks.
And now here you come,
bill of sale in your hand
and surprise in your eyes
that we're lacking in thanks.
for the blessings of civilization
you've brought us
the lessons you've taught us,
the ruins you've wrought us
oh, see what our trust
in America's bought us.

My country, 'tis of thy people you're dying.

Now that the pride of the sires
receives charity

Now that we're harmless
and safe behind laws
Now that my life's to be known
as your heritage
Now that even the graves
have been robbed
Now that our own chosen way
is a novelty
Hands on our hearts,
we salute you your victory
choke on your blue, white, and scarlet
hypocrisy,
pitying the blindness
that you've never seen
that the eagles of war,
whose wings lent you glory,
they were never no more
than carrion crows,
pushed the wrens from the nest
stole their eggs, changed their story
the mockingbird sings it,
it's all that she knows.
Ah, what can I do
say a powerless few
with a lump in your throat
and a tear in your eye
can't you see that their poverty's
profiting you?

My country, 'tis of thy people you're dying.

Buffy Sainte-Marie, of Cree heritage, is a singer, songwriter, and educator familiar to many from her frequent appearances on Sesame Street. She has founded the Cradleboard Project (www.cradleboard.org), a program to develop a native studies curriculum for native schools on the internet; it has many links to other native sites of general interest.

This song is from her recording titled Little Wheel Spin and Spin (Vanguard, 1966).

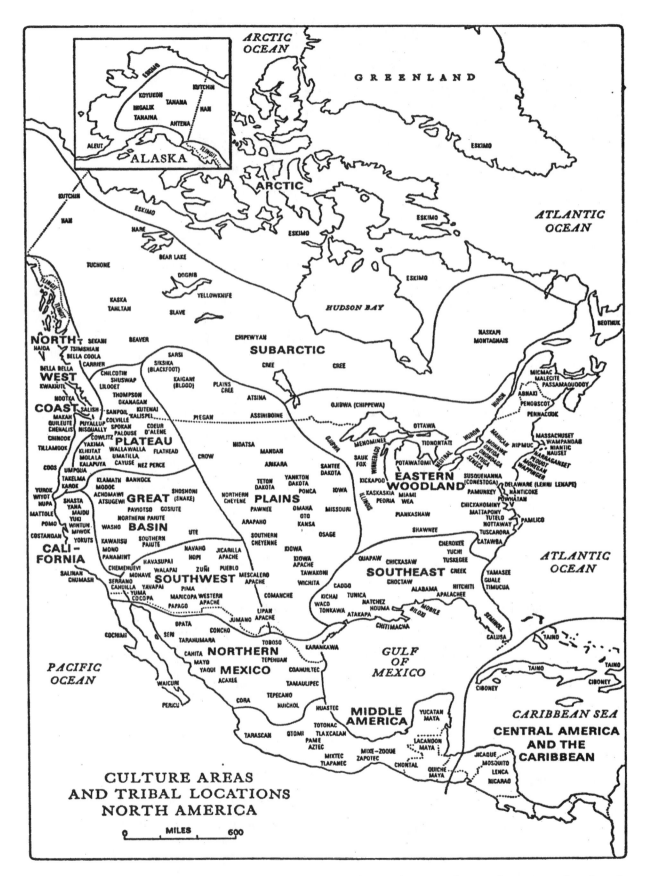

CULTURE AREAS
AND TRIBAL LOCATIONS
NORTH AMERICA

MILES
0   600

This map outlines thirteen culture areas — where distinct landforms, climate, and natural resources played a role in shaping the native cultures.

ELEMENTARY SCHOOL ISSUES

To invite students to question
the injustices embedded in texts
and children's books
is implicitly to invite them to question
the injustices embedded in society itself.

Isn't it about time
we used the Columbus myth
to allow students to begin discovering
the truth?

WHAT NOT TO TEACH
About Native Americans

BY JUNE SARK HEINRICH

Don't use alphabet cards that say A is for apple, B is for ball, and I is for Indian.

The matter may seem to be a trivial one, but if you want your students to develop respect for Native Americans, don't start them out in kindergarten equating Indians with things like apples and balls. Stay away from "I-is-for-Indian."

Don't talk about Indians as though they belong to the past.

Books often have titles like "How the Indians Lived," as though there aren't any living today. Today, about two million Native Americans live in what is now the United States, many on reservations and many in cities and towns. They are in all kinds of neighborhoods and schools and in all walks of life. Too many live today in conditions of poverty and powerlessness, but they are very much a part of the modern world. If the people who write books mean "How (particular groups of) Native Americans Lived Long Ago," then they should say so.

Don't lump all Native Americans together.

There were no "Indians" before the Europeans came to America — that is, no people called themselves "Indians." They are Navajo or Seminole or Menominee, etc. The hundreds of native groups scattered throughout the U.S. are separate peoples, separate nations. They have separate languages and cultures and names. Native Americans of one nation are as different from Native Americans of another nation as Italians are from Swedes, Hungarians from Irish, or English from Spanish. When teaching about Native Americans, use the word "Indians" — or even "Native American" — as little as possible. Don't "study the Indians." Study the Hopi, the Sioux, the Nisqually, the Apache.

Don't expect Native Americans to look like Hollywood movie "Indians."

Some Native Americans tell a story about a white "American" woman who visited a reservation. She stopped and stared at a young man, then said to him, "Are you a real Indian? You don't look Indian."

Whatever it is that people expect Native Americans to look like, many do not fit those images. Since they come from different nations, their physical features, body structure, and skin colors vary a great deal — and none has red skin. Of course, Native and non-Native Americans have intermarried, so many Native Americans today have European, African, or other ancestry. Don't expect all Native Americans to look alike, any more than all Europeans look alike.

Don't let TV stereotypes go unchallenged.

Unfortunately, TV programs still show the "savage warrior" or occasionally, the "noble savage" stereotypes. Discuss with children the TV programs they watch. Help them understand the meaning of the word "stereotype." Help them understand that,

Andrew Connors

from the Native American point of view, Columbus and other Europeans who came to this land were invaders. Even so, Native Americans originally welcomed and helped the European settlers. When they fought, they were no more "savage" than the Europeans and were often less so.

Help children understand that atrocities are a part of any war, as war itself is atrocious. At least, the Native Americans were defending land they had lived on for thousands of years. Native Americans were not "savage warriors," nor were they "noble savages." They were no more nor less noble than the rest of humanity.

Another common stereotype is the portrayal of the "Indian" as a person of few words, mostly "ugh." On the contrary, early European settlers often commented on the brilliance of Native American oratory and the beauty of their languages.

Stereotypes are sneaky. They influence the way we talk and live and play, sometimes without our knowing it. Don't say to your students, "You act like a bunch of wild Indians." Don't encourage or even allow children to play "cowboys and Indians." Be sensitive to stereotypes in everything you say and do.

Don't assume that Native American children are well acquainted with their heritage.

If you have Native American children in your class, you may expect that they will be good resource persons for your "unit on Indians." It is likely that such children will be proud of being Native American. Some may participate in traditional activities of their cultures. In general, however, native children today have much in common with other children in the U.S. They know far more about TV programs than about their own national ways of life. They eat junk food and want all of the things most children in our society want. If lost in a forest, they would not necessarily be able to manage any better than other children would. Like other children in the U.S., native children need to be taught about the native heritage which, in a very real sense, is the heritage of everybody living in the U.S. today.

Don't let students think that native ways of life have no meaning today.

Native arts have long commanded worldwide interest and admiration. But far more important for human and ecological survival are Native American philosophies of life. Respect for the land; love of every form of life, human and non-human; harmony between humans and nature rather than conquest and destruction of nature — these are vital characteristics of native ways of life. All people in the U.S. can and must learn to live in harmony with the natural world and with one another. That is one lesson native peoples can teach your students about "the Indians."

June Sark Heinrich formerly directed the Native American Committee's Indian School in Chicago. This piece is adapted from an article in Unlearning "Indian" Stereotypes, Council on Interracial Books for Children.

A FRIEND OF THE INDIANS
by Joseph Bruchac

A man who was known
as a friend of the Indians
spoke to Red Jacket one day
about the good treatment
the Senecas enjoyed
from their white neighbors.

Red Jacket walked with him
beside the river, then suggested
they should sit together
on a log next to the stream.

They both sat down.
Then Red Jacket slid closer
to the man and said, "Move Over."

The man moved over, but when he did
Red Jacket again slid closer.
"Move Over," he said.

Three times this happened
until the man had reached
the end of the log near the water.
Then, once more, he was told,
"Move Over."

"But if I move further
I shall fall in the water,"
the man pleaded,
teetering on the edge.

Red Jacket replied,
"And even so you whites
tell us to move on when
no place is left to go."

From Wounds Beneath the Flesh, ed. by Maurice Kenny
(Fredonia, NY: White Pine Press, 1987), first published in
Entering Onondaga, Cold Mountain Press, 1978. Joseph
Bruchac is a noted Abenaki poet, author, and scholar.
Red Jacket was an Iroquois leader of the late 1700s.

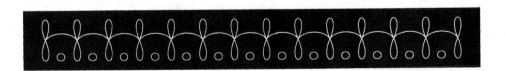

Jean-Claude Lejeune

COLUMBUS AND NATIVE ISSUES
in the Elementary Classroom

BY BOB PETERSON

Many of us grew up with the seemingly innocent refrain, "In fourteen hundred and ninety-two, Columbus sailed the ocean blue." Throughout our schooling, our understanding of Columbus didn't move much beyond this simple rhyme.

Unfortunately, the education of children today is not much different. While children's books, social studies texts, and the digital world may be more colorful, the approach is too often the same.

It is not easy for early childhood and elementary school teachers to challenge the Columbus myth in a way that doesn't just demonize Columbus. We need to help students understand Columbus' individual role in the context of European colonialism that sought wealth and land at the expense of the millions of Native Americans. Students should understand that many Native peoples resisted the European invasion and, despite a history of near genocide, have survived. Also, teachers should strive to have their students understand that Native

people live in all 50 states and in all countries of the Americas and continue to resist discrimination and oppression.

To do this requires first that teachers themselves are well educated or, in many cases, reeducated on these issues. Howard Zinn's *A People's History of the United States* and Hans Koning's *Columbus, His Enterprise* are good places to start. Equally, if not more important is to learn from Native people in your area. Take the time to check out local Native organizations and events, ask them for advice on what might be most helpful for your own education and your students, and check with your local librarian for resources on the original and/or current Native inhabitants of your community.

Assess Your Students

How we approach issues such as Columbus and stereotypes depends on children's developmental levels. For a child of 4 or 5 years old, "history" is yesterday and the "future" is tomorrow. A 5th grader, on the other hand, might be more sophisticated—but often thinks Martin Luther King, Jr. fought against slavery and views historical figures uncritically. Even the youngest children, however, should begin to experiment with words such as "fair," "unfair," and "stereotype," just as we try to teach them the meaning of "respect" and "cooperate."

One way to start studying Columbus and Native Americans is to assess what students already know. Ask them who were the original inhabitants of the land where their school is located and what they know of them. Ask what they know about Christopher Columbus (or an early European settler who first came to your state or community).

Another approach is to have students as a homework assignment interview family members about what they know and think about Columbus and Columbus Day. At the multiracial school where I work, 1st-grade teachers use this assignment to learn what parents think and to demonstrate that there are multiple views about Columbus.

Responses from families and students vary. Occasionally, they are completely incorrect or based on stereotypes. When a student says, for example, "My dad said, 'Columbus was great because he was one of the few people of his time who thought the world

was round'"—a false statement—I respond, "Well, that's what I was taught in school too. We're going to research that to see if that's correct."

Sometimes in early discussions of Native Americans a student might comment about people wearing feathers or living in a tipi. Such statements are based on stereotypes and should be challenged. I point out that such ideas are "stereotypes." I write the word on the board and review its meaning, if we've already covered this concept during the school year, or ask students what they think it means if we have not. I explain that a stereotype is an untrue statement about a whole group of people. If I haven't introduced the concept prior I say something like, "This is an important word and idea that we are going to learn about, and in fact we are going to hear from Native children what they think about stereotypes."

An Anti-Stereotype Curriculum

When stereotypes are out in the open, it's crucial they be dealt with. You might work with colleagues to build an "anti-stereotype curriculum." Here are some activities and class discussion starters that might be useful:

• Show the filmstrip *Unlearning "Indian" Stereotypes*, by the Council on Interracial Books for Children (available in DVD format through Rethinking Schools), and discuss it with your students. For younger children, show it in three or four parts and discuss each separately.

• Ask students what the Native children in *Unlearning "Indian" Stereotypes* identified as stereotypes about Native Americans and how the Native children felt when they saw such stereotypes in the books.

• Show *Unlearning "Indian" Stereotypes* a second time and ask your students to remember as much as they can about how the Native children described the history of their people and the unfair things that happened to them.

• Ask students if anyone in their extended family or friends of their family has Native American heritage. I have this conversation as part of a larger unit when students write autobiographies. Often children proudly talk about their own or their relatives' Native heritage.

• At a separate time, revisit the word "stereotype" and help students recall the definition—as a mistaken idea about how a whole group of people think, behave, or dress. Give examples that do not relate to American Indians, such as the view by some that girls can't be good baseball players, or boys can't cook, or that all elderly people are frail. Ask students: What is wrong with stereotypes? How could these be hurtful? Use one of the above examples: If a coach thought that all girls couldn't play baseball, whom might that hurt and how? Students will likely point

Stereotype Checklist

The book *Through Indian Eyes*, edited by Slapin and Seale, has a checklist to evaluate children's books. The checklist examines both blatant stereotypes and more subtle biases. Some of the many questions raised:

• In ABC books, is "E" for Eskimo or "I" for Indian? In picture books are children shown "playing Indian"?

• Are Native people shown as savages or primitive people rather than as human beings who are members of highly complex societies?

• Are Native people always shown the same, without regard for the cultural, religious, and language differences among tribes?

• Are Native people described with racist imagery, such as "half-naked," "brutal," or "bloodthirsty"? Do the Native people speak in short, inarticulate sentences such as "Me go. Soldier make fire. We now hide."?

• Is Native culture depicted in a condescending way in which, for example, religious beliefs are "superstitions"? Is there a paternalistic distinction between "them" and "us"?

Students and a Native elder drum together.

out that stereotypes like this could easily lead to the coach discriminating against and not letting girls be on the team. It can also prevent girls from having the opportunity to play and practice, making the stereotype self-fulfilling.

• Describe some stereotypes about Native Americans, and try to make analogies with children's own experiences. Ask the children how their family dresses for special occasions and ceremonies, such as weddings. Point out that it's a stereotype to think that all people of their ethnic background always dress as if they were at a wedding. Likewise, it's a stereotype to think that all Indians dress with feathers all the time.

• As an extension activity for *Unlearning "Indian" Stereotypes*, have students become "stereotype detectives." Collect some stereotypical materials—greeting cards, old alphabet and counting books, history books, or children's books on Columbus. (The success of this activity depends on locating fairly obvious stereotypes. I have a box in my classroom closet where I store books with stereotypes that I've collected from library discards, rummage sales, and second-hand book stores.) Model how to identify a stereotype using one of your collected materials writing what it is and why it is a stereotype. In groups, have students examine materials that you have collected. Some of the most common stereotypes are found in alphabet books that have "I for Indian," or in children's favorites such as *Clifford's*

Halloween by Norman Bridwell, in which Clifford uses a feather headdress to dress up as an Indian; or Maurice Sendak's *Alligators All Around,* in which the alligators are "imitating Indians" by wearing feather headdresses, carrying tomahawks, and smoking pipes. Also look at stereotypes in society at large, such as in the names of sports teams or cars or mascots for schools. Talk about the Cleveland Indians, or the Jeep Cherokee, or Winnebago motor homes. Ask students what other cars or sports teams named after nationality groups. Have students reflect on how such stereotypes hurt Indians and distort other people's images of them and their cultures.

• Use the article (p. 131) on people fighting against Indian "mascots" to start a discussion on what people can do to fight stereotypes.

• Point out and discuss stereotypes in books students read in class. As we model such thinking and give children the opportunity to think on their own—"Did you notice any stereotypes in that story?"—children will improve their ability to think critically.

• Use quality books to show how contemporary Native people live and look. *Children of Native America Today,* by Yvonne Wakim Dennis and Arlene Hirschfelder (Charlesbridge, 2003) is a wonderful collection of photos and brief descriptions of Native children today.

• Invite Native American adults into your classroom to talk about their jobs and families and how they feel about how Native Americans have been treated.

• Have children think about a time in their lives when they fought against something that wasn't fair. Explain how Native peoples have fought for what is "fair"—their land and way of life.

Taking Action

As children become aware of how unfair stereotypes are, teachers might encourage them to not only complain about them, but to take action. Educating others, writing to publishers and stores, and talking to librarians are all possibilities. One time after a discussion of Indian stereotypes, my 5th-grade students seemed particularly angered by what they had learned. The next day they talked about how their siblings in 1st grade had come home with construction-paper headdresses with feathers.

"That's a stereotype!" the students proudly proclaimed.

In ABC books, is "E" for "Eskimo"?
From Reed & Oswald, **My Little Golden Dictionary.**

"What did you do about it?" I asked.

"I ripped it up." "I slugged him," came the chorus of responses. Cringing and making a mental note to strengthen my conflict resolution curriculum, I initiated a discussion. "What else might you have done with your brother? Why do your brothers and sisters have feather headdresses and how do we learn such things?"

Finally the students decided there were more productive things they could do. They first scoured the school library for books with stereotypes. Since they didn't find many, they decided to investigate the 1st-grade room of one of their siblings. They wrote a letter to the teacher asking permission, and then went in armed with clipboards, paper, and pens. They found a picture of an Indian next to the letter "I" in the alphabet strip on the wall. They came back and decided they wanted to teach the 1st graders about stereotypes. I was skeptical, but agreed, and after much rehearsal, they entered the 1st-grade classroom to give their lesson. Later they reflected on it and two students wrote in our school newspaper:

We have been studying stereotypes of Native Americans. What is a stereotype? It's when somebody says something that's not true about another group of people. For example, it is a stereotype if you think all Indians wear feathers or say "HOW!" Or if you think that all girls are delicate. Why? Because some girls are strong.

Columbus Revisited

To find out what your students know about Columbus, have them draw or write what they have learned previously. Based on what they know, different approaches might be tried.

Even for very young children, teachers can talk about concepts such as fairness, discovery, and culture. Through dramatization and discussion, children can recognize that if someone was living in their house and some one else came up and "discovered" it, it wouldn't be fair for the new person to kick the current resident out. A similar dramatization about Columbus can dispel the myth of the "discovery of the new world."

The "discovered" purse exercise—where a teacher "discovers" and claims a student's purse or backpack—is a great way to start a discussion (see article, p. 17). I do it every year with my students as an introduction to our social studies unit on Columbus.

Helping Young Children Critique Columbus Books

As part of an "anti-stereotype curriculum," it is useful to have children break into groups and examine books on Columbus. The following questions can be written as a chart and can help children recognize the subtle ways in which books present stereotypes and distort information.

1. How many times did Columbus talk?
2. How many times did we get to know what he was thinking?
3. How many times did the Native people have names?
4. How many times did the Native people talk?
5. How many times did we get to know what the Native people were thinking?
6. What do you learn about Columbus's life?
7. What do you learn about Native people's lives?
8. Does the book describe the Native people's feelings?
9. Does the book describe how Columbus treated the Native people?

After such activities, a good next step is reading or talking about accurate accounts of Columbus. Do the children know, for example, that few of the Native children who witnessed Columbus' arrival in the Americas ever grew to adulthood? Or that Columbus and the Spaniards purposefully used attack dogs against Native peoples, not to mention more gruesome tactics such as cutting off hands and burning Native people alive? That Columbus initiated the trans-Atlantic slave trade when he sent hundreds of Native people back to Spain on his second voyage, to be sold as slaves?

By such dramatization and questions, I spark interest in Columbus, highlighting that this was not only a huge conflict between invading Europeans and Native peoples 500 years ago, but remains a conflict today in terms of how we sum up this history.

I use Jane Yolen's book, *Encounter,* as a way to help kids imagine what a Taíno view might have been towards the first Europeans. I contrast that to a traditional children's book on Columbus that glorifies his role.

I also have children read, discuss, illustrate their own books about Columbus, either using the story written by Tina Thomas (see p. 42) or selections from other books which I usually read aloud. I read selections from books such as *Taínos: The People Who Welcomed Columbus* by Francine Jacobs, and *Columbus and the World Around Him* by Milton Meltzer.

After the initial introduction to my unit, I play the song "1492" (see box p. 41) by Nancy Schimmel and use the song to explain some of the many Native American nations that existed at the time of Columbus. Later, I use Buffy Sainte-Marie's powerful song, "My Country, 'Tis of Thy People You're Dying" (see p. 28), to contrast the treatment of Native peoples to our nation's leaders' professed adherence to democratic ideals. I also stress the positive through using the alphabet of things that Native Americans gave to the world (see p. 75). I have kids choose an item from the list and use mime to get the other students to guess it. As a homework assignment, they need to list 15 different things at home that have origins in the Americas.

Textbook Detectives

As children become familiar with details of the Columbus story, they often ask questions such as,

> As children become familiar with details of the Columbus story, they often ask questions such as, "Why do some books not tell the truth?" "Why was I told something else at home or last year in school?"

"Why do some books not tell the truth?" "Why was I told something else at home or last year in school?" "My mom says Columbus was a brave man and a hero."

These are good questions without easy answers. I have found that only by integrating such questions throughout my entire curriculum do children begin to realize that the content of TV and textbooks is often shaped to serve interests of the status quo and those who most benefit by the way society is organized. By starting with a critical examination of Columbus, I set the stage for similar examinations later in the year—for example, when we look at how a handful of rich, white, male property owners elected our first president or when we examine a news article on the economy that quotes only business or government leaders and ignores ordinary workers or union leaders.

I show students Bill Bigelow's slide-show on children's books on Columbus (see Resources, p. 187) and we discuss the omissions and lies of many children's books still in publication. I then tell my kids I want them to be textbook detectives and to critically examine various children's books on Columbus. In cooperative groups, kids brainstorm what they should look for to see if the books on Columbus are accurate. Each group shares their ideas, and overnight I consolidate their ideas into a "Textbook Detective" sheet (see box, p. 38). The next day, working in pairs, the students evaluate different books. They share their findings with the whole class, and we brainstorm what can be done. Ideas range from writing authors (or suing them!) to talking to librarians.

One girl wrote to Ann McGovern, author of *Christopher Columbus* (Scholastic, 1992): "The kids of La Escuela Fratney are reading your book as an experiment. We think that it does not tell the whole truth. I don't want to be mean or pushy, but it doesn't say that Columbus forced six Taínos to go with him on his first trip back. He wanted gold and sometimes he killed Taínos to get it. The book doesn't say anything about him killing Taínos, or even that there were Taínos. It says 'Indian.'"

Another student reflected on another book, "I think if a teacher made me read this book I really would think Columbus was great, but he wasn't so great. All the little kids who read this book are going to get messed up. The kids of today need to dig deep so they get the truth."

Rarely do authors or publishers respond. A couple times, my students elected to write additions or notes of caution for those books and asked the librarian to put them with the biased books.

Role-Play Trial

As a culminating activity, the class holds a trial of Columbus (see pp. 87-93) which I have adapted for my 5th graders (see p. 94). The students examine evidence, learn about trial procedures, practice making arguments and counterarguments, write speeches, and ultimately hold a lively trial in which Columbus, his men, the King and Queen of Spain, and the Taínos are all charged with contributing to the violence against the Taínos.

Other Activities

A host of other activities on this subject are possible. Children might develop questions and interview people in their families and community. They could also ask "What do you think about Christopher Columbus?" and "When, where, and how did you learn about him?" The responses could then be charted and discussed in class or small groups.

Host a debate in your classroom over the question of whether Columbus Day, the federal holiday, should be abolished, changed to commemorate Native Americans or revised in some other way.

As children gain a new understanding of Columbus and the damaging effects of stereotypes, they often want to do something about it. I encourage them to make their own stories, poems, dramas, murals, videos, or drawings about Columbus and Native peoples. Using Paul Fleischman's "Honeybees" dialogue poem (p. 55 in *Rethinking Our Classrooms, Vol. 1*, Rethinking Schools, 2007) as a model, I often have children work in pairs and write a dialogue poem between Columbus and a Taíno.

One year my students created a drama for a school program on Columbus Day that had a space invader "discover" the entire planet earth and claim it for his own. First I gave the children a cartoon drawing of Columbus' landfall with Taíno people looking on. I asked them to write what both groups might have been thinking. I asked them to write a skit either about the interaction between Columbus

Osceola, Seminole leader, led a successful resistance of Native Americans and escaped African slaves against U.S. troops.

and the Taínos, or about why some Native people don't like to celebrate Columbus Day.

As a class we combined the ideas from the small groups and came up with a play that had some children explaining to their classmates why they weren't going to celebrate the holiday. They used the space invader analogy as a way to explain the issue to the audience. It ended with the aliens taking slaves back to their own galaxy and "settling" our planet.

Important Reminders

In discussing such issues, two points are especially important. First, both the Native Americans and Africans fought valiantly, sometimes successfully, for their own freedom. One of the most moving examples in U.S. history involves the Seminole Wars in Florida in the early to mid-1800s, in which Seminole Indians united with runaway and free African Americans to fight the U.S. army. Each year in my reading group we read the children's story called *Night Bird* by Kathleen V. Kudlinski (Scholastic, 1993), and I tell them the story of Osceola, the Seminole leader during the second Seminole War, whose African wife was kidnapped by slave traders. Henrietta Buckmaster's book, *The Seminole Wars*, is another good source of information. Written at a 5th-grade reading level, selections of the book can be read to a whole class or by children in groups. The story of cooperation between Native American and Africans who freed themselves lends itself to provocative role plays and discussions about the need for multiracial unity, then and today.

Second, not all Europeans supported the barbarous acts against people of color. Even in Columbus's era, there were forceful critics of the mistreatment of Native peoples, such as Bartolomé de las Casas and Antonio de Montesinos (see p. 103). And while the Founding Fathers of the United States were writing a constitution that made slavery legal, Thomas Paine eloquently wrote against such a view.

It is also important to link the myths surrounding Columbus to other myths of U.S. history. In particular, it is essential to expose the truth about the colonization of the Americas—its effect on the Native populations and how it led to the enslavement of millions of people from Africa. By critically evaluating U.S. history as presented in most social studies books, we can help children learn to think critically and independently.

Not Just History

Children must understand that when we discuss Native Americans, it is not only history. Native peoples have survived despite the European conquest, and live and work in all strata of society. They continue their cultural traditions, and still seek the justice they have been long denied.

By using various books, maps, and pictures, teachers can help children understand that there are hundreds of different nations of Native peoples living today in the Americas who speak different languages and have different cultures. One way of doing this is to refer to a particular people or nation by name (e.g., Cherokee, Hopi, or Yakama.)

It is essential to introduce political concepts such as the importance of treaty rights. Children should learn that tribes are independent governments with a special relationship to the federal government. They should learn of the hundreds of treaties that the U.S. government signed with Native peoples and then broke. They should be familiar with Native struggles to save their land and protect their resources. They should learn of indigenous views toward the environment and respect for Mother Earth.

For example, in 1855, Northwest Indians were acknowledged to have rights to fish "as long as the sun would shine," and yet in recent years they have had to struggle to protect their fishing rights. As part of the 4th-grade social studies curriculum, students could examine how Native peoples were pushed out of their state, investigating what treaties were signed and if they've been broken.

To deal with contemporary issues, children may want to write some of the organizations listed in Resources (beginning on p. 182) or invite local Native Americans to speak at school.

While information on political struggles is hard to come by, there is a growing body of Native American folk tales and poetry for young children. One of the best collections, which also suggests dozens of related activities for the elementary school curriculum, is *Keepers of the Earth, Native American Stories and Environmental Activities for Children*, by Michael J. Caduto and Joseph Bruchac.

As teachers build an anti-stereotype curriculum, it is important to include parents. The curriculum can be an important way to help educate parents, and to encourage parental involvement in the classroom. Parents, in turn, often have important perspectives to offer and can suggest how to carry an anti-stereotype approach into the home.

Teachers should prepare parents for alternative views of Columbus Day and Thanksgiving. Teachers should also use Halloween as a way to educate around stereotypes, explaining to parents why dressing up like an "Indian" perpetuates stereotypes and is insulting to Native people.

The best way to approach the Columbus issue is to use it as a catalyst for change. Perhaps it will help us reexamine approaches to teaching not only about Native Americans and Columbus, but about other oppressed and "silenced" people as well.

And as children awaken to the true and rich history of the Americas, we can help them become more inquisitive and responsible for their future in the Americas.

Bob Peterson (repmilw@aol.com) teaches elementary school in Milwaukee, Wisconsin, and is an editor of Rethinking Schools.

1492

A Song
by Nancy Schimmel (Sisters' Choice)

In fourteen hundred and ninety two
Columbus sailed the ocean blue.
It was a courageous thing to do,
But someone was already here.

Chorus:
The Inuit and Cherokee,
the Aztec and Menominee,
Onondaga and the Cree (clap, clap)
Columbus sailed across the sea,
But someone was already here.

Columbus knew the world was round,
So he looked for the East
      while westward bound,
But he didn't find
      what he thought he found,
And someone was already here.
Chorus

It isn't like it was empty space,
Caribs met him face to face.
Could anyone discover the place,
When someone was already here?
Chorus

So tell me who discovered what?
He thought he was in a different spot.
Columbus was lost,
      the Caribs were not.
They were already here.
Chorus

Recorded by Sally Rogers on the CD, Rainbow Sign *(Rounder, 1992).*

The Untold Story

BY TINA THOMAS

The following story can be used by teachers as a model of student writing and/or as a text that can be assembled and illustrated by young children. The story is printed in large type so teachers can cut out sentence strips, place them on the bottom of a page, and duplicate copies for students to illustrate and read together. The author, Tina Thomas, of Cherokee and African-American heritage, wrote this as an imaginative writing project while a student at Jefferson High School in Portland Oregon.

Once upon a time a group of people lived on an island, Hayti (now called Hispaniola), in the Caribbean. These people, whom I consider my people, were proud of their island. They built beautiful farms and villages from dirt and rock. They respected the plants and animals. Many people lived on Hayti. They called themselves Taínos.

One day, some of my people saw three boats far off in the ocean. They gathered around and watched as the boats came closer and closer. When the boats reached land, strange-looking people got off.

These people were not like us. Their skin was pink, their hair the color of sand, and their eyes the color of the open sea. They wore strange items that covered their bodies, even though it was very hot.

Their leader was a man called "Christopher Columbus." He immediately put a cross and flag down and acted as if the land were now his. This was odd. We did not believe anyone could own the land. Besides, we were already living there.

Through motions and gestures, it became clear Columbus wanted gold. He wanted us to find it for him.

We tried to explain there was little gold on our land, just a few small pieces gathered from the water. "We have no gold. There is no gold here," a man said in the Taíno language.

Columbus appeared very angry and walked away. My people were afraid of his anger. They wondered what he planned to do next.

After several months, Columbus returned to our island for a second visit. He brought hundreds of people on 17 boats. Before he left this time, he captured many of my people; over 500 were forced onto his boats. We later heard they had been taken to Spain to be sold as slaves. Many died on this voyage to Spain. Their bodies were thrown into the ocean.

During this second visit, Columbus again told my people to bring him gold. "If you do not," he warned, "we shall slay your people."

Our people had to bring him gold, even though it was very difficult to find. Columbus made us wear buttons to show we had brought him gold. If we didn't have our buttons, my people's hands were cut off and they bled to death.

My people formed an army. But we did not have the guns, swords and vicious dogs used by Columbus and his crew. We were defeated.

My people ran for their lives into the mountains. Those who were caught were hung or burned to death. Many others killed themselves. Two years had passed and over half of the Taíno people of Hayti were dead.

My people's peaceful and proud land was taken over and destroyed. These newcomers cut down all the forests. They let their pigs and cows eat all the grass. Thousands of my people's lives were destroyed for these people's pleasure.

Before long, the conquerors killed almost all the Taínos. Other native peoples in the Americas were also attacked, some with weapons, some with terrible new diseases. But not all were destroyed. My people have survived.

We have little to show our children as proof of what happened to the Taínos. But we have our stories, told from generation to generation. The stories tell of the cruel genocide of my people, hundreds of years ago:

"Once upon a time, in an untold story..."

THE SACRED BUFFALO

Sharon White

BY ROSALIE LITTLE THUNDER

In the winter of 1996-97, 1100 buffalo of the Yellowstone National Park herd were shot as they migrated out of the park. Ranchers feared a disease, brucellosis, might be passed to their cattle — although expert veterinarians noted that in the last 80 years, Yellowstone bison have never transmitted it to cattle. Nor had bison in nearby Grand Teton National Park, where cattle and bison have grazed side by side for 40 years.

Native peoples were concerned because they view bison as sacred — and because of memories related to the historical slaughter of bison. Last century, U.S. General Phil Sheridan knew that the survival of buffalo was essential to the survival of the Plains Indian tribes. In a strategic move to bring the tribes to their knees, he launched a campaign to wipe out the bison herds. When it was over, 60 million buffalo lay dead.

To protect today's Yellowstone herd, native peoples and wildlife preservationists staged a public protest. In a letter, Lakota elder Rosalie Little Thunder explained why she was willing to be arrested.

Why I Got Arrested

I will share with you my own beliefs about the buffalo.

You must know that Native American people hold buffalo sacred and for good reason. They were the center of our existence; we depended upon them in extremely harsh conditions for survival.

Buffalo provided every essential, from shelter to clothing and food. Nothing was wasted. The tongue and the calcium of bone marrow provided the nutrition for the elders to maintain their strength. Liver was reserved for pregnant mothers. Sharpened bones served as knives and awls. The porous hump bones were used for painting, making a record of our history. Bladders were water containers.

Even the dewclaws and hooves were used for artistic decoration. Art is all about honoring the beauty of the natural world, in spite of all the hardships. What little remained was not cast aside as "trash," but buried, returned to the Earth in prayer and gratitude for Creator's gifts.

The buffalo's greatest teaching was to show us how to live in balance with nature. Because we depended so much upon them for survival, we followed them in their migration path, never staying in one place long enough to destroy. The buffalo has great lessons on contributing to the health of the ecosystem — turning up the earth with its sharp hooves, fertilizing it, carrying seeds — and in its interdependencies with other species.

The buffalo, through its instinctive wisdom, had a sophisticated social system that we adopted. There were no "single parents" — grandmothers, grandfathers, aunts, uncles, mothers, second mothers, fathers, sisters, brothers, all actively contributed to the well-being of the young. We call this "Tiospaye." It takes a village to raise a child. It takes a herd to raise a good buffalo calf.

And because the buffalo played such a significant role in survival, is it no wonder that they are held in such spiritual reverence?

The pipe and its moral teachings were brought to us by the White Buffalo Calf Woman. Most religions have a parallel figure who brought moral teachings to the people. The Christians have Moses. Capitalists have Santa Claus. And we believe in the White Buffalo Calf Woman just as deeply as Christians (many of my relatives) believe in Jesus Christ.

In our own dependence upon the buffalo for sustenance, the killing was with proper ceremony, asking for forgiveness of the Creator and asking for the buffalo's surrender. There is also prayer for the release of the spirit, that it may live again. These rituals provided the necessary checks and balances against reckless and unnecessary killing.

I will further share some oral family history that contributed to my feelings. In 1855, the Little Thunder band, including the Hollow Horn Bear, the Iron Shell, and the Spotted Tail families were camped near the North Platte River, within treaty territory. General Harney and his troops approached the camp. Chief Little Thunder met him with a white flag, as they were instructed to do during the 1851 Ft. Laramie Treaty talks, in which he participated.

A grandmother stood watching with her ten-year-old grandson at her side. She sensed danger and instructed her grandson to hide in a burrow near her feet. She tossed her shawl over him to hide him. The army offered *aguyapi suta* (hard tack) and *wasin ska* (salt pork).

Then the firing started. The grandmother, shot,

For sport and to eliminate the herds, visitors shot buffalo from trains.

threw her body over the hole and her blood dripped through her shawl onto him. He did not move until there were no sounds and it was dark. He traveled from the death scene, north to the Black Hills, two hundred miles away.

Prayer Day

My own ten-year-old grandson stood by my side as we watched the butchering of more buffalo on the Royal Teton Ranch, their only crime for the death sentence was to be hungry and in search of food.

We had organized the National Prayer Day for the Buffalo to at least, in the aftermath of the slaughter, pray for the release of their spirits and seek Creator's help to prevent more deaths of our relatives. We even prayed for those responsible for the killing. The announcement and call for prayers went worldwide. Local people, park rangers, media, and native people from hundreds of miles away prayed together that day.

Let me ask you this: What do you hold as sacred? I feel so inadequate in explaining those feelings. But think of sacredness and loss.

I also remember my ten-year-old grandson's tiny voice, "Grandma, how old do you have to be to get arrested?" and my overwhelming sense of fear for him. (Call it "historical deja vu.") He was, in the innocence of his youth, willing to stand his ground.

Yes, I stood on bloody ground that day. And yes,

A Cold Wind Blew...

"A cold wind blew across the prairie when the last buffalo fell ... a death wind ... for my people." Those words are attributed to Sitting Bull. It is not easy to grasp the deep reverence that Lakota people had for the buffalo. Our creation story says we are the Buffalo Nation and, as that, we dwelled within the earth. We emerged (at Wind Cave in the Black Hills) and began our frail lives as two-legged beings. Those that remained as buffalo nourished and sustained us. We did not kill the buffalo carelessly, but only in times of need, with proper spiritual ceremonies. Forgiveness was sought from the Great Spirit and surrender from the Buffalo Spirit.

— *Rosalie Little Thunder,*
Lakota elder

The Plains Indian style of hunting buffalo to sustain their people.

I did not back down. I was arrested for trespassing. In the court of law, under oath, I told no lies and I have no regrets for my actions. It seems to me that all the religious rights of every faith in this country were gained only through refusal to remain oppressed, yes?

My involvement did not end that day. Just as I am a survivor of massacre, so too are the Yellowstone buffalo survivors of massacres. Just as I could not retreat from the horrendous injustice inflicted upon our relatives, the buffalo... we cannot retreat from the persecution of the buffalo until the threat of death is lifted.

Rosalie Little Thunder is a Lakota elder. For more information on the threats to the Yellowstone buffalo herd, see www. buffalofieldcampaign.org.

Additional background:

Culleton, Beatrice. Spirit of the White Bison. *Book Publishing Co., 1989. Grades 4 and up. The story of the deliberate destruction of the bison.*

Testa, Matthew. The Buffalo War. *Produced by Buffalo Jump Pictures. 2001. 57 min. Grades 7 and up. (Available from www.oyate.org.) The story of how the U.S. government waged war on Plains Indian peoples by wiping out the buffalo herds.*

The results of another style of hunting — note the enormous pile of buffalo bones stacked behind these travelers.

ONCE UPON A GENOCIDE
Columbus in Children's Literature

BY BILL BIGELOW

Children's biographies of Christopher Columbus function as primers on racism and colonialism. They teach youngsters to accept the right of white people to rule over people of color, of powerful nations to dominate weaker nations. And because the Columbus myth is so pervasive — Columbus's "discovery" is probably the only historical episode with which all my students are familiar — it inhibits children from developing democratic, multicultural, and anti-racist attitudes.

Almost without exception, children's biographies of Columbus depict the journey to the New World as a "great adventure" led by "probably the greatest sailor of his time." It's a story of courage and superhuman tenacity. Columbus is brave, smart and determined.

But behind this romanticized portrayal is a gruesome reality. For Columbus, land was real estate and it didn't matter that other people were already living there; if he "discovered" it, he took it. If he needed guides or translators, he kidnapped them. If his men wanted women, he captured sex slaves. If the indigenous people resisted, he countered with vicious attack dogs, hangings, and mutilations.

On his second voyage, desperate to show his royal patrons a return on their investment, Columbus rounded up some 1,500 Taíno Indians on the island of Hispaniola and chose 500 as slaves to be sold in Spain. Slavery did not show a profit as almost all the slaves died en route to Spain or soon after their arrival. Nonetheless, he wrote, "Let us in the name of the Holy Trinity go on sending all the slaves that can be sold."

Columbus decided to concentrate on the search for gold. He ordered every

Columbus kneels in pious glory in de Kay's **Meet Christopher Columbus.**

Victor Mays/Random House

Columbus "calm and alone," in **Columbus** *by the D'Aulaires.*

Indian 14 years and older to deliver a regular quota of gold. Those who failed had their hands chopped off. In two years of the Columbus regime, perhaps a quarter of a million people died.

This article follows Columbus as he sails through eight children's biographies [see box next page], comparing the books with the historical record, then analyzing how these accounts may influence young readers.

Portrait of Columbus

Why did Columbus want to sail west to get to the Indies? The answer offered to children in today's books hasn't changed much since I was in 4th grade. I remember my teacher, Mrs. O'Neill, asking our class this question. As usual, I didn't have a clue, but up went Jimmy Martin's hand. "Why do men want to go to the moon?" he said triumphantly. Mrs. O'Neill was delighted and told us all how smart Jimmy was because he answered a question with a question. In other words: just because — because he was curious, because he loved adventure, because he wanted to prove he could do it — just because. And for years I accepted this explanation (and envied Jimmy Martin).

In reality, Columbus wanted to become rich.

It was no easy task convincing Queen Isabella and King Ferdinand to finance this highly questionable journey to the Indies, partly because his terms were outrageous. Columbus demanded 10% of all the wealth returned to Europe along the new trade route to Asia (where Columbus thought he was headed) — that's 10% of the riches brought back by everyone, not just by himself. And he wanted this guaranteed forever, for him, for his children, for their children, in perpetuity. He demanded that he be granted the titles, "Viceroy" and "Admiral of the Ocean Sea." He was to be governor of all new territories found; the "Admiral" title was hereditary and would give him a share in proceeds from naval booty.

As for Queen Isabella and King Ferdinand, curiosity, adventure, and "exploration" were the last things on their minds. They wanted the tremendous profits that could be secured by finding a western passage to the Indies.

The books acknowledge — and even endorse — Columbus's demands and readily admit that securing "gold and spices" was an objective of the Enterprise. "Of course [Columbus] wanted a lot! What was wrong with that?" James de Kay's *Meet Christopher Columbus* tells 2nd graders. But this quest for wealth is downplayed in favor of adventure. "Exploration" meant going to "strange cities" where "many wonderful things" could be seen [de Kay]. Travel was exciting: Columbus "felt the heady call of the open sea. 'I love the taste of salt spray in my face,' he told a friend, 'and the feel of a deck rising and falling under my feet...'" [Monchieri]

According to these eight biographies, the major reason Columbus wants to sail west is because of his deep faith in God. Columbus thought "that the Lord had chosen him to sail west across the sea to find the riches of the East for himself and to carry the Christian faith to the heathens. His name was Christopher. Had not the Lord chosen his name-sake, Saint Christopher, to carry the Christ Child across the dark water of a river?" [D'Aulaire]

Religion, curiosity, adventure — all those motives are given preference in the Columbus biographies. But each of these motives pales before the Spanish empire's quest for wealth and power. In burying these more fundamental material forces, the Columbus books encourage students to misunderstand the roots of today's foreign policy exploits. Thus students are more likely to accept platitudes — "We're involved in the Middle East for freedom and democracy" — than to look for less altruistic explanations.

The Kind and Noble Columbus

None of the biographies I evaluated — all still on the shelves of school and public libraries and widely available — disputes the ugly facts about

Columbus and the Spanish conquest of the Caribbean. Yet the sad irony is that all encourage children to root for Columbus. "It was lucky that Christopher Columbus was born where he was or he might never have gone to sea." [Fritz] "There once was a boy who loved the salty sea." [D'Aulaire] Some of the books, particularly those for younger readers, refer to Columbus affectionately, using his first name. Unlike the people he will later exterminate, Columbus is treated as a real human being, one with thoughts and feelings. "When Christopher Columbus was a child, he always wanted to be like Saint Christopher. He wanted to sail to faraway places and spread the word of Christianity." [Osborne]

The series title of Robert Young's *Christopher Columbus and His Voyage to the New World* sums up the stance of most biographies: "Let's Celebrate."

The books cheer Columbus on towards the Indies. Each step on the road to "discovery" is told from his point of view. When Columbus is delayed, this is the "most unhappy part of his great adventure." [de Kay] Every successful step is rewarded with exclamation marks: "Yes, [the Queen] would help Columbus!" [Osborne] "After all these years, Columbus would get his ships!" [de Kay]

Columbus's devout Christianity is a theme in all the books — and is never questioned. The most insistent of these, and the worst of the lot in almost every respect, is Sean J. Dolan's *Christopher Columbus: The Intrepid Mariner*. By the second page in Dolan's reverent volume we're reading about Columbus's attachment to his leather-bound Bible. Dolan is constantly dipping us into the Admiral's thoughts. Usually these meditations run deep and pious: "[He] believed that the awe-inspiring beauty that surrounded him could only be the handiwork of the one true God, and he felt secure in his Lord and Savior's protection. If only my crewmen shared my belief, Columbus thought." And this is only on the third page — Dolan's narrative goes on like this for 114 more. The reader is practically strangled by Columbus's halo.

Jean Fritz's *Where Do You Think You're Going, Christopher Columbus?* is the only book somewhat skeptical about religion as a motive. Fritz tells her readers that Queen Isabella "was such an enthusiastic Christian that she insisted everyone in Spain be a Christian too.... Indeed, she was so religious that if she even found Christians who were not sincere Christians, she had them burned at the stake. (Choir boys sang during the burning so Isabella wouldn't have to hear the screams.)"

This is pretty strong stuff, but the implied critique would likely be lost on the book's targeted readers, upper elementary students.

The close association between God and Columbus in all the books, with the possible exception of Jean Fritz's, discourages children from criticizing Columbus. "Columbus marveled at how God had arranged everything for the best," the D'Aulaires write. Well, if God arranged everything, who are we, the insignificant readers, to question?

No book even hints that the Indians believed in their own God or gods who also watched over and cared about them. The Columbus expedition may be the first encounter between two peoples — Us and Them — where children will learn that "God is on our side."

Books Reviewed in this Article:

Christopher Columbus and His Voyage to the New World
(Let's Celebrate Series)
By Robert Young
Silver Press, 32 pp. (2nd grade)

Meet Christopher Columbus
By James T. de Kay
Random House, 72 pp. (2nd grade)

Christopher Columbus
(Great Tales Series)
By Jan Gleiter and Kathleen Thompson
Ideals, 32 pp. (3rd grade)

Columbus
By Ingri and Edgar Parin D'Aulaire
Doubleday, 59 pp. (5th grade)

Where do you think you're going, Christopher Columbus?
By Jean Fritz
G.P. Putnam's Sons, 80 pp. (Upper elementary)

Christopher Columbus
By Lino Monchieri (trans. by Mary Lee Grisanti)
Silver Burdett, 62 pp. (Upper elementary)

Christopher Columbus:
Admiral of the Ocean Sea
By Mary Pope Osborne
Dell, 90 pp. (Upper elementary/middle school)

Christopher Columbus:
The Intrepid Mariner
(Great Lives Series)
By Sean J. Dolan
Fawcett Columbine, 117 pp. (Middle school)

Evils? Blame the Workers

Columbus's journey across the Atlantic was not easy, according to most of the books, because his crew was such a wretched bunch. The sailors are stupid, superstitious, cowardly, and sometimes scheming. Columbus, on the other hand, is brave, wise and godly. These characterizations, repeated frequently in many of the books, protect the Columbus myth; anything bad that happens, like murder and slavery, can always be blamed on the men. Columbus, the leader, is pure of heart.

Taken together, the books' portrayals serve as a kind of anti-working class pro-boss polemic. "Soon [Columbus] rose above his shipmates, for he was clever and capable and could make others carry out his orders."[D'Aulaire] Evidently, ordinary seamen are not "clever and capable," and thus are good merely for carrying out the instructions of others. "Soon [Columbus] forgot that he was only the son of a humble weaver," the D'Aulaires write, as if a background as a worker were a source of shame. The books encourage children to identify with Columbus's hardships, even though his men worked and slept in horrible conditions while the future Admiral slept under a canopy bed in his private cabin. The lives of those who labored for Columbus are either ignored or held in contempt.

The "Discovery"

At the core of the Columbus myth—and repeated by all eight books — is the notion that Columbus "discovered" America. Indeed, it's almost as if the same writer churned out one ever so slightly different version after another.

James T. de Kay describes the scene in *Meet Christopher Columbus*:

The sailors rowed Columbus to the shore. He stepped on the beach. He got on his knees and said a prayer of thanks.

Columbus named the island San Salvador. He said it now belonged to Ferdinand and Isabella.

He tried to talk to the people on San Salvador. But they could not understand him.

Of course he couldn't understand them, either. But de Kay attributes the inability to understand solely to the Indians. Is it these Indians' implied ignorance that justifies heavily armed men coming onto their land and claiming it in the name of a kingdom thousands of miles away? In *Christopher Columbus and His Voyage to the New World*, Robert Young doesn't even tell his young readers of the people on these islands. Young's Columbus found "lands" but no people; in illustrations we see only palm trees and empty beaches.

Why don't any of the books ask students to think about the assumptions that underpinned this land grab? Naively, I kept waiting for some book to insert just a trace of doubt: "Why do you think Columbus felt he could claim land for Spain when there were already people living there?" or "Columbus doesn't write in his journal why he felt entitled to steal other people's property. What do you think?"

This scene of Columbus's first encounter with the Indians — read in school by virtually every child — is a powerful metaphor about relations between different countries and races. It is a lesson not just about the world 500 years ago, but about the world today. Clothed, armed, Christian, white men from a more technologically "advanced" nation arrive in

Whose side do you feel you're on in this illustration from **Meet Christopher Columbus** *by de Kay?*

a land peopled by darker-skinned, naked, unarmed, non-Christians — and take over. Because no book indicates which characteristic of either group necessitates or excuses this kind of bullying, students are left alone to puzzle it out: Might makes right. Whites should rule over people who aren't white. Christians should control non-Christians. "Advanced" nations should dominate "backward" nations. Each and every answer a student might glean from the books' text and images invariably justifies colonialism and racism.

In Columbus's New World "adventures," the lives of the Indians are a kind of "muzak" — insignificant background noise. Only one book, *Where do You Think You're Going, Christopher Columbus?*, tries to imagine what the Indians might have been thinking about the arrival of the Spaniards. Still, the point here seems more to gently poke fun at Columbus and crew than to seriously consider the Indians' point of view: "...if the Spaniards were surprised to see naked natives, the natives were even more surprised to see dressed Spaniards. All that cloth over their bodies! What were they trying to hide? Tails, perhaps?" Jean Fritz's interior monologue for the Indians makes fun of the explorers but in the process trivializes the Indians' concerns.

Not a single Columbus biography ever asks children: "What might the Indians have thought about the actions of Columbus and his men?"

The silent Indians in Columbus stories have a contemporary consequence. The message is that white people in "developed" societies have consciousness and voice, but Third World people are thoughtless and voiceless objects. The books rehearse students in a way of looking at the world that begins from the assumption: they are not like us. A corollary is that we are more competent to determine the conditions of their lives: their social and economic systems, their political alliances and so on. Intervention in Vietnam, subversion of the government headed by Salvador Allende in Chile, the invasions of Grenada and Panama, the attempted overthrow by proxy of the Nicaraguan and Angolan governments: our right to decide what's best for *them* is basic to the conduct of this nation's foreign policy. As most children's first exposure to "foreign policy," the Columbus myth helps condition young people to accept the unequal distribution of power in the world.

Theft, Slavery and Murder

Columbus's genocidal policies towards the Indians were initiated during his second journey. The three books aimed at children in early elementary grades, Gleiter and Thompson's *Christopher Columbus*, de Kay's *Meet Christopher Columbus*, and Young's *Christopher Columbus and His Voyage to the New World*, all conveniently stop the story after his first journey. The Columbus myth can take root in young minds without the complications of the slavery and mass murder to come.

After his first trip, Columbus returned to a hero's welcome in Spain. He also arrived telling all kinds of lies about gold mines and spices and unlimited amounts of wealth. The admiral needed royal backing for a second trip, and had to convince his sponsors that the islands contained more than parrots and naked heathens.

During his second voyage, in February of 1495, Columbus launched the slave raids against the Taínos of Hispaniola. Four of the eight books I reviewed — the ones aimed at older children — admit that Columbus took Indians as slaves. [Monchieri, Fritz, Osborne, and Dolan.] Their critique, however, is muted. No account tells children what slavery meant for its victims. One of the books, Monchieri's *Christopher Columbus*, says that taking slaves was "a great failing of Columbus.... He saw nothing wrong with enslaving the American Indians and making them work for Spanish masters.... Missionaries protested against this policy, but they were not listened to." End of discussion.

Mary Pope Osborne in *Christopher Columbus: Admiral of the Ocean Sea*, writes that "this terrible treatment of the Indians was Columbus's real downfall." Still, Osborne is unable to offer even this minimal critique of the admiral without at the same time justifying his actions: "Since Columbus felt despair and disappointment about not finding gold in the Indies, he decided to be like the African explorers and try to sell these Indians as slaves."[Osborne] Neither book ever describes the character of slave life — or slave death.

The other two biographies offer Columbus's justifications for taking slaves: "African explorers were always sending Africans back to Spanish slave markets, Columbus told himself. Besides, the natives were all heathens. It wasn't as if he were selling Christians into slavery." [Fritz] Dolan at one point blames it all on the men: "Given the attitude of the men at large, however, [Columbus] had little choice but to give his approval to the slaving sorties."

Imagine, if you will, Nazi war crimes described in this way — nothing about the suffering of the victims, tepid criticism of the perpetrators, the horrendous crimes explained by the rationalizations of Hitler and his generals. How long would these books last in our schools?

From the beginning, locating gold was Columbus's primary objective. In one passage, not included in any of the children's books, Columbus wrote: "Gold is a wonderful thing! Whoever owns it is lord of all he wants. With gold it is even possible to open for souls the way to paradise." Two of the eight authors, Fritz and Dolan, describe Columbus's system for attempting to extract gold from the Indians. Dolan writes that Columbus instituted "a system of forced tribute: each Indian was to provide a certain amount of gold each year. Penalties for failure to comply with this rule included flogging, enslavement, or death." Nothing here about cutting people's hands off, which is what Columbus did, but still it's pretty explicit. Fritz writes simply that Indians who didn't deliver enough gold "were punished." She concludes that "between 1494 and 1496 one-third of the native population of Hispaniola was killed, sold, or scared away." The passive voice in Fritz's version — "was killed, sold, or scared away" — protects the perpetra-

tors: exactly who caused these deaths?

More significantly, these accounts fail to recognize the Indians' humanity. The books' descriptions are clinical and factual, like those of a coroner. What kind of suffering must these people have gone through? How did it feel to have their civilization completely destroyed in just a few years? What of the children who watched their parents butchered by the Spanish gold-seekers? These books show no passion or outrage — at Columbus or at the social and economic system he represented. This devastation happened to several hundred thousand human beings, maybe more. Why don't the writers of these books get angry?

I find the most "honest" books about Columbus's Enterprise — those that admit slavery and other crimes — the most distressing. They lay out the facts, describe the deaths, and then move on to the next paragraph with no look back. These books foster a callousness toward human suffering — or is it simply a callousness toward people of color? Apparently students are supposed to value bravery, cunning, and perseverance over a people's right to life and self determination.

Contempt for Native Resistance

Given that Columbus biographies scarcely consider Indians as human beings, it's not surprising that native resistance to the Spaniards' atrocities is either barely acknowledged or treated with hostility. Gleiter and Thompson's *Christopher Columbus* notes that in future trips Columbus "fought with the natives." In a sentence, Lino Monchieri writes, "The Indians became rebellious because [Columbus] compelled them to hand over their gold." At least here the author credits the Indians with what might be a legitimate cause for revolt, though offers no further details. Mary Pope Osborne buries the cause of resistance in non-explanatory, victimless prose: "But the settlers had run into trouble with the Indians, and there had been

A racist drawing in the D'Aulaires' Columbus, *still on the shelves of many libraries. They state that some of the Indians were cannibals who ate their enemies, but offer no historical evidence.*

Ingri and Edgar Parin D'Aulaire

a lot of fighting."

Some writers choose to portray Indian resistance not as self-defense, but as originating from the indigenous people's inherently violent nature. In *Meet Christopher Columbus*, "unfriendly Indians" surprise the innocent Spaniards: "Suddenly more than 50 Indians jumped out from behind the trees. They had bows and arrows. They attacked the men. The men fought back." Thus, Indian resistance to the Spaniards' invasion and land grab is not termed "freedom fighting," but instead is considered "unfriendly." The violence of the Spaniards is described as self-defense. Note that in this quote, the Spaniards are "men" and the Indians are, well, just Indians.

The books which bother to differentiate between groups of Indians single out the Caribs for special contempt. Caribs are presented as cannibals, even though no historical evidence exists to corroborate such a claim. The Caribs lived on islands "so wild and steep, it seemed as if the waterfalls came tumbling out of the clouds. The Indians who lived there were wild too. They were cannibals who ate their enemies." [D'Aulaire]

In Dolan's *Christopher Columbus: The Intrepid Mariner*, Columbus sends an armed contingent to "explore" the island that today is St. Croix. Because Caribs attack the Spaniards, Dolan considers this resistance sufficient to label the Caribs as ferocious. In fact, according to the eyewitness account of Dr. Diego Alvarez Chanca, the Indians attacked only when the Spaniards trapped them in a cove. In today's parlance, the Caribs were "radicals" and "extremists" — in other words, they tenaciously defended their land and freedom.

The books condition young people to reject the right of the oppressed to rebel. We have a right to own their land, and they should not protest—at least not violently. Those who do resist will be slapped with a pejorative descriptor—cannibal, savage, communist, militant, radical, hard-liner, extremist—and subdued. The Columbus biographies implicitly lead students to have contempt for contemporary movements for social justice. Obviously, they leave children ill-prepared to respect current Indian struggles for land and fishing rights.

Columbus's Legacy

I expected each book to end with at least some reflection on the meaning of Columbus's voyages. None did. In fact, only one book, *Meet Christopher Columbus*, even suggests that today's world has anything to do with Columbus: Thanks to the Admiral,

"Thousands of people crossed the ocean to America. This 'new world' became new countries: the United States, Canada, Mexico, Brazil, and many others."

It's much simpler for the authors to ignore both short and long term consequences of Columbus's Enterprise. Instead of linking the nature of Columbus's Spain to 20th century America, each book functions as a kind of secular Book of Genesis: In the beginning there was Columbus — he was good and so are we.

This is a grave omission. In addition to the genocide of native peoples in the Caribbean, the most immediate effect of Columbus's voyages was the initiation of the Atlantic slave trade between Africa and America (see stories p. 22 and p. 24).

Colonialism and slavery: this was the "new world" Columbus did not so much discover as help to invent. In the emerging commercial ethos of his society, human beings were commodities whose value was measured largely in monetary terms. The natural environment was likewise cherished not for its beauty but for the wealth that could be extracted.

Columbus's Enterprise and the plunder that ensued contributed mightily to the growth of the nascent mercantile capitalism of Europe. His lasting contribution was to augment a social order that confronts the world in commercial terms: How much is it worth? — that appreciates markets rather than cultures.

> The books condition young people to reject the right of the oppressed to rebel.

Asking Why?

Why are Columbus biographies characterized by such bias and omission? I doubt any writers, publishers or teachers consciously set out to poison the minds of the young. The Columbus story teaches important values, some would argue. Here was a young man who, despite tremendous adversity, maintained and finally achieved his objectives. Fear and narrow-mindedness kept others from that which he finally accomplished.

But in the Columbus biographies, these decent values intermingle seamlessly with deep biases against working class people, people of color, and Third World nations. The blindness of writers and educators to these biases is simply an indication of how pervasive they are in the broader society. The seeds of imperialism, exploitation and racism were planted with Columbus's first trans-Atlantic Enterprise — and these seeds have taken root.

Without doubt, ours is a very different world than Spanish America in the 15th and 16th centuries, but there is a lingering inheritance: the tendency for powerful groups to value profit over humanity; racial and cultural differences used to justify exploitation and inequality; vast disparities in living conditions for different social classes; economically and militarily strong nations attempting to control the fates of weaker nations. Hence, life amidst injustice in today's United States inures many of us to the injustice of 500 years earlier. Characteristics that appear to someone as natural and inevitable in the 21st century will likely appear as natural and inevitable in the descriptions of the world five centuries ago.

The Biographies' Pedagogy

The Columbus stories encourage passive reading, and never pose questions for children to think about. Did Columbus have a right to claim Indian land in the name of the Spanish crown? Were those Indians who resisted violently justified in doing so? Why does the United States commemorate a Columbus Day instead of a Genocide Day? The narratives require readers merely to listen, not to think. The text is everything, the reader nothing. Not only are young readers conditioned to accept social hierarchy — colonialism and racism — they are also rehearsed in an authoritarian mode of learning.

By implication, in this review essay I suggest the outlines of a more truthful history of Columbus and the "discovery" of America. First, the indigenous peoples of America must be accorded the status of full human beings with inalienable rights to self-determination. The tale of "discovery" needs to be told from their perspective as well as from the Europeans'. Although there is little documentation of how the Indians interpreted the Spaniards' arrival and conquest, readers could be encouraged to think about these events from the native point of view. Columbus's interior monologue should not be the only set of thoughts represented in the story.

A more accurate tale of Columbus would not simply probe his personal history but would also analyze the social and economic system he represented. And children might be asked to think about how today's world was shaped by the events of 1492. Above all, young readers must be invited to think and critique, not simply required to passively absorb others' historical interpretations.

Until we create humane and truthful materials, teachers may decide to boycott the entire Columbus canon. The problem with this approach is that the distortions and inadequacies characterizing this literature are also found in other children's books.

A better solution is to equip students to read critically these and other stories — inviting children to become detectives, investigating their biographies, novels and textbooks for bias. In fact, because the Columbus books are so bad, they make perfect classroom resources to learn how to read for social as well as for literal meaning. After students have been introduced to a critical history of Columbus, they could probe materials for accuracy. Do the books lie outright? What is omitted from the accounts that would be necessary for a more complete understanding of Columbus and his encounters with native cultures? What motives are given Columbus, and how do those compare with the actual objectives of the admiral and the Spanish monarchs? Whom does the book "root" for, and how is this accomplished? What role do illustrations play in shaping the view of Columbus? Why do the books tell the story as they do? Who in our society benefits and who is hurt from these presentations?

Teachers could assign children to write their own Columbus biographies — and some of these could be told from Indians' points of view. Or youngsters might take issues from their own lives suggested by the European invasion of America — fighting, fairness, stealing, racism — and write stories drawn from these themes.

Significantly, to invite students to

In this typical illustration, young Chris sits and dreams — a sympathetic image to young readers today. From **A Picture Book of Christopher Columbus,** *by David A. Adler (New York: Holiday House, 1992).*

John C. and Alexandra Wallner

question the injustices embedded in text material is implicitly to invite them to question the injustices embedded in the society itself. Isn't it about time we used the Columbus myth to allow students to begin discovering the truth?

Bill Bigelow (bbpdx@aol.com) teaches at Franklin High School in Portland, Oregon, and is an editor of Rethinking Schools.

Additional Reading:

Zinn, Howard. A People's History of the United States. *New York: Harper and Row, 1980.*

Sale, Kirkpatrick. The Conquest of Paradise: Christopher Columbus and the Columbian Legacy. *New York: Knopf, 1990.*

Davidson, Basil. The African Slave Trade: Precolonial History 1450-1850. *Boston: Little, Brown, 1961.*

For additional readings, see Resources, page 182.

Dear Diary...

I, Columbus: My Journal — 1492-3, edited by Peter and Connie Roop, illustrated by Peter E. Hanson (New York, Walker and Co., 1990), 57 pp.

Diaries are a seductive form of literature. "This is the real thing," we imagine as we sit down to read. A silent bargain is struck with the writer: You let me into your private thoughts and I'll try to look at the world through your eyes.

This is the danger of the Roops' book. *I, Columbus* invites children into the colonialist mind — and leaves them there. The very structure of the book encourages children to view colonial conquest from the standpoint of the white European conqueror. Youngsters buddy-up to Columbus and ride along on his "voyage to the unknown," as the Roops call it.

Clearly the book is intended to foster an admiration for Columbus. The Roops write in their acknowledgments: "Most of all we express our awe of Columbus himself, a man with a vision and the determination to accomplish it."

The Roops selected passages from Columbus's journal that portray him at his most appealing. Indeed the Roops' Columbus is more saint than conqueror. For example, on first encounter with the indigenous people of Guanahaní the Roops' Columbus is strict with his crew and kind to the Indians: "I warned my men to take nothing from the people without giving something in exchange." They neglect to include a passage from Columbus's journal that foreshadows his massive slave raids: "They [the Indians] should be good servants and of quick intelligence, since I see that they very soon say all that is said to them...."

The Roops' October 14 diary entry acknowl-edges that Columbus "captured" Indians, but fails to include a later passage from that day that places this act in a broader context. Columbus wrote: "... I caused [the Indians] to be taken in order to carry them off that they may learn our language and return. However, when Your Highnesses so command, they can all be carried off to Castile or held captive in the island itself, since with fifty men they would be all kept in subjection and forced to do whatever may be wished."

Columbus's captives resist, by attempting to escape, sometimes successfully. The Roops edit this resistance out of their book, as they also omit Columbus's further kidnappings. On November 12, Columbus describes the kidnap of "seven head of women, small and large, and three children."

As in the traditional myth, *I, Columbus* largely ignores the Taíno people. On October 29, Columbus enters Taíno homes which "were well swept and clean, and their furnishing very well arranged; all were made of very beautiful palm branches." None of this appears in the Roop version. And on December 16, Columbus says of the Taínos, "They are the best people in the world and beyond all the mildest...." Again, none of this appears in the Roop version. Columbus even refers to some Taíno leaders, like the Hispaniola *cacique* (leader), Guacanagarí, by their given names. The Roops' Indians have no names.

I, Columbus follows the same cheerleading pattern as other biographies. However, unlike other biographical accounts, the journal structure more easily excuses the Roops from prompting students to question the myth. We're only letting Columbus tell his own story, they can claim. Even more effectively than other biographies, the Roops' diary silences the perspectives of the "discovered."

GEORGE WASHINGTON
An American Hero?

George Washington had a personal interest in driving native peoples from their lands. This article can be shared with students during Washington's birthday celebrations in February to help balance the myth of him as an honest, unselfish hero.

Financial Interests in Native Lands

Before the American Revolution, George Washington fought for the British against the Indians in the "French and Indian War." As payment, he received thousands of acres of native peoples' land on the south bank of the Ohio River — land given him by the British, not by the native people who lived on the land.

He also owned shares in the Mississippi Company, a land speculation group that "held" 2.5 million acres of native land in the Ohio Valley. Native people still lived there and had never given it to the Company.

Like other large plantation owners (when he died in 1799, he held 317 black people in slavery), Washington was often in debt to British merchants. He and many others speculated in (bought and sold) native lands, as a way of making quick profits. Because much of the land in the original 13 colonies was already in large estates, people who wanted to start new farms and villages were encouraged to "settle" west of the Alleghenies. They "bought" this land from the speculators (who made handsome profits), while the native people, whose land it was, received nothing and were forced to move.

In 1763, the great leader of the Ottawa nation, Pontiac, united 18 native nations to fight this white invasion of their lands. The confederacy he formed

At age 16, George Washington became a surveyor for a wealthy Englishman, Lord Fairfax. In 1748, young Washington traveled west of the Blue Ridge Mountains and into the Shenendoah Valley to survey some of the five million acres of native land the British king had "granted" to Lord Fairfax. Washington soon learned the ways of land speculation for himself, laying claim to native lands; he later claimed the Indians were "consenting to our occupying the lands."

almost defeated the British. To stop the fighting, the British King issued the Proclamation of 1763. It agreed that no more white settlements could go west of the Allegheny mountains — and demanded that white settlements already there "remove themselves."

This action clearly threatened the financial interests of Washington and other wealthy colonists (like

Patrick Henry and Benjamin Franklin) who had bought land in the forbidden area. But the King's Proclamation didn't stop Washington. He employed a surveyor to secretly locate more valuable land for him.

Washington wrote to a friend: "Between ourselves, [the British restrictions should be viewed] as a temporary expedient to quiet the minds of the Indians.... Any person, therefore who neglects the present opportunity of hunting out good lands ... will never regain it."

With the American Revolution, the King's Proclamation was thrown out and Washington was free to profit from his illegal land deals. At his death, Washington "owned" 40,000 acres of Native American land west of the Alleghenies.

A Cruel Campaign Against the Iroquois

Most of the Six Nations of the Iroquois Confederacy sided with the British in the Revolutionary War. In retaliation, George Washington ordered a harsh military campaign launched. On May 31, 1779, Washington wrote to General Sullivan:

Joseph Brant, Iroquois (above), fought in vain to defend his nation against Washington's troops.

The great Ottawa leader, Pontiac (left).

The expedition you are appointed to command is to be directed against the hostile tribes of the Six Nations of Indians with their associates and adherents. The immediate object is their total destruction and devastation and the capture of as many persons of every age and sex as possible.

It will be essential to ruin their crops now on the ground, and prevent their planting more....

Parties should be detached to lay waste all settlements around ... that the country may not be merely overrun, but destroyed....

Washington's men obeyed. Their records of destruction report: "The force under Col. Daniel Brodhead burned 11 towns, containing about 165 houses, which for the most part were constructed of logs and framed timber.

"They destroyed more than 500 acres of cultivated land, and took loot estimated at $30,000. Many homes were large and beautifully painted, with architecture that impressed the officers."

As General Sullivan wrote in his official report: "The quantity of corn destroyed might amount to 160,000 bushels, with vast quantities of vegetables of every kind....

"We have not left a single settlement or field of corn in the country of the Five Nations, nor is there even the appearance of an Indian on this side of the Niagara."

Adapted from Unlearning "Indian" Stereotypes, *Council on Interracial Books for Children. Based in part on documents in* The Writings of George Washington, *edited by John C. Fitzpatrick, and from Charles A. Beard's* An Economic Interpretation of the Constitution.

SCALPING: FACT & FANTASY

By Philip Martin

Stereotypes are absorbed from popular literature, folklore, and misinformation. For instance, many children (and adults) incorrectly believe that fierce native warriors were universally fond of scalping early white settlers and soldiers. In fact, when it came to the bizarre practice of scalping, Europeans were the ones who encouraged and carried out much of the scalping that went on in the history of white/native relations in America.

Scalping had been known in Europe, according to accounts, as far back as ancient Greece ("the cradle of Western Civilization"). More often, though, the European manner of execution involved beheading. Enemies captured in battle — or people accused of political crimes — might have their heads chopped off by victorious warriors or civil authorities. Judicial systems hired executioners, and "Off with their heads!" became an infamous method of capital punishment.

In some places and times in European history, leaders in power offered to pay "bounties" (cash payments) to put down popular uprisings. In Ireland, for instance, the occupying English once paid bounties for the heads of their enemies brought to them. It was a way for those in power to get other people to do their dirty, bloody work for them.

Europeans brought this cruel custom of paying for killings to the American frontier. Here they were willing to pay for just the scalp, instead of the whole head. The first documented instance in the American colonies of paying bounties for native scalps is credited to Governor Kieft of New Netherlands.

By 1703, the Massachusetts Bay Colony was offering $60 for each native scalp. And in 1756, Pennsylvania Governor Morris, in his Declaration of War against the Lenni Lenape (Delaware) people, offered "130 Pieces of Eight [a type of coin], for the Scalp of Every Male Indian Enemy, above the Age of Twelve Years," and "50 Pieces of Eight for the Scalp of Every Indian Woman, produced as evidence of their being killed."

Massachusetts by that time was offering a bounty of 40 pounds (again, a unit of currency) for a male Indian scalp, and 20 pounds for scalps of females or of children under 12 years old.

The terrible thing was that it was very difficult to tell a man's scalp from a woman's, or an adult's from a child's — or that of an enemy soldier from a peaceful noncombatant. The offering of bounties led to widespread violence against any person of Indian blood, male or female, young or old.

Paying money for scalps of women and even children reflected the true intent of the campaign — to reduce native populations to extinction or to smaller numbers so the natives could not oppose European seizure of Indian lands.

Scholars disagree on whether or not scalping was known in America before the arrival of Europeans. For instance, in 1535, an early explorer, Jacques Cartier, reportedly met a party of Iroquois who showed him five scalps stretched on hoops, taken from their enemies, the Micmac. But if scalping in pre-European America occurred, it was fairly rare, certainly not an organized government practice done for money.

Regarding the philosophy of many native tribes, note the following quote, from a man, Henry Spelman, who lived among the Powhatan people and described their approach to warfare: "they might fight seven years and not kill seven men" (in Kirkpatrick Sale, *The Conquest of America*, p. 319). Many native societies did not engage in wars of any kind. Native scholar Darcy McNickle estimates that 70% of native tribes were pacifist (in Allen, *Sacred Hoop*, p. 266).

By anyone's standards, the Europeans were more skilled and deadly in the practice of war. Paying bounties for scalps was just one of many ways in which the Europeans took warfare to new levels of violence.

Popular literature and newspapers loved to describe any Indian attack in great detail in a bloodthirsty, sensational manner. Readers easily believed that Indians were all "savages" — as that is what the newspapers said. And this helped the government justify its practice of driving native families off tribal lands or killing them.

Almost every fictional account of scalping blames the Indians. The European involvement is overlooked. But it is wrong to do so. Oral history collected from native peoples differs greatly in the interpretation of who was the most cruel, why conflicts were started, or who was defending their family homes from whom.

But it is the victors who write the official history books, and it is the white viewpoint which has dominated our image of the American past.

From information in Unlearning "Indian" Stereotypes *(Council on Interracial Books for Children) and other sources. Philip Martin is a folklorist.*

By His EXCELLENCY

WILLIAM SHIRLEY, Esq;

Captain-General and Governor in Chief, in and over His Majesty's Province of the *Massachusetts-Bay*, in *New-England,* and Vice-Admiral of the same, and Major-General in His Majesty's Army.

A PROCLAMATION.

HEREAS the Indians of *Norridgewock, Arresagun a ook, Weweenock* and *St. John's* Tribes, and the Indians of the other Tribes inhabiting in the Eastern and Northern Parts of His Majesty's Territories of *New-England,* the *Penobscot* Tribe only excepted, have, contrary to their solemn Submission unto His Majesty long since made and frequently renewed, been guilty of the most perfidious, barbarous and inhuman Murders of divers of his Majesty's *English* Subjects; and have abstained from all Commerce and Correspondence with His Majesty's said Subjects for many Months past; and the said *Indians* have fully discovered an inimical, traiterious and rebellious Intention and Disposition;

I have therefore thought fit to issue this Proclamation, and to Declare the Indians of the Norridge- wock, Arresaguntacook, Weweenock and St. John's Tribes, and the Indians of the other Tribes new or late inhabiting in the Eastern and Northern Parts of His Majesty's Territories of New-England, and in Alliance and Confederacy with the above-recited Tribes, the Penobscots only excepted, to be enemies, Rebels and Traitors to his Most Sacred Majesty: And I do hereby require His Majesty's subjects of this Province to embrace all Opportunities of pursuing, captivating, killing and destroying all and any of the aforesaid Indians, the Penobscots excepted.

AND WHEREAS the General Court of this Province have voted, That a Bounty or Encouragement be granted and allowed to be paid out of the Publick-Treasury to the marching Army that shall be employed for the Defence of the Eastern and Western Frontiers from the Twenty-fifth of this Month of *June* until the Twenty-fifth of *November* next;

I have thought fit to publish the same; and I do hereby promise, That there shall be paid out of the Province-Treasury to all and any of the said Forces, over and above their Bounty upon Enlistment, their Wages and Subsistence, the Premiums or Bounties following, viz.

For every Male Indian Prisoner above the Age of Twelve Years, that shall be taken and brought to *Boston, Fifty Pounds.*

For every Male Indian Scalp, brought in as Evidence of their being killed, *Forty Pounds.*

For every Female Indian Prisoner, taken and brought in as aforesaid, and for every Male Indian Prisoner under the Age of Twelve Years, taken and brought in as aforesaid, *Twenty-five Pounds.*

For every Scalp of such Female Indian or Male Indian under Twelve Years of Age, brought as Evidence of their being killed, as aforesaid, *Twenty Pounds.*

GIVEN under my Hand at Boston, *in the Province aforesaid, this Twelfth Day of* June, 1755, *and in the Twenty-eighth Year of the Reign of our Sovereign Lord* GEORGE *the Second, by the Grace of* GOD, *of Great-Britain, France, and Ireland,* KING, *Defender of the Faith, &c.*

By His Excellency's Command,
J. WILLARD, Secr'y.

"Courtesy Pioneer Historical Society"

GOD Save the KING.

W. Shirley.

BOSTON: Printed by *John Draper,* Printer to His ' the Honourable His Majesty's COUNCIL. 1755.

British 1755 proclamation offering 40 pounds for the scalp of an adult Indian male, 20 pounds for the scalp of an Indian woman or child.

INDIAN LAND FOR SALE

GET A HOME

OF

YOUR OWN

✳

EASY PAYMENTS

PERFECT TITLE

✳

POSSESSION

WITHIN

THIRTY DAYS

FINE LANDS IN THE WEST

IRRIGATED IRRIGABLE   GRAZING   AGRICULTURAL DRY FARMING

IN 1910 THE DEPARTMENT OF THE INTERIOR SOLD UNDER SEALED BIDS ALLOTTED INDIAN LAND AS FOLLOWS:

Location.	Acres.	Average Price per Acre.	Location.	Acres.	Average Price per Acre.
Colorado	5,211.21	$7.27	Oklahoma	34,664.00	$19.14
Idaho	17,013.00	24.85	Oregon	1,020.00	15.43
Kansas	1,684.50	33.45	South Dakota	120,445.00	16.53
Montana	11,034.00	9.86	Washington	4,879.00	41.37
Nebraska	5,641.00	36.65	Wisconsin	1,069.00	17.00
North Dakota	22,610.70	9.93	Wyoming	865.00	20.64

FOR THE YEAR 1911 IT IS ESTIMATED THAT **350,000** ACRES WILL BE OFFERED FOR SALE

For information as to the character of the land write for booklet, "INDIAN LANDS FOR SALE," to the Superintendent U. S. Indian School at any one of the following places:

CALIFORNIA:
 Hoopa.
COLORADO:
 Ignacio.
IDAHO:
 Lapwai.
KANSAS:
 Horton.
 Nadeau.

MINNESOTA:
 Onigum.
MONTANA:
 Crow Agency.
NEBRASKA:
 Macy.
 Santee.
 Winnebago.

NORTH DAKOTA:
 Fort Totten.
 Fort Yates.
OKLAHOMA:
 Anadarko.
 Cantonment.
 Colony.
 Darlington.
 Muskogee, DEPT. OF UNION AGENCY.
 Pawnee.

OKLAHOMA—Con.
 Sac and Fox Agency.
 Shawnee.
 Wyandotte.
OREGON:
 Klamath Agency.
 Pendleton.
 Roseburg.
 Siletz.

SOUTH DAKOTA:
 Cheyenne Agency.
 Crow Creek.
 Greenwood.
 Lower Brule.
 Pine Ridge.
 Rosebud.
 Sisseton.

WASHINGTON:
 Fort Simcoe.
 Fort Spokane.
 Tekoa.
 Tulalip.
WISCONSIN:
 Oneida.

WALTER L. FISHER,
Secretary of the Interior.

ROBERT G. VALENTINE,
Commissioner of Indian Affairs.

"Perfect Title?" By warfare, treaties, and deceit, the U.S. government acquired and re-sold Native lands, in return for promises made to Native peoples — many of which were quickly broken.

A BARBIE-DOLL POCAHONTAS

BY CORNEL PEWEWARDY

Disney's Pocahontas has a Barbie-doll figure, an exotic model's glamour, and an instant attraction to a distinctively Nordic John Smith.

Yet historians agree that Pocahontas and John Smith had no romantic contact. In short, Disney has abandoned historical accuracy in favor of creating a marketable New Age Pocahontas who can embody dreams for wholeness and harmony.

This New Age Pocahontas is in line with shifts in stereotypes about Native Americans. For half a century or more, the dominant image of Indians was that of "savages," of John Wayne leading the U.S. Cavalry against the Indians.

Today the dominant stereotype has shifted to that of the noble savage, which portrays Indians as part of a once-great but now dying culture that could talk to the trees (like Grandmother Willow) and the animals (like Meeko and Flit that protected nature). Such contradictory views of Indians, from terrifying and evil to gentle and good, stem from a Eurocentric ambivalence toward an entire race of people that they attempted to exterminate.

Pocahontas is rooted in the "Indian princess" stereotype, which is typically expressed through characters who are maidenly, demure, and deeply committed to some white man. As writer Gail Guthrie Valaskakis notes:

The dominant image of the Indian princess appeared in the 1920s. She is a shapely maiden with a name like Winona, Minnehaha, Iona — or even Hiawatha. She sits posed on a rock or in a canoe, seemingly suspended, on a mountain-rimmed, moonlit lake, wearing a tight-fitting red tunic and headband with one feather; and she has the perfect face of a white female.

Disney's Pocahontas is a 1990s version of the red-tunic lady. She combines the sexually alluring qualities of innocence and availability.

Walt Disney Company

"Pocahontas captures the excitement and adventure of this nation's origins." — Walt Disney Pictures press release.

But perhaps the most obvious manifestations of the racism in Pocahontas is in the movie's use of terms such as "savages," "heathens," "pagans," "devils," and "primitive." These terms reflect something wild and inferior, and their use implies a value judgment of white superiority. By negatively describing Native lifestyle and basing the movie on a "we-they" format, there is a subtle justification of the subjugation of Indian tribes by so-called "advanced" cultures in the name of progress.

The movie makes little reference to the European greed, deceit, racism, and genocide that were integral to the historical contacts between the Indians and Jamestown settlers.

Cornel Pewewardy, of Comanche and Kiowa heritage, is a professor at the University of Kansas in Lawrence. This is excerpted from an article on Disney's Pocahontas that appeared in Rethinking Schools, *Fall 1995.*

GOOD INTENTIONS ARE NOT ENOUGH
Recent Children's Books on the Columbus-Taíno Encounter

BY BILL BIGELOW

Books Reviewed:

Michael Dorris, **Morning Girl,**
Hyperion, 74 pp. 1992.

Jean Fritz, et al., **The World in 1492,**
Henry Holt, 168 pp., 1992.

Francine Jacobs, **The Taínos: The People Who Greeted Columbus,**
G.P. Putnam's Sons, 107 pp., 1992.

Piero Ventura, **1492: The Year of the New World,**
G.P. Putnam's Sons, 93 pp., 1992.

Jane Yolen, **Encounter,**
Harcourt, Brace, Jovanovitch, (unpaginated), 1992.

Stephano Vitale/The Trumpet Club

Asia as depicted in **The World in 1492.**

For many educators and publishers, the 1992 Columbus Quincentenary was a period of profound rethinking of long-held truths and curricular approaches to history.

A number of children's books were published in that flurry of interest. While on-balance a cause for celebration — because the books crack open new doors of inquiry — together they suggest both the possibilities and pitfalls of what is fast becoming a mass-market multiculturalism.

Many of the new books provide a broader context within which to view the European invasion of the Americas. Authors make special efforts to portray Native American societies as worthwhile and also to include discussions of other cultures heretofore ignored in the 1492 canon. For the first time, commercially-published books attempt to draw children into the world of the Taínos, the first Americans encountered by Europeans.

Unfortunately, many of these books maintain a deeply Eurocentric bias in their descriptions of non-Western societies. In describing a wider world in 1492, the books admire stratified and unjust societies, and downplay or ignore important divisions within societies. While many of the works are peppered with the heroic deeds of elites, they dismiss the creativity and struggles of the vast majority. Most of the books ignore popular resistance to injustice. And women appear mostly as bit players. Finally, because all of these books fail to link history to contemporary social problems, they never attempt to answer the most important question of a critical multicultural curriculum: How does history help us understand and improve our world today?

The World in 1492
The World in 1492 begins with promise: "Though the history of European civilization is a grand one, it's not the only one...." Nonetheless, in five essays, European values are by and large the standards

against which the achievements of non-European societies are measured. Assorted cultures earn praise by out-dueling Europe in an implicit competition. For example, the Ming Dynasty scores worthy civilization points in Katherine Paterson's contribution to the book: "In contrast to Columbus's three tiny ships with total crews of ninety men, Cheng Ho captained fleets of fifty-two ships to 317 ships, some more than four hundred feet long. Columbus's largest ship, the Santa Maria, was only 117." Likewise, under Yung Lo, the third Ming emperor, "the Chinese experienced their own age of discovery," thus keeping up with the European Joneses. One joint Korean-Mongol military enterprise "was the greatest naval flotilla the world had ever known." In this volume, cultures win respect to the extent that they manifest similarities with Europe.

Jamake Highwater suggests a hierarchy of Native American civilizations, from those which have reached their "highest glory" — complex imperial states with powerful militaries, social classes, often slavery — to those at the bottom which are "just beginning" — presumably climbing inexorably towards militarism and imperialism, just like their European brethren. The mound builders of North America are honored because "they were a very complicated group of tribal communities" who "lived under the control of unbelievably powerful chiefs." The "highest glory" societies receive page after page; the Plains Indians, lamentably "unconcerned with appointing high priests or producing temples and cities," earn exactly one paragraph. But why focus on empires? Why not focus on less hierarchical, more communal, more democratic societies? Why should inequality and domination be the hallmarks of praiseworthy civilizations?

Katherine Paterson admires the power and wealth of Kublai Khan and quotes the descriptions of a reverent Marco Polo: "In respect to number of subjects, extent of territory, and amount of revenue, he surpasses every sovereign that has heretofore been or that now is in the world; nor has any other been served with such implicit obedience by those whom he governs." Overwhelmingly, what is valued in the societies described in *The World in 1492* derives from a European paradigm of domination. To rule lots of people is good. To gain control through violence is good. To have a hierarchy is good.

A contempt for the lives of "lesser" groups — women, workers, peasants, slaves — necessarily accompanies the glorification of kings and emperors. Usually this contempt is revealed in silence: the non-wealthy, non-powerful are invisible. Sometimes they're pitied in a line here or there: "The common people of Mexico were born, they worked, and then they died. They had little opportunity for education

England is a busy, industrious place in Ventura's book, **1492: The Year of the New World.**

or advancement."

Ironically, although the writers acknowledge class stratification, they say little about its implications. It's as if they want to suggest that each culture, each nation, is just one big, happy, stratified family. In one of the most curious passages, Jean Fritz writes that Florence "managed to be a democracy ... even when they had a dictator...." And later: "[N]o matter how miserable conditions may have been for some, they shared, rich and poor, a sense of brotherhood." One would like a little evidence here.

Celebrating lifestyles of the rich and famous cuts children off from a much richer multicultural inheritance: knowledge of, and identification with, the strivings of ordinary people to lead dignified lives. Why praise the slave owners and militarists of their day when there are equally gripping stories to tell about those who struggled for a different, more just society?

1492: The Year of the New World

The structure of Piero Ventura's *1492: The Year of the New World* suggests to children that 500 years ago there was more to the world than just Spain and the Indies. Through a series of personal vignettes — seven

European, seven Native American, and one Ottoman —eleven males and four females introduce readers to different societies. While each narrative purports to offer a sympathetic account of the culture it describes, unfortunate stereotypes mar the effort.

As with *The World in 1492*, despite its multicultural veneer, Ventura's work is deeply Eurocentric. Europe is hustle and bustle, "a whirlwind of mercantile activity." Predictably, almost all the European protagonists come from families of means: Thomas's parents own an inn; Karl belongs to a rich merchant's family; Joanna is the daughter of Ferdinand and Isabella; Lucia's grandfather is one of the richest merchants in Genoa. Almost entirely ignored are the vast numbers of people not born with silver spoons in their mouths.

These chapters promote a money-makes-the-world-go-'round multiculturalism. Commerce is the world's great unifier. Portugal draws African people closer to Europe, as "this enterprising nation...began to explore the interior of Africa, with expeditions to Timbuktu and its treasures." And later: "The Portuguese have established good, advantageous relations with the powerful African realms along the immense Gulf of Guinea." Amazingly, Ventura describes Portugal's "conquering new markets" in Africa without one mention of slavery.

Despite a clever first-person narrative that hops from society to society, the book's European chapters focus not on people, but on things. Jan of Flanders

> While Europe busies itself with God's work of creating wealth, the Third World Others squabble, scalp, and plunder.

admires "the many arched bridges over the canals, the facades of the lovely, solidly-built houses with their stepped gables [and] the impressive palaces...." Martin of France "looks with a touch of envy at the grand Hotel de Cluny...." William, a shipwright, and young Thomas of England spend time discussing "how to choose the right wood [which sometimes comes from as far as Norway]..."

By contrast, non-European societies are consumed with thoughts and fears of war. Sa'adi, of the Ottoman Empire, is an "old soldier" who "can

barely remember the details of all the battles he has been in...." But he remembers well "the slaughter and sacking" of Constantinople. Young readers learn that in the Middle East, a ruler dines with "women in his harem," and cavalrymen "fight at full gallop while wielding a lance and a bow," after which they take "war captives and slaves of Christian origin." Similarly, halfway across the world, "the Maya are no longer the same people as of old. Now they love war, and the caste of noble warriors is almost more important than the priests." The Hopis, who are "by nature, a reserved, peaceful, moderate people... neither too curious nor too emotional," fear the Apaches who "love war and plunder...." (Notice the book maintains the friendly Indian/unfriendly Indian dichotomy.)

Thus, without saying so directly, the book confirms Europe's moral supremacy. While Europe busies itself with God's work of creating wealth, the Third World Others squabble, scalp, and plunder. Certainly, though perhaps unintentionally, the book promotes an ideological framework that coincides handily with contemporary justifications for U.S. global interventions: Left to themselves, the hot-blooded, lusty, quick-tempered foreigners make a mess of everything, and so require the guidance of cooler, wiser heads.

Encounter

Jane Yolen's groundbreaking *Encounter* is a well-crafted, poignant tale about the arrival of Columbus, told from the point of view of a Taíno boy in the Caribbean. David Shannon's illustrations are both beautiful and eerie.

Whereas the traditional discovery tale presents the initial encounter between Columbus and "natives" as a carefree, happy occasion, Yolen foreshadows the coming tragedy. Her young Taíno protagonist sees Columbus's men as:

Strange creatures, men but not men. We did not know them as human beings, for they hid their bodies in colors, like parrots. Their feet were hidden, also.

And many of them had hair growing like bushes on their chins. Three of them knelt before their chief and pushed sticks into the sand.

Then I was even more afraid.

Or compare Columbus as described in most children's books with Yolen's Columbus-through-Taíno eyes:

So I drew back from the feast, which is not what one should do, and I watched how the sky strangers touched our golden nose rings and our golden armbands but not the flesh of our faces or arms. I watched their chief smile. It was the serpent's smile — no lips and all teeth.

Yolen imagines these first meetings from the viewpoint of the soon-to-be-conquered. This invitation to stand the old Eurocentric, pro-colonialist story on its head represents the book's great achievement.

Despite *Encounter*'s importance, the story is seriously flawed. Ultimately, Yolen blames the Taínos for their own demise. The Taíno boy, through his dreams and observations, sees the deadly designs of the strangers. However, the adults, captivated by the trinkets offered and desiring the Spaniards' swords and mirrors, pay no attention. Two assumptions underpin Yolen's narrative. First, the Taíno community is so age-fractured that adults ignore the pleadings and insights of children. Maybe she's right. Or maybe she wrongly projects our own society's contempt for children backward in history. And second, the Taínos were so obsessed with acquiring the goodies of Western Civilization that they lost sight of their need for self-preservation. Again, Yolen may be right. Or maybe life in a society suffering from the disease of consumerism skews her historical imagination.

In any event, her narrative is hardly fair to the Taíno elders. Missing from Yolen's story is any reference to Taíno resistance to Spanish colonialism: Caonabó's attack on the 39 men Columbus left at La Navidad in January 1493, the Taíno refusal to plant crops for the Spaniards, suicide attacks on individual Spanish soldiers, guerrilla warfare carried on from

Gold makes Columbus very happy, in this illustration from Jane Yolen's **Encounter**.

mountain bases, etc. True, she's writing a children's book, which no one expects to be an encyclopedia of popular resistance. Still, Yolen could have included something, anything, to indicate that the Taínos did not passively accept their fate.

Even the closing monologue in *Encounter* drips with self-blame: "So it was *we* lost our lands to the strangers from the sky. *We* gave our souls to their gods. *We* took their speech into our mouths, forgetting our own." [emphasis added]

The tale quickly jumps to the defeated old man the Taíno narrator has become, repeating his "warning to all the children and all the people in every land." But what led to this sad conclusion? The book's ultimate cynicism derives from its erasure of resistance and its failure to adequately link past and present.

Nonetheless, with parent and teacher guidance, *Encounter* will help children critique the traditional Eurocentric tales and imagine a more complete history.

Morning Girl

Of all the children's books reviewed here, the novella by the late Michael Dorris, *Morning Girl*, most effectively re-centered attention on the people who were here first, those so thoroughly neglected in the traditional Columbus canon. Dorris chose a different focus than Yolen, locating his story just before the Spanish/Taíno encounter in the summer and early fall of 1492 on the island of Guanahaní. Star Boy and Morning Girl, brother and sister, trade narration as they describe how their sibling rivalry slowly matures into a relationship of camaraderie. Sadly, Dorris's portrayals of the children conform to stereotypical sex roles: Star Boy is a mischievous boy: he's too loud, runs when he should sit, digs holes and kicks dirt where Morning Girl has swept. Morning Girl is sweet and, well, sugar and spice and everything nice. The story is not heavy on plot, but thoughtfully probes the inner lives of children and is richly metaphorical.

Despite Dorris's commitment to explore the world of the forgotten Others, and thus to recast the act of "discovery," he has checkered success in abandoning the assumptions absorbed from life in contemporary U.S. society. In fairness to Dorris, it's worth remembering that to capture the experiences and world-view of the Taínos 500 years past is almost purely speculative, as they left no written records.

Given the limitations, the children Dorris describes seem at least somewhat plausible, their inner monologues filled with vivid images drawn from nature: "The day welcomed me, brushed my hair with its breeze, greeted me with its songs." "But Morning Girl's words were a splashing stream that found its way between my fingers, no matter how tightly I pressed them together." Much of the family life of Morning Girl, Star Boy, and their parents is also convincing. Children learn how to act from clues and examples provided by their parents, not through force or formal training. Without being sappy or sentimental, Morning Girl's parents really listen to the children. Their family is a haven of tender solidarity.

On the other hand, Dorris ignores or scorns the larger community. And it's this contrast between his paean to the nuclear family and contempt for communal values that may reveal Dorris's contemporary blinders. We're halfway through the book before hearing that Star Boy has even one friend; we never do find out about Morning Girl's friends. The siblings learn and play alone, with each other, or with Mama and Papa. Morning Girl's loneliness is so acute, her imagination reincarnates the baby sister her mother miscarried some time before; the invented girl then

becomes Morning Girl's confidant, She Listens.

Even though the real Taínos lived in villages (and some of them in huge dwellings with lots of people), Morning Girl experiences a communal gathering following a hurricane as a fearful event. She wishes she could "do whatever I wanted with no aunt's or uncle's eyes to correct me or to embarrass Mother by staring at me too hard." Star Boy acts silly in public and she sees "all around him those terrible looks, pointed at him." Such tension sets up a bonding opportunity for Star Boy and his sister, a touching act of love as Morning Girl deflects attention from him to herself, but its inclusion makes other people seem mean-spirited.

Oddly, Dorris has invented a society of enormous individual freedom, but a freedom largely cut off from the broader community. Instead, group life is filled with apprehension. It's doubly unfortunate: First, because Dorris missed an opportunity to portray lives characterized both by personal freedom *and* social responsibility; second, because he leaves readers ill-equipped to reflect on the full range of social consequences initiated by Columbus's arrival on Guanahaní. Dorris's desire to tell a simple brother/sister story is understandable, but he fails to suggest how a richer community life could nurture such a relationship. In this respect Dorris shares the common commercial multicultural ailment: failing to imagine a world fundamentally different than contemporary U.S. society.

The book's epilogue consists entirely of an ominous passage taken directly from Columbus's journal, which concludes: "They should be good servants, for I see that they say very quickly everything that is said to them.... Our Lord pleasing, at the time of my departure I will take six of them from here to Your Highnesses in order that they may learn to speak."

There it ends: Columbus's arrogance, set against the backdrop of Taíno family life, foreshadowing the Taínos' victimization. And the Taínos were victims. But as mentioned, they also left a legacy of resistance to domination. A critical multiculturalism needs to invite children to draw inspiration from historic struggles against oppression. It's part of youngsters' cultural inheritance. Knowledge of the Taíno response to Spanish colonialism could help students locate themselves as part

> Oddly, Dorris has invented a society of enormous individual freedom, but a freedom largely cut off from the broader community.

of a tradition of caring and commitment — even if they don't have a drop of Taíno blood.

The Taínos

In her nonfiction book, *The Taínos*, Francine Jacobs takes European observers at their word: "The writings of Christopher Columbus and others who accompanied and followed him to the 'New World' also provide a rich source of information...." Jacobs fails to warn readers to be suspicious of these documents, since they were all written as part of a colonial enterprise to dominate and exploit. For example, according to Jacobs, the Taínos in the Lucayan islands [the Bahamas] "timidly welcomed the visitors, convinced that these white strangers were gods dropped from Heaven." Says who? These people left nothing in writing, and when Columbus described the Taíno reactions, he'd been in the "New World" for a grand total of two days.

Nonetheless, Jacobs' book is by and large a fine and sympathetic account of the colonial brutality that transformed the "once prosperous districts" of the Taínos into "zones of famine, disease and despair." Unlike so many of the much-to-admire, nothing-to-get-upset-about traditional tales of discovery, Jacobs' narrative is pointed and passionate: "The Spanish called the native Indians 'dogs,' and they had come to regard them as little more than animals."

Jacobs punctuates her account with numerous examples of Taíno resistance: attacks on Spanish garrisons, Taínos chewing through each other's bonds to escape their captors; armies raised by caciques Guatiguana, Behechio, and Guarionex; and non-violent attempts to negotiate deals, postpone confrontations, or make alliances to disrupt the Spaniards' unity. She also mentions important instances of ecclesiastic resistance in the early 16th century from churchmen

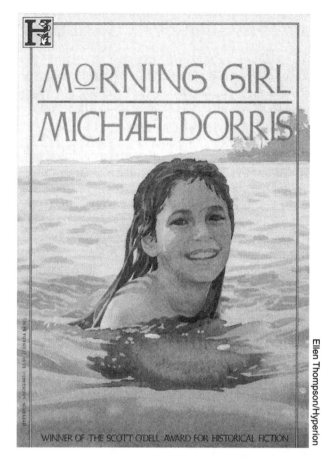

WINNER OF THE SCOTT O'DELL AWARD FOR HISTORICAL FICTION

Ellen Thompson/Hyperion

Antonio de Montesinos and Bartolomé de las Casas. Jacobs' inclusion of these episodes helps alert children that even those born to privilege can choose to side with the oppressed.

Unfortunately, she misses the most important point of telling the story. In three short concluding paragraphs, Jacobs dismisses the legacy of colonial-

Patrick Collins,
The Taínos,
G.P. Putnam's Sons

ism as ancient history and waxes romantic about contemporary Caribbean life:

Today the riches of the Indies are once again their people, a different people, generously welcoming thousands of vacationers from around the world. Tourism is one of the islands' most important industries. Visitors travel to the West Indies for vacations in the sun.

This is a wretched end to a worthwhile book. For one thing, the bulk of Jacobs' account is about the land today called Haiti. Hardly a tourist paradise, Haiti is one of the poorest countries in the hemisphere. Those Haitians lucky enough to have jobs eke out a living as agricultural laborers tending export crops like coffee or cacao for wealthy landowners. Or they might labor in hazardous conditions at starvation wages, assembling baseballs for multinational corporations. These Haitians have more urgent concerns than "generously welcoming thousands of vacationers."

There is something unsettling about a North American writer's discovery of the "Indies' riches" of today in Caribbean people welcoming and serving descendants of the original colonizing countries. Is there nothing else to tell a North American audience about modern Caribbean life?

A Critical Multiculturalism

Inadequacies aside, the literature examined here is important and suggests worthwhile routes of exploration for writers and teachers. In the space of just a couple of years, a number of books were published on the European/American encounter and the origins of the modern world, unlike any produced in previous decades. Taken together, these books urged children to stretch their historical imaginations and encouraged them to approach the world through perspectives of people long ignored.

Perhaps inevitably, this literature could not escape the hierarchical, elitist, and individualistic attitudes so embedded in today's society. The shortcomings of the new commercial multculturalism indicate some vital considerations for all concerned with developing a more accurate, critical, and inclusive curriculum. — and to succeed, these need to be understood as part of a wider movement for social change:

1. A humane pedagogy must value the lives of ordinary people. The narrowness of the traditional Eurocentrism, which invites children to imagine a world where only white European military, political, or economic leaders matter, should not be replaced by a similarly elitist multiculturalism. It makes no difference if the celebrated aristocracy is African, Asian, or Native American. A genuine multiculturalism should help children discover their connection to a broader humanity, and help them create a much more profound "we."

2. Highlighting the efforts of those individuals and groups throughout history who struggled for greater equality will encourage children's respect for equality. Conversely, books which admire history's royal thugs, "discoverers," and captains of industry encourage children to hold domination in high esteem. A multicultural curriculum should be a rainbow of resistance, reflecting the rich diversity of people from all cultures who tried to make a difference, many of whom did so at great sacrifice. Students should be allowed to learn about and feel connected to this legacy of defiance. However, we should also equip our students to evaluate the relative effectiveness of different forms of resistance.

3. While not abandoning their own ethical, critical standards, children should be encouraged to approach different cultures in the terms of those cultures. We should avoid projecting our own presumptions about "human nature," derived from our own experiences, onto other cultures, past and present. Let's allow ourselves and our students to be startled at how very differently other people live and understand the world.

4. The aim of a multicultural curriculum should be to help empower young people to make the world a better place. Thus, writers and teachers have to pose the big "why" questions. Why is there hunger and poverty? Why is there racism? Why is there sexism? What are the roots of social conflicts? That a series of "multicultural" books such as those reviewed here should concern itself with the birth of the modern world and pay no attention to these vital questions is unfortunate.

5. A critical multicultural classroom should be an activist classroom, characterized by an ethos of caring and equity. Multiculturalism demands more than passive contemplation. Children must be encouraged to act on their new understandings. To avoid a debilitating cynicism, kids need an opportunity to flex their utopian imaginations. They need the opportunity to make their dreams real.

Bill Bigelow (bbpdx@aol.com) teaches at Franklin High School in Portland, Oregon, and is an editor of Rethinking Schools. *A version of this article appeared first in* The New Advocate, *Vol. 7, No. 4, Fall 1994.*

ELEMENTARY SCHOOL ISSUES

The following teaching ideas are in addition to those in other sections of this book. We encourage you in particular to check out those contained in the article "Columbus and Native Issues in the Elementary Classroom" p. 35, and "People vs. Columbus, et al." role-play trial on p. 87.

Indian Claims Italy
New York Times Article (p. 16)

Read the news article to the children or have them read it in pairs. Ask them to imagine other cases where someone might "discover" another place or thing. In small groups, have them either write up or act out such scenarios.

My Country, 'Tis of Thy People You're Dying
Song by Buffy Sainte-Marie (p. 28)

Introduce the song to your students by telling them that it might be different than most music they listen to, but that the singer is a Native American (Cree) who has a powerful message she wants people to hear. After listening to the song, examine with your students the meaning of some of the images. Have students in pairs or groups read the song together and list how Native Americans have been mistreated throughout history. Use such lists for the basis for further research or school projects (e.g., boarding schools, use of smallpox-infested blankets, etc.). Have class discussions around questions such as: Why does she say the "Liberty Bell rang with a thud?" She mentions school textbooks twice. What does she think about them?

North American Tribal Locations
Map (p. 30)

Make copies of the map for your students. Tell them that such "boundaries" for where Native nations lived were not permanent. Have students count the number of nations listed on the map, to give them a sense of the diversity of the Native peoples in the Americas. Have students identify the names of Native nations closest to their community. Do research to find out what happened to the original inhabitants of your community.

A Friend of the Indians
Poem by Joseph Bruchac (p. 34)

Distribute copies of the poem to students. In groups of three, have them read and act out the poem using two chairs placed together. Explain what a metaphor is, and ask the students how this metaphor reflects the accuracy of the way Native Americans were removed from their lands. Have them try to come up with other metaphors that would depict this removal, and write a poem or story about that.

1492
Song by Nancy Schimmel (p. 41)

Locate a recording of the song and duplicate the words for your students. This is a fast-moving song that kids like to sing. Have them find the original locations of the Native nations mentioned in the song. Ask the students to describe the message. Ask them if it tells the whole story. Use the song as an introduction to presentations your students do to other classes about "Breaking the Columbus Myth."

The Untold Story
Story by Tina Thomas (p. 42)

Read and discuss the story together. Working in pairs or small groups, have students cut the story into strips, glue the strips on the bottom of tag board, and illustrate the story. Bind the pages into booklets.

Students might be inspired by Tina's story to write their own stories or poems about the Taíno-Spaniard encounter — from the point of view of the "discovered." See other ideas in "Talking Back to Columbus" (p. 115) for poems and imaginative story-writing from a Taíno perspective.

If students write their own books, make arrangements for volunteers to take them to read in other classrooms. Encourage them to explain how, and why, their self-made books are different from traditional tales of discovery. Laminate the books and add them to your school library collection.

Students might use Tina's story as a framework and add more detail. What do the Taínos say to each other, as Columbus's invasion begins to destroy their culture? What do they think and feel?

Bring in commercially published books on Columbus. Have students compare the perspective of their self-made books to those books. See "Helping Young Children Critique Columbus Books" (p. 38).

The Sacred Buffalo
by Rosalie Little Thunder (p. 44)

Read the article and select sections of it to share with your class. Using children's books on the buffalo, have children draw a picture list of how Plains Indians used all parts of the buffalo.

Make an overhead of the picture and caption on p. 45 and show it to the class. Have the students figure out the average number of buffalo that were killed each day between 1870 and 1883 [7,000,000 ÷ (13 yrs. x 365 days) = 1464 per day]. Have students compare this number with something they are familiar with (e.g., number of kids in your school, etc.) The caption says the buffalo were slaughtered by white men for hides and sport. Ask the children if they think that was justified. Ask them if there are things today in our society that are done for purposes of making money and sport that might have negative impacts on the natural world.

Have students investigate other endangered animals or those now extinct because of the actions of people (e.g., passenger pigeon, mountain lion, wolves, polar bear, eagle.) Have students investigate what put these animals in danger and what, if anything, can be done to help those animals.

Once Upon a Genocide
Article by Bill Bigelow (p. 47)

Students might critique books in the school library for race, sex, and class bias. They could tally all the biographies in the library by these categories. They could evaluate specific books about Native Americans, Columbus, and other "explorers." Ask them to write up their findings, maybe as a "report card" on various textbooks or library books. (See "Unlearning the Myths that Bind Us," by Linda Christensen in *Rethinking Our Classrooms*, listed in Resources, p. 182.) Their findings could be distributed to parents, other teachers, other classes, librarians, the school district's curriculum department, or the school board. They might also want to meet with local Native American organizations to share their report card with them and to find out native perspectives on their work.

George Washington
Background Article (p. 56)

Read and discuss this article with your students. As a class or in small groups, have the students compare children's books on Washington to the information presented here. Imagine that you are Iroquois. Why might the Proclamation of 1763 lead you to support the British and oppose the American revolution? Have students survey parents, neighbors, and other staff and students to see if they know about this aspect of George Washington's life.

Scalping
Background Article (p. 58)

Ask students what they know about scalping. Have them ask their parents or neighbors. Duplicate the poster and read it aloud to your class. Ask students why they think many whites portrayed the Native Americans as savages. What role does racism play in such perspectives?

Indian Land for Sale
Historical Poster (p. 60)

Who is selling the land? How did they acquire the land? How do you think Native people felt regarding this land sale? Write a critique of this poster from a Native standpoint. Design an alternative "ad" or poster replying to the land sale. Write a poem or letter to someone who is considering buying Indian land.

Pocahontas
by Cornel Pewewardy (p. 61)

Disney Films provide ample opportunity to develop students' critical, anti-stereotype skills. The depiction of Native peoples in Disney's *Peter Pan* cartoon video, for example, is so racist and stereotypical that it is fairly easy to critique. Show a short selection of Peter Pan and/or Pocahontas, and have children brainstorm about stereotypes in the movie. Ask them how they think it might make Native people feel. Ask them why they think such stereotypes are in the films, and who benefits by them. Refer to Linda Christensen's article, "Looney Tunes and Peter Pan," (p. 133).

RETHINKING THANKSGIVING

And they shall look to the earth as their mother
And they shall say, "It is she who supports us."
You said that we should always be thankful
For our earth and for each other
So it is that we are gathered here...

—Seneca Thanksgiving Prayer

THE DELIGHT SONG OF TSOAI-TALEE

BY N. SCOTT MOMADAY

I am a feather in the bright sky.

I am the blue horse that runs in the plain.

I am the fish that rolls, shining, in the water.

I am the shadow that follows a child.

I am the evening light, the lustre of meadows.

I am an eagle playing with the wind.

I am a cluster of bright beads.

I am the farthest star.

I am the cold of the dawn.

I am the roaring of the rain.

I am the glitter on the crust of the snow.

I am the long track of the moon in a lake.

I am a flame of the four colors.

I am a deer standing way in the dusk.

I am a field of sumac and the poome blanche.

I am an angle of geese upon the winter sky.

I am the hunger of a young wolf.

I am the whole dream of these things.

You see, I am alive, I am alive.

I stand in good relation to the earth.

I stand in good relation to the gods.

I stand in good relation to all that is beautiful.

I stand in good relation to the daughter of Tsen-tainte.

You see, I am alive, I am alive.

— *from* Angle of Geese and Other Poems
(Boston: D.R. Godine, 1974).

Momaday is a Kiowa and winner of a Pulitzer Prize for his novel, A House Made of Dawn *(New York: Harper & Row, 1985).*

GIVING THANKS
The Story of Indian Summer

BY JOSEPH BRUCHAC

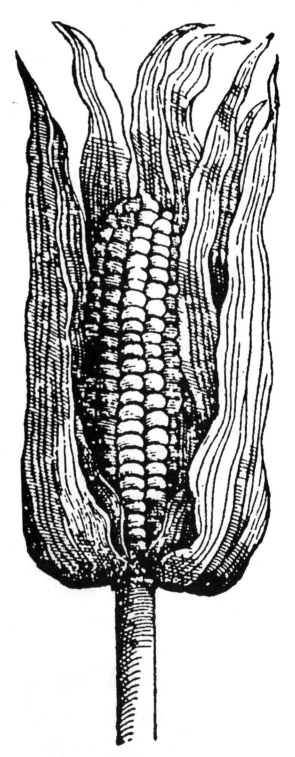

There is a man who is a very great farmer. He always has great success. He always gives thanks to the Creator and to the plants.

And he always shares whatever he grows with everyone in the village and in his family. They really rely on him. Without the food he grows, they would not survive.

But what happens is that one year, everything goes wrong. He plants his crops and a freeze comes and kills them. But he has kept more seeds, so he plants a second time. This time, hard rains wash away the seeds. A third time, the insects and birds come and eat all the plants. Then he plants a fourth time and now the sun is so hot and the rain does not fall, so the plants dry out and die.

Now it is too late to plant and he has used up all his seeds. The leaves are falling from the trees and the weather is real cold. He is afraid that he and his people will starve.

But instead of complaining, he again gives thanks to the Creator.

That night when he goes to bed, he has a dream in which he hears a beautiful voice saying to him, "You have always been thankful and so I will reward you by giving you special seeds and a special time to plant them."

When he wakes the next morning, there is a basketful of seeds by his bed. Giant seeds.

He goes outside and the sun is shining and it is as warm as summer.

When he plants those seeds, they grow up and produce a harvest within the space of a few days so that he and his people do not starve. As soon as they've harvested the crops, the cold weather comes back and again the snow begins to come. The summer is gone.

We no longer have those special seeds, but as long as we are thankful each year, the Creator will give us that special time.

In Abenaki, we have a name for that time of year, that time of warmth that comes in the fall. We call it *nibun alnoba*, which means a person's summer.

But you know it as Indian summer.

That is a thanksgiving story that explains why we have Indian summer every year.

Joseph Bruchac is an Abenaki poet, storyteller, and author of more than sixty books for adults and children.

THANKING THE BIRDS

BY JOSEPH BRUCHAC

One day 30 years ago, Swift Eagle, an Apache man, visited some friends on the Onondaga Indian Reservation in central New York. While he was out walking, he heard sounds of boys playing in the bushes.

"There's another one. Shoot it!" said one of the boys.

When he pushed through the brush to see what was happening, he found that they had been shooting small birds with a BB gun. They had already killed a chickadee, a robin, and several blackbirds. The boys looked up at him, uncertain what he was going to do or say.

There are several things that a non-Indian bird lover might have done: given a stern lecture on the evil of killing birds; threatened to tell the boys' parents on them for doing something they had been told not to do; or even spanked them. Swift Eagle, however, did something else.

"Ah," he said, "I see you have been hunting. Pick up your game and come with me."

He led the boys to a place where they could make a fire and cook the birds. He made sure they said a 'thank you' to the spirits of the birds before eating them, and as they ate he told stories. It was important, he said, to be thankful to the birds for the gifts of their songs, their feathers, and their bodies as food. The last thing he said to them they never forgot — for it was one of those boys who told me this story many years later: "You know, our Creator gave the gift of life to everything that is alive. Life is a very sacred thing. But our Creator knows that we have to eat to stay alive. That is why it is permitted to hunt to feed ourselves and our people. So I understand that you boys must have been very, very hungry to kill those little birds."

Similarities Among Native People

I have always liked that story, for it illustrates several things. Although there was a wide range of customs, lifeways and languages — in pre-Columbian times more than 400 different languages were spoken on the North American continent — many close similarities existed between virtually all of the Native American peoples. Thus ideas held by an Apache from the Southwest fitted into the lives and traditions of Onondagas in the Northeast.

One of these ideas, expressed in Swift Eagle's words to the boys, was the continent-wide belief that mankind depended on the natural world for survival, on the one hand, and had to respect it and remain in right relationship with it, on the other.

As the anecdote about Swift Eagle also shows, the children were taught the values of their cultures through example and stories. Instead of scolding or lecturing them, Swift Eagle showed the boys how to build a fire and cook the game they had shot, giving the songbirds the same respect he would have given a rabbit or deer. He told stories that pointed out the value of those birds as living beings. The ritual activity of making the fire, thanking the spirits of the birds, hearing the stories, and then eating the game they had killed taught the boys more than a hundred stern lectures would have done, and the lesson stayed with them all their lives.

Excerpted from the afterword to Keepers of the Earth, Native American Stories and Environmental Activities for Children, *by Michael J. Caduto and Joseph Bruchac (Golden, CO: Fulcrum, 1988).*

ALPHABET OF THE AMERICAS
Things That the Americas Gave to the World

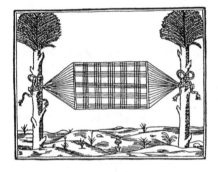

A	avocado, amaranth, asphalt
B	buffalo (bison), beaver pelts, black bears, barbeque
C	canoe, corn, caucus, chocolate, cocoa, cassava, chicle, cotton, cashews, chayotes, catfish, chilis, cayenne, cranberries
D	democracy, dyes, dog sleds
E	ecology
F	fertilizer, food preservation
G	gum, guano deposits, grits
H	hammock, hominy, hickory nuts
I	impeachment, ipecac, igloo, iguana
J	jerky, Jerusalem artichoke
K	kidney beans, kayaks
L	libraries, long pants, llamas
M	milpa, moccasins, manioc, medicines, maple syrup
N	nuts, names (half of the state names in USA)
O	Oklahoma
P	potatoes, parrots, pumpkins, peanuts, popcorn, pineapple, passenger pigeon, pear cactus, parkas, peppers, pomegranate, passion fruit, papaya, pecan, paprika, persimmons, prairies
Q	quinine, quinoa
R	rubber, raccoons
S	squash, silver, sisal, sunflowers, sweet potatoes, succotash, sorghum molasses, snowshoes
T	turkey, tapioca pudding, tomatoes, tortillas, tobacco, tar, tamales, tipi
U	USA constitution (influenced by Iroquois)
V	vanilla
W	wild rice, witch hazel, words (several thousand words in English and Spanish), white potatoes, wigwam
X	xylophone (the marimba is of both African and American origin)
Y	yams
Z	zero, zucchini

WHY I'M NOT THANKFUL FOR THANKSGIVING

BY MICHAEL DORRIS

Native Americans have more than one thing not to be thankful about on Thanksgiving. Pilgrim Day, and its antecedent feast Halloween, represent the annual twin peaks of Indian stereotyping. From early October through the end of November, "cute little Indians" abound on greeting cards, advertising posters, in costumes and school projects. Like stock characters from a vaudeville repertoire, they dutifully march out of the folk-cultural attic (and right down Madison Avenue!) ughing and wah-wah-wahing, smeared with lipstick and rouged; decked out in an assortment of "Indian suits" composed of everything from old clothes to fringed paper bags, little trick-or-treaters and school pageant extras mindlessly sport and cavort.

Considering that virtually none of the standard fare surrounding either Halloween or Thanksgiving contains an ounce of authenticity, historical accuracy, or cross-cultural perception, why is it so apparently ingrained? Is it necessary to the American psyche to perpetually exploit and debase its victims in order to justify its history? And do Native Americans have to reconcile themselves to forever putting up with such exhibitions of puerile ethnocentrism?

It's Never Uncomplicated

Being a parent is never uncomplicated. One is compelled, through one's children, to re-experience vicariously the unfolding complexities of growing up, of coping with the uncomprehended expectations of an apparently intransigent and unaffectable world, of carving a niche of personality and point of view amidst the abundance of pressures and demands which seem to explode from all directions. Most people spend a good part of their lives in search of the ephemeral ideal often termed "identity," but never is the quest more arduous and more precarious — and more crucial — than in the so-called "formative years."

One would like, of course, to spare offspring some of the pains and frustrations necessarily involved in maturation and self-realization, without depriving them of the fulfillments, discoveries, and excitements which are also part of the process. In many arenas, little or no parental control is — or should be — possible. Learning, particularly about self, is a

According to this coloring book, the only one who doesn't like Thanksgiving is the turkey.

struggle, but with security, support and love it has extraordinary and marvelously unique possibilities. As parents, our lot is often to watch and worry and cheer and commiserate, curbing throughout our impulse to intervene. The world of children interacting with children is in large part off-limits.

Passivity ends, however, with relation to those adult-manufactured and therefore wholly gratuitous problems with which our children are often confronted. We naturally rise against the greed of panderers of debilitating junk foods; we reject dangerous toys, however cleverly advertised; and we make strict laws to protect against reckless motorists. We dutifully strap our children into seatbelts, keep toxic substances out of reach, and keep a wary eye for the molesting or abusive stranger.

With so many blatant dangers to counter, perhaps it is unavoidable that some of the more subtle and insidious perils to child welfare are often permitted to pass. The deficiencies of our own attitudes and training may be allowed to shower upon our children, thus insuring their continuation, unchallenged, into yet another generation. Much of what we impart is unconscious, and we can only strive to heighten our own awareness and thereby circumvent a repetition ad infinitum of the "sins of the fathers" (and mothers).

And of course, we all make the effort to do this, to one degree or another. It is therefore especially intolerable when we observe other adults witlessly, maliciously, and occasionally innocently, burdening our children with their own unexamined mental junk. Each of us has undoubtedly amassed a whole repertoire of examples of such negative influences, ranked in hierarchy of infamy according to our own values and perspectives. Even with the inauguration of certain broad controls, Saturday morning cartoon audiences are still too often invited to witness and approve violence, cruelty, racism, sexism, ageism, and a plethora of other endemic social vices.

Attitudes pertinent to "racial" or "sex-role" identity are among the most potentially hazardous, for these can easily be internalized — particularly by the "minority" child. Such internalized attitudes profoundly affect self-concept, behavior, aspiration, and confidence. They can inhibit a child before he or she has learned to define personal talents, limits, or objectives, and tend to regularly become self-fulfilling prophesies. Young people who are informed that they are going to be under-achievers do underachieve with painful regularity.

Indian Fakelore

The progeny of each oppressed group are saddled with their own specialized set of debilitating — and to parents, infuriating — stereotypes. As the father of three Native American children, aged ten, six and three, I am particularly attuned (but not resigned) to that huge store of folk Americana presuming to have to do with "Indian lore." From the "One little, two little..." messages of nursery school, to the ersatz pageantry of boy scout/campfire girl mumbo jumbo, precious, ridiculous and irritating "Indians" are forever popping up.

Consider for a moment the underlying meanings of some of the supposedly innocuous linguistic stand-bys: "Indian givers" take back what they have sneakily bestowed in much the same way that "Indian summer" deceives the gullible flower bud. Unruly children are termed "wild Indians" and a local bank is named "Indian Head (would you open an account at a "Jew's hand," "Negro ear" or "Italian toe" branch?). Ordinary citizens rarely walk "Indian file" when about their business, yet countless athletic teams, when seeking emblems of savagery and bloodthirstiness, see fit to title themselves "warriors," "braves," "redskins," and the like.

On another level, children wearing "Indian suits," playing "cowboys and Indians" (or, in the case of organizations like the Y-Indian Guides, Y-Indian Maidens and Y-Indian Princesses, simply "Indians"), or scratching their fingers with pocket knives (the better to cement a friendship) are encouraged to shriek, ululate, speak in staccato and ungrammatical utterances (or, conversely, in sickeningly flowery metaphor) — thus presumably emulating "Indians." With depressing predictability, my children have been variously invited to "dress up and dance," portray Squanto (Pocahontas is waiting in the wings: my daughter is only three), and "tell a myth."

Not surprisingly, they have at times evidenced some unwillingness to identify, and thus cast their

Clifford dresses up like an Indian for Halloween.

Norman Bridwell/Clifford's Halloween/Scholastic

lot, with the "Indians" which bombard them on every front. My younger son has lately taken to commenting "Look at the Indians!" when he comes across Ricardo Montalban, Jeff Chandler or the improbable Joey Bishop in a vintage TV western. Society is teaching him that "Indians" exist only in an ethnographic frieze, decorative and slightly titillatingly menacing. They invariably wear feathers, never crack a smile (though an occasional leer is permissible under certain conditions), and think about little besides the good old days. Quite naturally, it does not occur to my son that he and these curious and exotic creatures are expected to present a common front — until one of his first grade classmates, garbed in the favorite costume of Halloween (ah, the permutations of burlap!) or smarting from an ecology commercial, asks him how to shoot a bow, skin a hamster, or endure a scrape without a tear. The society image is at the same time too demanding and too limiting a model.

What Does One Do?

As a parent, what does one do? All efficacy is lost if one is perceived and categorized by school officials as a hyper-sensitive crank, reacting with horror to every "I-is-for-Indian" picture book. To be effective, one must appear to be super-reasonable, drawing sympathetic teachers and vice-principals into an alliance of the enlightened to beat back the attacks of the flat-earthers. In such a pose, one may find oneself engaged in an apparently persuasive discussion with a school librarian regarding a book titled something like *Vicious Red Men of the Plains* ("Why, it's set here for 20 years and nobody ever noticed that it portrayed all Indi...uh, Native Americans, as homicidal maniacs!") while at the same time observing in silence a poster on the wall about "Contributions of the Indians" (heavy on corn and canoes, short on astronomy and medicine).

Priorities must be set. One might elect to let the infrequent coloring book page pass uncontested in favor of mounting the battlements against the visitation of a traveling Indianophile group proposing a "playlet" on "Indians of New Hampshire." These possibly well-intentioned theatricals, routinely headed by someone called "Princess Snowflake" or "Chief Bob," are among the more objectionable "learning aids" and should be avoided at all costs. It must somehow be communicated to educators that no information about native peoples is truly preferable to a reiteration of the same old stereotypes, particularly in the early grades.

"The Indians Had Never Seen Such a Feast!"

A year ago my older son brought home a program printed by his school; on the second page was an illustration of the "First Thanksgiving," with a caption which read in part: "They served pumpkins and turkeys and corn and squash. The Indians had never seen such a feast!"

On the contrary! The Pilgrims had literally never seen "such a feast," since all foods mentioned are exclusively indigenous to the Americas and had been provided, or so legend has it, by the local tribe.

Thanksgiving could be a time for appreciating Native American peoples as they were and as they are, not as either the Pilgrims or their descendant bureaucrats might wish them to be.

If there was really a Plymouth Thanksgiving dinner, with Native Americans in attendance as either guests or hosts, then the event was rare indeed. Pilgrims generally considered Indians to be devils in disguise, and treated them as such.

And if those hypothetical Indians participating in that hypothetical feast thought that all was well and were thankful in the expectation of a peaceful future, they were sadly mistaken. In the ensuing months

and years, they would die from European diseases, suffer the theft of their lands and property and the near-eradication of their religion and their language, and be driven to the brink of extinction.

Thanksgiving, like much of American history, is complex, multi-faceted, and will not bear too close a scrutiny without revealing a less than heroic aspect. Knowing the truth about Thanksgiving, both its proud and its shameful motivations and history, might well benefit contemporary children. But the glib retelling of an ethnocentric and self-serving falsehood does not do one any good.

Parents' major responsibility, of course, resides in the home. From the earliest possible age, children must be made aware that many people are wrongheaded about not only Native Americans, but about cultural pluralism in general.

Children must be encouraged to articulate any questions they might have about "other" people. And "minority" children must be given ways in which to insulate themselves from real or implied insults, epithets, slights, or stereotypes. "Survival humor" must be developed and positive models must, consciously and unconsciously, be available and obvious. Sadly, children must learn not to trust uncritically.

Protecting children from racism is every bit as important as insuring that they avoid playing with electrical sockets. Poison is poison, and ingrained oppressive cultural attitudes are at least as hard to antidote, once implanted, as are imbibed cleaning fluids.

No one gains by allowing an inequitable and discriminatory status quo to persist. It's worth being a pain in the neck about.

In preparing this essay on stereotyping and Native American children, I did not concern myself with overt or intentional racism. Native American young people, particularly in certain geographical areas, are often prey to racial epithets and slurs — and to physical abuse — just by being who they are. No amount of "consciousness-raising" will solve this problem; it must be put down with force and determination.

Author of award-winning novels for adults and for children, the late Michael Dorris was of Modoc heritage. This essay originally appeared in the Bulletin of the Council on Interracial Books for Children, *Vol. 9, No. 7. Section headings have been added.*

Anson Lowitz/Lerner

"And when it was all over, the Indians gave three cheers for the Pilgrims. Never before had they eaten such wonderful food," according to this popular children's book, **The Pilgrims' Party, A Really True Story,** *by Sadyebeth and Anson Lowitz.*

PLAGUES & PILGRIMS
The Truth about the First Thanksgiving

BY JAMES W. LOEWEN

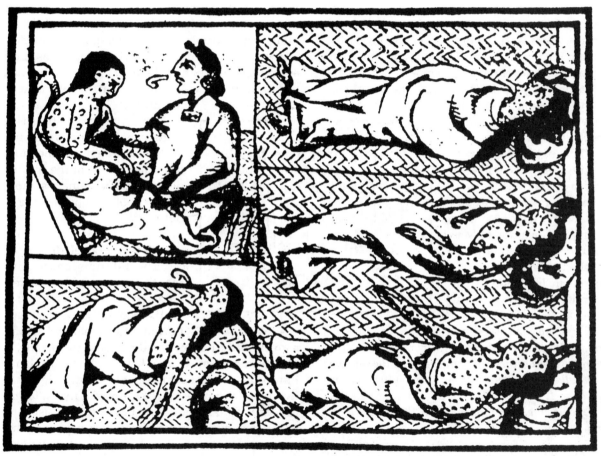

Native peoples had no immunity to smallpox.

Textbooks spin happy yarns about the Pilgrims and the "First Thanksgiving." Here is the version in one high-school history, *The American Tradition*:

After some exploring, the Pilgrims chose the land around Plymouth Harbor for their settlement. Unfortunately, they had arrived in December and were not prepared for the New England winter. However, they were aided by some friendly Indians, who gave them food and showed them how to grow corn. When warm weather came, the colonists planted, fished, hunted, and prepared themselves for the next winter. After harvesting their first crop, they and their Indian friends celebrated the first Thanksgiving.

I teach first-year college students, the products of American high schools. And when I ask my students about the plague, they stare back at me. "What plague?"

For a variety of reasons, Native Americans were "a remarkably healthy race" before Columbus. Ironically, their very health now proved their undoing, for they had built up no resistance, genetically or through childhood diseases, to the microbes Europeans and Africans now brought with them. In 1617, just before the Pilgrims landed, the process started in southern New England. Today we think it was the bubonic plague, although pox and influenza are also candidates.

British fishermen had been fishing off Massachusetts for decades before the Pilgrims landed. After filling their hulls with cod, they would set forth on land to get firewood and fresh water and perhaps capture a few Indians to sell into slavery in Europe. On one of these expeditions they probably transmitted the illness to the people they met.

Whatever it was, within three years this plague wiped out between 90 percent and 96 percent of the inhabitants of southern New England. The Indian societies lay devastated. Only "the twentieth person is scarce left alive," wrote British eyewitness Robert Cushman, describing a death rate unknown in all previous human experience. Unable to cope with so many corpses, survivors fled to the next tribe, carrying the infestation with them, so that Indians died who had never seen a white person.

During the next fifteen years, additional epidemics, most of which we know to have been smallpox, struck repeatedly.

The English Separatists, already seeing their lives as part of a divinely inspired morality play, inferred that they had God on their side. John Winthrop, Governor of Massachusetts Bay Colony, called the plague "miraculous." To a friend in England in 1634, he wrote:

But for the natives in these parts, God hath so pursued them, as for 300 miles space the greatest part of them are swept away by the smallpox which still continues among them. So as God hath thereby cleared our title to this place, those who remain in these parts, being in all not fifty, have put themselves under our protection....

God, the original real estate agent!

Many Indians likewise inferred that their God had abandoned them. Cushman reported that "those that are left, have their courage much abated, and their countenance is dejected, and they seem as a people affrighted." After all, neither they nor the Pilgrims had access to the germ theory of disease. Indian healers offered no cure, their religion no explanation. That of the whites did. Many Indians surrendered to alcohol or began to listen to Christianity.

These epidemics constituted perhaps the most important single geopolitical event of the first third of the 1600s, anywhere on the planet. They meant that the British would face no real Indian challenge for their first fifty years in America. Indeed, the plague

helped cause the legendary warm reception Plymouth [the Pilgrims] enjoyed in its first formative years from the Wampanoags. Massasoit, the Wampanoag leader, needed to ally with the Pilgrims because the plague had so weakened his villages that he feared the Narragansetts to the west.

Moreover, the New England plagues exemplify a process which antedated the Pilgrims and endures to this day. The pestilence continues, now killing Indians in the interior of the Amazon Basin in northern Brazil and southern Venezuela.

Europeans were never able to "settle" China, India, Indonesia, Japan, or most of Africa because too many people already lived there. Advantages in military and social technology would have enabled Europeans to dominate the Americas — as they eventually dominated China and Africa — but not to "settle" the New World. For that, the plague was required.

Thus, except for the European invasion itself, the pestilence was surely the most important event in the history of America. Nonetheless, most high-school textbooks leave it out.

> The antidote to feel-good history is not feel-bad history, but honest and inclusive history.

It was a Lovely Site

The Pilgrims chose Plymouth because of its cleared fields, recently planted in corn, "and a brook of fresh water [that] flowed into the harbor." It was a lovely site for a town. Indeed, until the plague, it had been a town. Everywhere in the hemisphere, Europeans pitched camp right in the middle of native populations — Cuzco, Mexico City, Natchez, Chicago. Throughout New England, colonists appropriated Indian cornfields, which explains why so many town names — Marshfield, Springfield, Deerfield — end in "field."

Inadvertent Indian assistance started on the Pilgrims' second full day in Massachusetts. A colonist's journal tells us:

We marched to the place we called Cornhill, where we had found the corn before. At another place we had seen before, we dug and found some more corn, two or three baskets full, and a bag of beans .... In all we had about ten bushels, which will be enough for seed. It was with God's help that we found this corn, for how else could we have done it, without meeting some Indians who might trouble us.... The next morning, we found a place like a grave. We decided to dig it up. We found first a mat, and under that a fine bow.... We also found bowls, trays, dishes, and things like that. We took several of the prettiest things to carry away with us, and covered the body up again.

A place "like a grave"!

Squanto

More help came from a live Indian, Squanto. What do the textbooks leave out about Squanto? First, how he learned English. As a boy, along with four Penobscots, he was probably stolen by a British captain in about 1605 and taken to England. There he probably spent nine years, two in the employ of a Plymouth merchant who later helped finance the Mayflower. At length, the merchant helped him arrange a passage back to Massachusetts.

He was to enjoy home life for less than a year, however. In 1614, a British slave raider seized him and two dozen fellow Indians and sold them into slavery in Malaga, Spain. Squanto escaped from slavery, made his way back to England, and in 1619 talked a ship captain into taking him along on his next trip to Cape Cod.

It happens that Squanto's fabulous odyssey provides a "hook" into the plague story. For now

Squanto walked to his home village, only to make the horrifying discovery that "he was the sole member of his village still alive. All the others had perished in the epidemic two years before." No wonder he throws his lot in with the Pilgrims, who rename the site of his original village, "Plymouth." Now that is a story worth telling!

Compare the pallid account in a high-school textbook, *Land of Promise*. "He had learned their language from English fishermen." What do we make of books that give us the unimportant details — Squanto's name, the occupation of his enslavers — while omitting not only his enslavement, but also the crucial fact of the plague? This is distortion on a grand scale.

Embarrassing Facts

Should we teach the truths about Thanksgiving? Or, like our textbooks, should we look the other way? Thanksgiving is full of embarrassing facts. The Pilgrims did not introduce the Native Americans to the tradition; Eastern Indians had observed autumnal harvest celebrations for centuries. Our modern

Anson Lowitz/Lerner

"The Pilgrim army drilled," a curious thing to do for guests at the 1621 Thanksgiving feast — unless the goal was to impress the visiting Wampanoag leader, Massasoit, with the Pilgrims' military power. Illustration from the book **The Pilgrims' Party, A Really True Story,** *by Sadyebeth and Anson Lowitz.*

celebrations date back only to Abraham Lincoln in 1863; not until the 1890s did the Pilgrims get included in the tradition.

Plymouth Rock itself achieved legendary status only in the 19th century, when some enterprising residents of the town moved it down to the water so its significance as the "holy soil" the Pilgrims first touched might seem more plausible.

Indians are marginalized in this civic ritual. Our archetypal image of the first Thanksgiving portrays the groaning boards in the woods, with the Pilgrims in their starched Sunday best and the almost naked Indian guests. This exemplifies what art historians call "hieratic scale," as in "hierarchy." It is silly once thought about, for depending on the weather, either the Indians were very cold or the Pilgrims were very hot. But we aren't supposed to think about it.

Thanksgiving silliness reaches some sort of zenith in the handouts that school children have carried home for decades, with captions like, "They served pumpkin and turkeys and corn and squash. The Indians had never seen such a feast!"

When his son brought home this "information" from his New Hampshire elementary school, Native American novelist Michael Dorris pointed out "the *Pilgrims* had literally never seen 'such a feast' since all foods mentioned are exclusively indigenous to the Americas and had been provided by [or with the aid of] the local tribe."

I do not suggest a "bash the Pilgrims" interpretation, emphasizing only the bad parts. I have emphasized untoward details only because our histories have suppressed everything awkward for so long. The Pilgrims' courage in setting forth in the late fall to make their way on a continent new to them remains unsurpassed. In their first year, like the Indians, they suffered from diseases. Half of them died. The Pilgrims did not cause the plague and were as baffled as to its true origin as the stricken Indian villagers.

The antidote to feel-good history is not feel-bad history, but honest and inclusive history.

Because our Thanksgiving holiday has roots in both Anglo and Native cultures, and because of the interracial cooperation the first celebration enshrines, it might yet develop into a holiday that promotes tolerance and understanding.

But to glorify the Pilgrims is dangerous. The genial omissions and false details our texts use to retail the Pilgrim legend promote Anglocentrism, which only handicaps us when dealing with all those whose culture is not Anglo.

James Loewen is the author of Lies My Teacher Told Me: Everything Your American History Textbook Got Wrong *(New Press, 1995), from which this excerpt is modified.*

The Wampanoag leader, Massasoit, had a son, Metacom, also known as King Philip, who became the leader of an alliance of several tribes worried about the spread of European settlements deeper into their lands. In 1675, war broke out between the Native peoples and the Pilgrim colonists. Within a year, the European immigrants crushed the resistance; Massasoit's heir, Metacom, was killed in battle and his wife and child captured and sold into slavery. Metacom's head was cut off and displayed on a pole in the town of Plymouth for the next 25 years.

RETHINKING THANKSGIVING

Teaching Ideas

Thanksgiving is a simple holiday: a time for joining hands and giving thanks. It is also a complicated U.S. national holiday, filled with murky myths, stereotypes, historical propaganda, and inane pageantry.

Below are some suggestions for how it could be approached in American schools. Following each general idea, specific teaching ideas are given for articles in this section on "Rethinking Thanksgiving."

Suggested Activities

A Day of Mourning

Many native peoples object to this holiday because it falsely represents American history, perpetuates stereotypes, and brings to mind, for them, the theft of land, religious oppression, grave robbing, and cultural suppression by European settlers. Some native peoples have called for this day to be renamed "Native American Day," to be used as a way to educate the public about their history.

Classroom ideas: Share with students information in this chapter and explain how some Native Americans are offended by Thanksgiving celebrations. Brainstorm with your class how they could teach others in your school the truth about Thanksgiving.

A Day of Giving Thanks

Thanksgiving can be defined broadly. In most societies for thousands of years, there have been harvest festivals in celebration. These celebrations are often intended to thank the deities that the people believed to have been responsible for their harvest — and wish to honor through activities such as speeches, ceremonies, preparation of special foods, etc.

Classroom ideas: Have students research harvest festivals in different countries and share what they find. Ask them to consider questions like: How are we related to the natural world? Where does our food come from? What family, friends, and neighbors do we have, and how can we get along better — given differences, and given similarities? Use the ideas given below for Bruchac's stories ("Indian Summer" and "Thanking the Birds").

A Day of Examination

The day could be used to critically examine Native American issues and how they are portrayed during this holiday.

Classroom ideas: Bring in Thanksgiving greeting cards and advertisements and have students look at them for stereotypes (see checklist on p. 36.) Have students look at their school bulletin boards to find stereotypes.

For older students pose these questions:

Why did Pilgrims and natives really gather in 1621? Why did they engage in warfare some years later in King Philip's War? What were the effects of the plague on Indian populations? What were native/white relations like then? Now? Why had Squanto been enslaved?

A Day of Communication

The day could be used to encourage students to listen to native voices.

Classroom ideas: Read to your class articles, stories, or poetry by native authors and activists. Bring into the classroom a Native American newspaper (see Resources, p. 182) and share it with students. Invite a local Native American in to speak about a concern that they have. Challenge students to find out what native people who live in your area are saying.

A Day *Not* to Do a Pageant About the "First" Thanksgiving

None of these suggestions involve putting on a pageant with Pilgrims and Indians. If you feel compelled to do a play, why not do one that shows the Pilgrims engaging in grave robbing, or the hostilities of King Philip's war, or Squanto's life in slavery? Unless a teacher is prepared to take students in depth into the real issues, it's probably better to do something else.

(continued on next page)

Additional Teaching Ideas

The Delight Song of Tsoai-Tselee
Poem by N. Scott Momaday (p. 72)

Ask students to write a poem about themselves, modeled after Momaday's. Begin with "I'm..." and complete the sentence. You might give them a specified number of descriptions — such as ten — that they need to list in their poem.

Giving Thanks
A Story by Joseph Bruchac (p. 73)

Read the story about the origin of the term "Indian summer." Young students could re-enact the story. Older students could write their own thanksgiving story that emphasizes respect for the earth and all living things.

Thanking the Birds
Story by Joseph Bruchac (p. 74)

Ask students to describe other positive attributes of animals and nature. Why might native people try to learn from animals? What do you do when you see animals or insects outdoors? What can we learn from them? Native leader, Chief Luther Standing Bear (p. 166) said that in Lakota, they have no word for "pest." What do you think of as "pests?" Why do you think the Lakota language has no word for "pest?"

Take your class on a walk around your school or to a nearby park. Ask children to notice all the living things they can. Talk about how we act when we see different living things.

When you read "Thanking the Birds" with your students, ask if they agree with how Swift Eagle dealt with the boys. If they had been the children in the story, how would they have responded to Swift Eagle?

Alphabet of the Americas
List of Native Contributions (p. 75)

Before passing out the list, do a mime of some of the items on the list and see if students can guess the item. Pass out the list, and read it with the students. Have students look up words that they don't know. Have students volunteer to mime other items on the list.

For homework, have students list at least ten items at home that have their origins in the Americas.

Ask questions such as: What ways did Native Americans affect European culture? How would students' lives be different without these things? Older students could be encouraged to write skits about native contributions and perform them for younger students.

Note: Charts of native contributions to the world often acknowledge foods like potatoes and chilis without emphasizing that these plants were not simply found in the Americas but that many varieties were developed by Native agriculturists. Also, in recognizing native contributions, we should not become complacent about the human costs of the exchange: "The 'exchange' is okay because 'they' gave 'us' something useful. We are okay because we are crediting them for this."

Plagues and Pilgrims: The Truth About the First Thanksgiving
by James W. Loewen (p. 79)

Have students find references to the Pilgrims and the first Thanksgiving in your school district textbooks or in library books at your school. After summarizing that point of view, read selections of "Plagues and Pilgrims" to your students. Ask: What are the differences in the versions of the events? In whose interest are each of the versions? What makes one version more believable than the other?

Older students can do additional research on Thanksgiving and write a more accurate Thanksgiving story to share with younger students.

Additional Resources

Highly recommended is a curriculum packet, "Teaching About Thanksgiving," developed for the Tacoma Public Schools, available on the website of the Fourth World Documentation Project (www. ewebtribe.com/thanksgiving/thanksgiving/ html).

With an introduction by Chuck Larsen (Seneca, Ojibwa, Métis), the packet carefully examines the interaction of the Pilgrims and the Wampanoag Indians who shared the famous thanksgiving feast of 1621. The packet includes study questions, recipes for native foods, and much more.

Also Recommended:

Keepers of Life: Discovering Plants Through Native American Stories and Earth Activities for Children, by Joseph Bruchac (Abenaki) and Michael K. Caduto. (Golden, CO: Fulcrum Publishing, 1994). Especially Chapter 4. An insightful, multi-layered look at giving thanks, rooted in traditional Seneca Thanksgiving customs. The chapter includes valuable questions and explorations for students — about giving thanks, celebrating, and living in balance with nature. Includes a round dance and other activities.

THE PEOPLE VS. COLUMBUS, et al.

A monstrous crime was committed
in the years after 1492,
when as many as three million Taínos
on the island of Hispaniola
lost their lives.

Who — or what —
was responsible
for this slaughter?

This is what we will
confront here today....

— from the role-play trial,
The People vs. Columbus, et al.

16th-century engraving of cruelties to the Taínos, by Theodore de Bry.

FOR THE SAKE OF GOLD

To fill the empty ships going back to Castile, to stop his detractors from talking, to prove his success, Columbus needed gold. And the following system was adopted for this end.

Every man and woman, every boy or girl of fourteen or older, in the province of Cibao (of the imaginary gold fields) had to collect gold for the Spaniards. As their measure, the Spaniards used those same miserable hawks' bells, the little trinkets they had given away so freely when they first came "as if from Heaven." Every three months, every Indian had to bring to one of the forts a hawk's bell filled with gold dust. The chiefs had to bring in about ten times that amount. In the other provinces of Hispaniola, twenty-five pounds of spun cotton took the place of gold.

Copper tokens were manufactured, and when an Indian had brought his or her tribute to an armed post, he or she received such a token, stamped with the month, to be hung around the neck. With that they were safe for another three months while collecting more gold.

Whoever was caught without a token was killed by having his or her hands cut off.

There were no gold fields, and thus, once the Indians had handed in whatever they still had in gold ornaments, their only hope was to work all day in the streams, washing out gold dust from the pebbles. It was an impossible task, but those Indians who tried to flee into the mountains were systematically hunted down with dogs and killed, to set an example for the others to keep trying.

From Columbus: His Enterprise, *by Hans Koning (New York: Monthly Review Press).*

THE PEOPLE VS. COLUMBUS, et al.

A Class Role Play

BY BILL BIGELOW

This role play begins with the premise that a monstrous crime was committed in the years after 1492, when perhaps as many as three million or more Taínos on the island of Hispaniola lost their lives. (Most scholars estimate the number of people on Hispaniola in 1492 at between one and three million; some estimates are lower and some much higher. By 1550, very few Taínos remained alive.)

Who — and/or what — was responsible for this slaughter? This is the question students confront here.

Materials Needed:

1. Some construction paper suitable for making name placards.
2. Colored markers.

Suggested Procedure:

1. In preparation for class, list the names of all the "defendants" on the board: Columbus, Columbus's men, King Ferdinand and Queen Isabella, the Taínos, and the System of Empire.

2. Tell students that each of these defendants is charged with murder — the murder of the Taíno Indians in the years following 1492. Tell them that, in groups, students will portray the defendants and that you, the teacher, will be the prosecutor. Explain that students' responsibility will be two-fold: a) to defend themselves against the charges, and b) to explain who they think is guilty and why.

One rule: They may plead guilty if they wish, but they cannot claim sole responsibility; they must accuse at least one other defendant. At this point, students sometimes protest that it's ridiculous to charge the Taínos for their own deaths, or they may show some confusion about the "system of empire." Tell them not to worry, that it's your job as prosecutor to explain the charges. Each group will receive a written copy of the charges against them.

3. Explain the order of the activity:

a. In their groups, they will prepare a defense against the charges contained in the indictments. It's a good idea for students to write these up, as they will be presenting these orally and may want to read a statement.

b. Before the trial begins, you will choose several students, who will be sworn to neutrality. These people will be the jury.

c. As prosecutor, you will begin by arguing the guilt of a particular group.

d. Those in the group accused by the prosecutor will then defend themselves and will state who they believe is guilty and why. [One option is to require that each group call at least one witness. For example, in one class, the group representing the King and Queen called one of the Taínos to the stand and asked, "Have you ever seen me before?" No. "Did I ever kill any of your people?" No. "Did I ever hurt any of your people?" No. "We have no further questions."]

e. The jury will then question that group, and others may also question the group and offer rebuttals.

f. This process is repeated until all the groups have been accused and have defended themselves. The jury will then decide guilt and innocence.

4. Ask students to count off into five groups of roughly equal numbers. To get things moving quickly, I like to tell students that the first group to circle up gets first pick of who they'll represent. Go around to each of the groups and distribute the appropriate "indictment" sheets. Remind students to read the indictment against them carefully and discuss

possible arguments in their defense.

As they discuss, I wander from group to group, making sure students understand their responsibilities — at times playing devil's advocate, at times helping them consider possible defenses. Also, at this point, I distribute a placard and marker to each group so that they can display which role they are portraying.

Sometimes students want to see the indictments against the other groups. I encourage them to read these because it will help students develop additional arguments. Also, students may want to use other "evidence" included throughout *Rethinking Columbus* — for example, from Columbus's diary (p. 96), the timeline (p. 99), or the Taínos (p. 106).

5. When each group appears ready — after perhaps a half hour, depending on the class — choose a jury: one member from each group (in a big class), or a total of three students in a smaller class. Publicly swear them to neutrality; they no longer represent the King and Queen, the Taínos, or anyone else.

6. The order of prosecution is up to you. I prefer: Columbus's men, Columbus, the King and Queen, the Taínos, and the System of Empire. I save the System for last as it's the most difficult to prosecute, and depends on having heard the other groups' presentations. As mentioned, the teacher argues the indictment for each group, the group defends, the jury questions, and other groups may then question. Then, the process repeats itself for each

indictment. The written indictments should be an adequate outline for prosecution, but I always feel free to embellish.

7. After each group has been charged and has made its defense, I ask the jury to step out of the classroom and deliberate. They can assign "percentage guilt," e.g., one party is 25% guilty, another 60%, etc. They also need to offer clear explanations for why they decided as they did. As they deliberate, I ask the rest of the class to step out of their roles and to do in writing the same thing the jury is doing.

8. The jury returns and explains its verdict and then we discuss. Here are some questions and issues to raise:

•Was anyone entirely not guilty? Did the prosecutor convince you that the Taínos were in part responsible for their own deaths?

•Why *didn't* the Taínos kill Columbus on his first voyage?

•How did you weigh responsibility between the "bosses" and the men they hired?

•Can you imagine a peaceful meeting between Europeans and Taínos? Or did European life — the "System of Empire" — make violence inevitable? How would Spain and other European countries have had to be different to have made a more peaceful outcome possible?

•What more would you need to know about the System of Empire to understand how it affected people's thinking and behavior?

•If the System of Empire is guilty, what should be the "sentence"? You can't put a system in prison.

Note: The time needed for this activity can vary considerably depending on the preparation and defenses mounted by students. Teachers should allocate at least two 50-minute periods for the role-play.

Theodore de Bry

Enslaved labor in the mines of Hispaniola.

The Indictment:
You are charged with the mistreatment and murder of thousands, perhaps millions, of Taíno Indians.

Your first act in the lands you "discovered" was to take possession of another people's territory in the name of an empire thousands of miles away.

From the very beginning of your time in the Indies you kidnapped Indians. Even when they attempted to escape, making it clear that they wished to leave, you refused to release them.

Your journal shows that your only wish in the Indies was to find gold. The only reason you showed any kindness to the Taínos on your first trip was so they would agree to show you the source of their gold.

On your second voyage to the Indies, you ordered your men to round up Indians and had over 500 shipped to Spain as slaves. You told your men to help themselves to the remaining Taíno captives, which they did. This act alone killed several hundred Taínos.

In 1495 you started the policy of forcing Indians, age 14 and older, to collect gold for you. Those who didn't return every three months with the amount of gold you demanded were punished by having their hands chopped off.

You ordered your men to spread "terror" among the Taínos when there was rumor

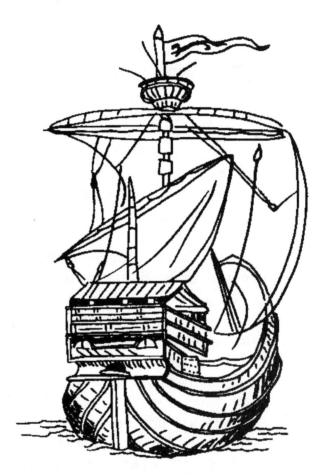

of resistance.

The list goes on. When you arrived on Hispaniola there may have been as many as a million or even three million Taínos on the island. According to one Spanish priest, by 1542 there were 200 Taínos left. There is no one to blame but you.

You were Admiral, you were Viceroy, you were Governor of the island.

—*from the role play,* The People vs. Columbus, et al.

COLUMBUS'S MEN

The Indictment:
You are charged with the mistreatment and
murder of thousands, perhaps millions, of Taíno Indians.

Without you, Columbus's orders to enslave and kill Taínos would have been empty words.

There is no evidence that Columbus personally captured slaves or killed anyone with his own hands. You are the ones responsible for the enslavement of first hundreds, then thousands, of Taíno Indians.

You did the dirty work. You raped women. You set dogs on infants. You cut the hands off Taínos who didn't deliver enough gold. You whipped Taínos if they didn't work hard enough in the mines.

Without you there were no crimes.

You may try to blame your superiors, Columbus or even King Ferdinand and Queen Isabella. But because someone orders you to commit a crime does not free you of the blame for committing it. You could have said no. There were Spaniards, like the priests Antonio de Montesinos and Bartolomé de las Casas, who refused to mistreat Indians and spoke out on their behalf. Why didn't you?

Without the soldier there is no war.

Without you there would have been no genocide.

—from the role play The People vs. Columbus, et al.

KING FERDINAND AND QUEEN ISABELLA

The Indictment:
You are charged with the mistreatment and murder of thousands, perhaps millions, of Taíno Indians.

Without your money, Columbus couldn't have launched his plan to find the East Indies by sailing west. Without you, he was an unemployed sailor.

You hired him to "discover" and claim new lands. Thus you are guilty of conspiracy to steal the territory of people you didn't even know, who had never bothered or harmed you.

When Columbus returned after his first voyage with several Indian captives, and you rewarded him, you became guilty of kidnapping. You could have ordered Columbus to stop kidnapping Indians. You could have punished him for this illegal act. By not doing anything to stop Columbus and his men, you legalized every crime they committed.

In his first letter to you, Columbus wrote that the Indians would make excellent slaves. Right away, you could have ordered him to take no slaves. You did no such thing, and thus became accomplices in all future slave taking. True, after a while you discouraged Columbus from taking slaves — they mostly died, anyway — but you never punished him for these crimes which killed hundreds of human beings.

Really, you didn't care what Columbus did, so long as you got rich. At times, you would order that the Indians should be treated humanely. But you took no action to stop the Indians from being forced to work in the mines. They were slaves in everything but name. Had you wanted the cruelty to stop, you could have ordered all your subjects home. But then you wouldn't have gotten any more gold. And that was what you wanted, right?

Because Columbus was unpopular with other Spaniards, you replaced him as governor. But you never punished him for the crimes committed against Taínos when he was governor. And these crimes continued under the next governor.

Because you were the bosses and because you paid the bills, you have more guilt than had you been the ones wielding the swords and hangmen's nooses.

— *from the role play,* The People vs. Columbus, et al.

TAÍNOS

The Indictment:
You are charged with the mistreatment and
murder of thousands, perhaps millions, of Taíno Indians.

While you are the victim of this crime, you are also guilty of committing it. You failed to fight back against the Spaniards. This meant that you brought the fate of slavery and death upon yourselves.

From the very beginning you must have known what Columbus meant to do. He took Indian captives from other islands and held them against their will. He claimed your land as his own. He was interested only in finding gold. When your people were cut by Spaniards' swords, he and his men showed no concern. All this you must have known.

Tragically, you let this greedy, violent man get away, so he could return. On his next trip, however, he brought 17 ships and between 1,200 and 1,500 men, all heavily armed. You allowed, even invited, this invasion.

Foolishly, your cacique (leader), Caonabó, killed the 39 men Columbus left behind. Why didn't Caonabó and the Taínos kill *all* the Spaniards — including Columbus — before they had a chance to return to Spain? Imagine the different outcome had the Taínos been smart enough to stop Columbus before he could launch the invasion.

Who knows why the Taínos of Hispaniola did not unite to throw out all the Spaniards? Had Taínos worked together they might have beaten the Spaniards even after Columbus returned. After all, the Spaniards numbered fewer than 2,000; Taínos numbered in the hundreds of thousands, possibly as many as three million.

However, as a result of this Taíno failure, all the Native peoples of the Americas suffered.

— *from the role play,* The People vs. Columbus, et al.

THE PEOPLE VS. COLUMBUS, ET AL.

THE SYSTEM OF EMPIRE

The Indictment:
You are charged with the mistreatment and murder of thousands, perhaps millions, of Taíno Indians.

Handout

This gets complicated. You are not a person, but a system. We like to blame crimes on people. But in this case, the real criminal is not human.

True, Columbus's men did the killing, Columbus gave the orders and King Ferdinand and Queen Isabella paid the bills —and took the profits. But what made them behave the way they did? Were they born evil and greedy? The real blame lies with a system that values property over people.

European society was organized so that an individual had to own property to feel secure. The more property one owned, the more security, the more control over one's destiny. There was no security without private ownership of property. If you were poor, you could starve. The Taínos were not perfect, but they had no "poor" and no one starved. Indians commented that Europeans' love of gold was like a disease. In fact, this attitude was a product of a diseased system.

In order to get more wealth, Columbus and his men took Indians as slaves, terrorized them into searching out gold and forced them to work on their farms and in their mines. They justified all this by telling themselves that the Indians weren't Christian, so "we" can control "their" land and labor. The European system saw only white Christians as full human beings.

It was life in a system that valued private property (especially gold), and approved of violence against foreigners and non-Christians to get it, that made Columbus and his men enslave and kill. Sane people do not kill hundreds of thousands of other human beings. It was a rotten, insane system that led Columbus and the others to behave the way they did. You, as the representatives of this system, are guilty for the genocide committed against Taínos.

As a final test to see who is guilty for the mass murder of the Taínos, ask yourself these questions:

• If it had been some other "explorer" besides Columbus to "discover America," would he have let the Taínos keep their land?
• Would he not have taken slaves?
• Would he not have made them search for gold and work in the mines?

You know the answer: Any European conqueror would have been every bit as bad as Columbus. Why? Because the system of empire was to blame, not any particular individual.

— *from the role play,* The People vs. Columbus, et al.

THE TRIAL
in the Elementary Classroom
(Some Tips)

BY BOB PETERSON

I've had great success with the Columbus role play in my 5th-grade classroom, adapting it in the following manner:

Background Preparation

1. I do it as the culmination of our Columbus/Native American/colonialism unit so that the children have sufficient background knowledge. I explain the main components of the trial and show portions of a videotape from a previous year to give students a sense of what it will be like. (Depending on the sophistication of the particular class, I sometimes omit "The System of Empire" group, or I simplify it to become "Bad Ideas" — how the love of gold and property, and a disrespect for native peoples, were responsible for the crimes against the Taínos.

2. We talk about the concept of evidence and I provide "evidence sheets" — each one numbered — for the kids to keep in their folders for future reference. Examples of such evidence sheets are a modified version of the Timeline on p. 99; examples of Taíno resistance, p. 111; Columbus's journal p. 96; the writings of las Casas, p. 103; background on the Taínos, p. 106. As a whole class, we read each evidence sheet and brainstorm how it might be used by the different groups.

3. We study important "courtroom" vocabulary such as witness, evidence, jury, etc.

4. I model and students practice statements such as, "I will present evidence to show..." or "How do you explain your statement ... given ...?"

5. I model how to take notes when someone is speaking and then develop arguments and counter-arguments to their statements.

6. After the above preparation, I have students choose in order of priority what group they'd like to be in. (Later I carefully divide the group so that there is a good mix in each group of strong readers and self-confident speakers).

Preparing Defense Statements

1. I post the list of students and groups early in the day. When the students break down to prepare their statements, witnesses, etc., they have explicit instructions to first read the "indictment" sheet, then brainstorm ideas, and finally write their own statements.

2. I provide each group with a special brainstorming sheet, and each student with a special sheet for them to write their own statement. The sheet provides a structure for the students — "Hello, my name is ... [the students think up an appropriate fictitious name]; I am ... [students describe their fictitious self and family]; I think ... [students write out their argument that they will present].

3. I suggest that each group decide who will be a lawyer and a witness.

4. I have students finish their speeches for homework.

5. The groups meet the following day to practice their speeches and the part that the lawyers and witness will play. Oftentimes I model the way a lawyer and witness might interact.

The Trial

1. I have a couple of students videotape the role play. This lends an air of importance to the trial.

2. I play the role of the prosecutor. I generally try to have another adult — a student teacher, parent, or volunteer — play the role of the judge. Between the two of us, we can usually keep order. I have the judge explain the idea of shared guilt, and use a percentage pie-chart to give examples of what a jury might decide in terms of responsibility.

3. When the jury is deliberating, I have each student fill out a role-play reflection sheet, in which they reflect on what they learned preparing for and participating in the role play. In the reflection sheet, they also write down who they think is guilty.

COLUMBUS'S DIARY
Reading Between the Lines

BY BILL BIGELOW

Columbus's journal of his first voyage to the Americas may or may not tell us much about the people he encountered. But it tells us lots about the attitudes and behaviors he brought with him.

This activity aims to prompt students to read deeply and critically by posing a series of questions for students to consider as they read Columbus's journal. A sharp reading of even these few passages reveals pretty clearly what Columbus's Enterprise (la empresa), as he called it, was all about.

One caveat: The Columbus journal that comes down to us today is a transcription of a transcription made by Spanish priest Bartolomé de las Casas after Columbus's death. Parts are missing, parts are condensations. However, the excerpts included here "are the actual words of the admiral," wrote las Casas, and most historians believe the transcription is probably accurate. The original journal has never been found.

Suggested Procedure:

1. Explain the document's background. It is a transcription of a transcription, but generally regarded as accurate. It is a portion of a much longer, several-months' journal. The Taíno people themselves left no written record which might either verify or contradict Columbus's account; nor did Columbus's men leave any writings.

2. Review the critical reading questions with students. I find that it's best to read aloud at least the first day's entry. In fact, we do almost a sentence by sentence reading, with me asking students to think carefully about what they can glean about Columbus's attitudes toward the Taínos: "What does it appear he wants from these people? Does he view them as equals? Why do you think Columbus gives stuff to the people?" Be sure students support their responses with evidence from Columbus's own words. From just this first day's entry, students can see that Columbus transforms difference into inferiority. I ask students why, if the "Indians" are so intelligent, does Columbus think they'll make good servants?

Draw students' attention to Columbus's comment, "They do not bear arms or know them, for I showed them swords and they took them by the blade and cut themselves through ignorance." Ask students what Columbus does not say about this incident. Some will notice that Columbus does not express remorse, that he fails to express regret that he caused people harm. Others notice that Columbus makes no mention that he tried to prevent Taínos from hurting themselves. I've always found this one sentence description a chilling harbinger of events to come.

3. Encourage students to work in small groups to begin answering the critical reading questions, then to finish them as homework.

4. A few questions to raise after students bring in their homework include:
   • Why does Columbus say that the people he meets are "deficient in everything"?
   • According to Columbus, what kind of people are the Taínos he encounters? In your opinion, how accurate are Columbus's descriptions of the Taínos? What clues are there that Columbus may be making some shaky assumptions? (I'm always amazed that although Columbus had been on "San Salvador" — what Taínos called Guanahaní — for only a couple of days, he believes that he can understand what they say. He writes, "One old man got into the boat, and all the rest, men and women, cried in loud voices: 'Come and see the men who have come from heaven...'" This year to demonstrate how preposterous Columbus's claim was, I wrote on a slip of paper, "Look at the stupid guy with the beard and funny clothes!" I asked Nghia, a Vietnamese student, if he would translate that phrase into Vietnamese and call it out to me across the room. I then asked other students to guess what Nghia had shouted. No one had a clue. I wanted kids to see that it would be similarly improbable for Columbus to have known what Taínos were shouting from the shore.)
   • If students don't bring it up, it's worth pointing out that the Taínos did not all passively accept Columbus's authority. Within the first few days, two of the Taíno captives threw themselves overboard and fled in a speedy canoe. Columbus's men went after them, but, according to Columbus, the Taínos "ran off like chickens."

THE FIRST FEW DAYS
The Journal of Christopher Columbus

Friday, October 12, 1492. In order that they might feel great friendship toward us, because I knew that they were a people to be delivered and converted to our holy faith by love rather than by force, I gave to some of them some red caps and some glass beads, which they hung round their necks, and many other things of little value. At this they were greatly pleased and became so entirely our friends that it was a wonder to see.

Afterwards they came swimming to the ships' boats, where we were, and brought us parrots and cotton thread in balls, and spears and many other things, and we exchanged them for other things, such as small glass beads and hawks' bells, which we gave to them. In fact, they took all and gave all, such as they had, with good will, but it seemed to me that they were a people very deficient in everything.

They all go naked as their mothers bore them, and the women also, although I saw only one very young girl. And all those whom I did see were youths, so that I did not see one who was over thirty years of age; they were very well built, with very handsome bodies and very good faces. Their hair is coarse almost like the hairs of a horse's tail and short; they wear their hair down over their eyebrows, except for a few strands behind, which they wear long and never cut. Some of them are painted black, and they are the color of the people of the Canaries, neither black nor white, and some of them are painted white and some red and some in any color that they find. Some of them paint their faces, some their whole bodies, some only the eyes, and some only the nose.

They do not bear arms or know them, for I showed them swords and they took them by the blade and cut themselves through ignorance. They have no iron. Their spears are certain reeds, without iron, and some of these have a fish tooth at the end, while others are pointed in various ways.

They are all generally fairly tall, good looking and well proportioned. I saw some who bore marks of wounds on their bodies, and I made signs to them to ask how this came about, and they indicated to me that people came from other islands, which are near, and wished to capture them, and they defended themselves. And I believed and still believe that they come here from the mainland to take them for slaves.

They should be good servants and of quick intelligence, since I see that they very soon say all that is said to them, and I believe that they would easily be made Christians, for it appeared to me that they had no creed. Our Lord willing, at the time of my departure I will bring back six of them to Your Highnesses, that they may learn to talk.

Saturday, October 13th. As soon as day broke, there came to the shore many of these men, all youths, as I have said, and all of a good height, very handsome people.... Their eyes are very lovely and not small. They are not at all black, but the color of Canarians.... Their legs are very straight, all alike; they have no bellies but very good figures.

They came to the ship in boats, which are made of a treetrunk like a long boat and all of one piece.

COLUMBUS'S JOURNAL
Reading Deeply

1. What attitudes does Columbus have about the people he encounters (the "Indians")? Summarize these and then give at least three quotes from his journal as evidence.

2. Based on what you read in his journal, what does it appear that Columbus cares about, what he wants? Give several quotes as evidence.

3. Based on Columbus's observations, what if anything can you tell about the kind of people the "Indians" are — what they value, how they treat other people, etc.? If you don't think you can tell anything about the Indians from Columbus's journal, give your reasons for why not.

European illustration of a Native dugout canoe.

They are very wonderfully carved, considering the country, and large, so that in some forty or forty-five men came. Others are smaller, so that in some only a solitary man came. They row them with a paddle, like a baker's peel, and they travel wonderfully fast. If one capsizes, everyone at once begins to swim and right it, baling it out with gourds which they carry with them.

They brought balls of spun cotton and parrots and spears and other trifles ... and they gave all for anything that was given to them. And I was attentive and labored to know if they had gold, and I saw that some of them wore a small piece hanging from a hole which they have in the nose, and from signs I was able to understand that, going to the south or going round the island to the south, there was a king who had large vessels of it and possessed much gold. I tried to make them go there, and afterwards saw that they were not inclined for the journey.

I decided to wait until the afternoon of the following day, and after that to leave for the south-west, for, as many of them indicated to me, they said that there was land to the south and to the southwest and to the northwest, and that those of the northwest often came to attack them. So I decided to go to the southwest, to seek the gold and precious stones....

The people also are very gentle and, since they long to possess something of ours and fear that nothing will be given to them unless they give something, when they have nothing, they take what they can and immediately throw themselves into the water and swim. But all that they do possess, they give for anything which is given to them, so that they exchange things even for pieces of broken dishes and bits of broken glass cups....

Sunday, October 14th. At dawn, I ordered the ship's boat and the boats of the caravels to be made ready, and I went along the island in a north-northeasterly direction, to see the other part, which lay to the east, and its character, and also to see the villages. And I soon saw two or three, and the people all came to shore, calling us and giving thanks to God. Some brought us water, others various eatables: others, when they saw that I was not inclined to land, threw themselves into the sea and came, swimming, and we understood that they asked us if we had come from heaven. One old man got into the boat, and all the rest, men and women, cried in loud voices: "Come and see the men who have come from heaven; bring them food and drink."

Many came and many women, each with something, giving thanks to God, throwing themselves on the ground and raising their hands to the sky, and then shouting to us that we should land. But I feared to do so, seeing a great reef of rocks which encircled the whole of that island, while within there is deep water and a harbor large enough for all the ships of Christendom, the entrance to which is very narrow....

And in order to see all this, I went this morning, that I might be able to give an account of all to Your Highnesses and also say where a fort could be built. I saw a piece of land, which is formed like an island although it is not one, on which there were six houses; it could be converted into an island in two days, although I do not see that it is necessary to do so, for these people are very unskilled in arms, as Your Highnesses will see from the seven whom I caused to be taken in order to carry them off that they may learn our language and return. However, when Your Highnesses so command, they can all be carried off to Castile or held captive in the island itself, since with fifty men they would be all kept in subjection and forced to do whatever may be wished....

Monday, October 15th. To this island I gave the name Santa Maria de la Concepcion, and about sunset, I anchored to learn if there were gold there, because those whom I had caused to be taken in the island of San Salvador told me that there they wore very large golden bracelets on the legs and arms.

I can well believe that all that they said was a ruse [a trick] in order to get away. It was nevertheless my wish not to pass any island without taking possession of it, although when one had been annexed [claimed], all might be said to have been. And I anchored and was there until today, Tuesday, when at dawn I went ashore in the armed boats and landed.

The people, who were many, were naked and of the same type as those of the other island of San Salvador; they allowed us to go through the island and gave us what we asked of them. And as the wind blew more strongly across from the southeast, I was unwilling to wait and went back to the ship.

A large canoe was alongside the caravel Niña, and one of the men of the island of San Salvador, who was in her, threw himself into the sea and went off in it, and during the evening before midnight the other threw himself overboard ... and went after the canoe, which fled so that there was not a boat that could have overtaken it, since we were a long way behind it. In the end it reached land and they left the canoe, and some of my company went ashore after them, and they all ran off like chickens....

These islands are very green and fertile and the breezes are very soft, and it is possible that there are in them many things, of which I do not know, because I did not wish to delay in finding gold, by discovering and going about many islands. And since these men give these signs that they wear it on their arms and legs, and it is gold because I showed them some pieces of gold which I have, I cannot fail, with the aid of Our Lord, to find the place it comes from.

Being in the middle of the channel between these two islands, that of Santa Maria and this large island, to which I gave the name Fernandina, I found a man alone in a canoe on his way from the island of Santa Maria to that of Fernandina. He was carrying with him a piece of their bread, about as large as the fist, and a gourd of water and a piece of brown earth, powdered and then kneaded, and some dried leaves, which must be a thing highly prized among them, since already at San Salvador they presented me with some of them....

He came alongside the ship. I made him come on board, as he asked to do so, and caused him to bring his canoe on board also and all that he had with him to be kept safe. I commanded that bread and honey should be given to him to eat, and something to drink, and thus I will carry him to Fernandina and will give him back all his belongings, in order to give him a good opinion of us, so that when, please God, Your Highnesses send here, those who come may receive honor and the Indians will give to us of all that they have.

From The Journal of Christopher Columbus, *ed. by Cecil Jane (New York: Bramhall House, 1960). Paragraph breaks have been added.*

TIMELINE:
Spain, Columbus, and Taínos

Approximately 13,000 B.C.: First known human beings live in the Caribbean.

Approximately 800 B.C.: The people who call themselves Taíno, or "men of good," arrive in the region. With great care for the earth, the Taínos are able to feed millions of people. No one in a community goes hungry. They play sports and recite poetry. They are great inventors and travel from island to island. One Spanish priest reported that he never saw two Taínos fighting.

There are frequent skirmishes between Taínos and Caribs on nearby islands, but these threaten neither civilization.

1451: Columbus is born probably in the Italian port city, Genoa. At the time of his birth, there may be as many as 70 to 100 million people living in what will one day be called the Americas. They are of many nationalities, speaking perhaps 2,000 different languages.

1453: Constantinople (now Istanbul) falls to the Ottoman Turks who make it the capital of their empire. For European merchants, trade with Asia becomes more difficult.

1455: Christian Castile [Spain] begins attacks on Granada in Andulasia, the last province under Arab/Islamic rule in Spain. The Arabs (called "Moors" by European Christians) had ruled the Iberian peninsula for eight centuries.

1471: About this time, Columbus first goes to sea on a Genoese ship.

1483: Under King Ferdinand and Queen Isabella, the Inquisition intensifies in the Christian-reconquered areas of Spain. The Inquisition aims at rooting out Muslims and Jews who had converted to Christianity but whose conversion the Inquisition deems insincere. Before it is over, three centuries later, thousands will die, with an estimated three million people driven into exile.

1484: Columbus first presents his idea to the king of Portugal for reaching the Indies by sailing west. The plan is rejected, not because the king's advisors don't believe the world is round, but because they think Columbus's estimate of the distance is way

Columbus sets sail from Spain.

too small.

1486: Columbus first proposes a western voyage to Queen Isabella, whose advisors postpone any recommendation.

1488: Columbus appeals again to the Portuguese king. At the same time, Bartolomé Dias claims Africa can be rounded by sea to get to the Indies. This eliminates Portugal's interest in looking for a westward route.

1490: Queen Isabella's advisors urge the queen to reject Columbus's proposal. But Isabella keeps Columbus on the royal payroll, offering him hope his proposal will eventually be granted.

Jan. 2, 1492: The Arab rulers and their court surrender in Granada. According to the surrender agreement, the inhabitants of Muslim Spain have until the beginning of 1495 to decide between living under Christian rule or exile. Those who choose to stay begin to feel the threat of the Inquisition immediately, and in 1498 official inquisitors come, and forced conversions to Christianity begin.

March 30, 1492: Ferdinand and Isabella order all Jews to leave Spain.

April, 1492: Ferdinand and Isabella agree to Columbus's westward voyage to the Indies. They also agree to his demands: 10% of all the wealth returned to Spain, the title of Admiral of the Ocean Sea, governor and viceroy of all the territory he discovers. All these titles are to be inherited by his heirs.

Dec. 9: Columbus sails into the harbor of the island the Taíno people call Hayti. Its plains are "the loveliest in the world" and remind Columbus of Spain. He calls the island Española.

Oct./Nov./Dec.: Columbus's every move is determined by where he believes he can find gold. On December 23 he writes in his journal: "Our Lord in His Goodness guide me that I may find this gold, I mean their mine, for I have many here who say they know it." Still, by mid-December Columbus has found very little gold.

Dec. 25: Columbus's ship, the Santa Maria, hits rocks off Española. He is forced to abandon it. The Taíno *cacique* (leader), Guacanagarí, weeps when he hears of the shipwreck. Taínos help unload the ship "without the loss of a shoe string." "They are," Columbus writes, "a people so full of love and without greed... I believe there is no better race or better land in the world."

Dec. 26: Realizing he will have to leave men behind, Columbus orders a fort and tower built. He writes that it is necessary to make the Indians realize that they must serve Spain's king and queen "with love and fear."

Jan. 2, 1493: Columbus prepares to leave Hayti. He leaves behind 39 men and orders them "to discover the mine of gold."

Jan. 13: First reported skirmish between Spaniards and Indians: After landing on an island to trade for bows, Columbus writes that many Indians prepared "to assault the Christians and capture them." The Spaniards "fell upon" them, "they gave an Indian a great slash on the buttocks and they wounded another in the breast with an arrow." Columbus believes that these people were "Carib and that they eat men [though he offers no evidence]." He regrets he didn't capture some to take back to Spain.

Feb. 15: Columbus returns with relatively little of value. In a letter written aboard ship, Columbus lies, saying that on Española, "there are many spices and great mines of gold and of other metals."

Mid-April: Columbus welcomed by Ferdinand and Isabella. They begin planning his second voyage. Of the six Indians brought to Spain, one would stay and die in two years. The others would leave with Columbus for Española and three would die enroute.

May 28, 1493: The king and queen confirm that Columbus, his sons and his heirs will be Admiral and Viceroy and Governor of the islands and mainland discovered "now and forever."

Approx. Sept./Oct. 1493: The men left behind at La Navidad brutally mistreat the Taínos. They steal, take slaves and rape women. In response, the Taíno cacique, Caonabó, kills all the Spaniards on the island.

Aug. 2, 1492: Deadline for Jews to leave Spain. Between 120,000 and 150,000 are forced out, able to take only what they can carry. They must leave all their gold, silver, jewels and money for the King and Queen.

Aug. 3, 1492: Columbus departs from Palos instead of the port of Cadiz, which is filled with ships taking some 8,000 Jews into exile.

Oct. 12, 1492: Juan Rodriguez Bermejo, a sailor on the Pinta, shouts, "Land, Land!" Columbus later claims he first spotted land and thus will collect the lifetime pension promised. The ships arrive at the island, Guanahaní, which Columbus claims for Ferdinand and Isabella. Columbus receives presents from the people he encounters and gives them some red caps, glass beads, and "many other things of little value."

The first thing he tries to ask the people is "if they had gold."

Oct. 14: Columbus's thoughts turn to slavery: "... When Your Highnesses so command, they [the Indians] can be carried off to Castile or held captive in the island itself, since with 50 men they would be all kept in subjection and forced to do whatever may be wished."

Nov. 12: Columbus kidnaps 10 Taínos: My men "brought seven head of women, small and large, and three children."

Nov. 17: Two of his captives escape.

Sept. 25, 1493: Columbus's second voyage begins. His fleet includes 17 ships and between 1200 and 1500 men (no women). Pressure is high for Columbus to make good on his promises. At least some of the money to finance the voyage comes from wealth taken away from Spanish Jews.

Nov. 3, 1493: Columbus lands on Dominica. On Guadeloupe, his men go ashore "looting and destroying all they found," according to Columbus's son, Fernando. They capture 12 "very beautiful and plump" teenage Taíno girls.

Mid-Nov.: Columbus's crew trap a small group of Caribs in a harbor at what is now St. Croix. In defense, the Indians shoot arrows at the Spaniards, killing one and wounding one. The Indians are caught, and one is horribly mutilated, then killed, by the Spaniards.

Nov. 28: Columbus finds the fort at La Navidad burned.

Early Feb. 1494: Columbus sends 12 of the 17 ships back to Spain for supplies. Several dozen Indian slaves are taken aboard — "men and women and boys and girls," he writes. He justifies this by writing that they are cannibals and thus slavery will more readily "secure the welfare of their souls."

Columbus recommends to the king and queen that supplies needed in the Indies could be paid for in slaves, "well made and of very good intelligence," and that slave shipments could be taxed to raise money for Spain. Spanish priest Bartolomé de las Casas later writes that claims of cannibalism are used to "excuse the violence, cruelty, plunder and slaughter committed against the Indians every day."

Feb./March: In Isabella, Spaniards are dying of disease, and there is less food everyday. Columbus uses violence against Spaniards who disobey his orders to work. Any Spaniard found hiding gold is "well whipped." Colonist Michele de Cuneo writes: "Some had their ears slit and some the nose, very pitiful to see." Many blame Columbus, governor of the island, for their problems. Demoralized, many want to leave.

Late March/early April: Columbus is told that Indians are leaving their villages and that the cacique, Caonabó, is preparing to attack the fort at Isabella. Las Casas writes that Columbus "ordered Alonso de Hojeda to lead a squadron by land to the fort of Santo Tomas and spread terror among the Indians in order to show them how strong and powerful the Christians were."

April 9, 1494: Hojeda takes 400 men inland, captures a cacique and some relatives, accuses one of theft and has his ears publicly cut off. When Hojeda returns to Isabella with these and other prisoners, Columbus orders a crier to announce their public decapitation. Las Casas comments, "What a pretty way to promote justice, friendship, and make the Faith appealing — to capture a King in his own territory and sentence him, his brother and his nephew to death, for no fault of their own!"

April 24, 1494: Columbus leaves Isabella to seek the mainland of the Indies.

Spring 1494: Columbus explores the coast of Jamaica. Andres Bernaldez, accompanying Columbus, writes of the island's "extreme beauty." Columbus sets loose a vicious dog against the Indians. Bernaldez writes that it "did them great damage, for a dog is the equal of 10 men against the Indians."

June 12, 1494: Columbus, off the coast of Cuba, believes he has reached the mainland. The next day he begins his return to Española.

Sept. 14: Columbus reaches the southern coast of Española. Instead of returning to Isabella, Columbus heads to Puerto Rico to raid for Carib slaves. However, he becomes ill and his officers return the ships to Isabella.

Nov. 1494: Returning to Spain, mutineers against Columbus complain to the king and queen. They say there is no gold and that the enterprise is a joke.

Feb. 1495: Columbus must be desperate to prove that his "enterprise" can be profitable. He rounds up

The governor, de Ovando, lures the Taíno leader Anacaona and her followers to a meeting; the Spaniards burn down the meeting house and hang her.

Theodore de Bry

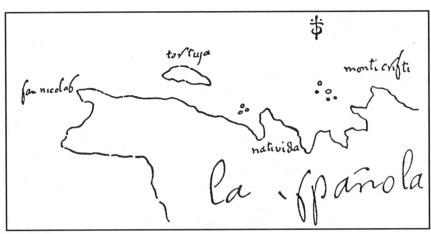

A sketch by Columbus of northwest Hispaniola.

1600 Taínos — the same people he had earlier described as "so full of love and without greed." Some 550 of them — "among the best males and females," writes colonist Michele de Cuneo — are chained and taken to ships to be sent to Spain as slaves. "Of the rest who were left," writes Cuneo, "the announcement went around that whoever wanted them could take as many as he pleased; and this was done."

1495: Columbus establishes the tribute system. Every Taíno, 14 or older, is required to fill a hawk's bell full of gold every 3 months. Those who comply are given copper tokens to wear around their necks. Where Columbus decides there is little gold, 25 pounds of spun cotton is required. The Spaniards cut the hands off those who do not comply; they are left to bleed to death. As las Casas writes, the tribute is "impossible and intolerable."

Columbus will soon replace the tribute system with outright slavery, though the Queen will rule that Indians forced to work must be paid "wages." It is called the encomienda system, in which colonists are simply granted land and numbers of Taínos.

March 24, 1495: Columbus, and his brothers Diego and Bartolomé, who had arrived earlier, send an armed force to the mountains to put down Taíno resistance to Spanish brutality. The force includes 200 soldiers in full armor, 20 vicious dogs and 20 mounted cavalry. The Spaniards confront a large number of Taínos in a valley 10 miles south of Isabella, attack them and, according to Columbus's son, "with God's aid soon gained a complete victory, killing many Indians and capturing others who were also killed."

Oct. 1495: Responding to reports of Columbus's misrule, the king and queen send an investigator to Española.

March 1496: Columbus departs for Spain. Two ships make the journey. Onto them, Columbus forces 30 Taíno prisoners, including the cacique, Caonabó, who led the first resistance to Spanish rule in Española. It takes 3 months to make the voyage. Caonabó dies enroute; no one knows how many others also die.

Columbus arrives and awaits an answer from the king and queen to his request for a third voyage.

July 1496: Ferdinand and Isabella agree to see Columbus. He sets out for Burgos with his Taíno slaves. Columbus promises to locate the mainland so that it will come under Spanish rather than Portuguese control. The king and queen will not agree to Columbus's plans for almost two years.

May 30, 1498: Columbus's third voyage begins. Three ships head directly for Española, another three, with Columbus, travel farther south.

July 31, 1498: Columbus sails past and names Trinidad. He saw what is today Venezuela, but didn't realize that it was the mainland.

Mid-Aug. 1498: Columbus lands in Española. The admiral finds Spanish colonists in rebellion against his brothers' rule. He backs down and offers amnesty to anyone who will return to Spain or will accept free land.

1500: By now the Spaniards have established at least seven forts in Española and at least 340 gallows.

Aug. 1500: The king and queen, upset over the negative reports of Columbus's bad government, though not his mistreatment of Taínos, send a commissioner to take charge in Española. The commissioner arrives amid another uprising against the Columbus brothers. He arrests them and in October sends them to Spain for trial.

Late Oct.: Columbus arrives in Cadiz in chains. A few months later, he presents his case to the king and queen. He demands he be reinstated governor. He will make one more voyage but will never regain his power.

May 20, 1506: Columbus dies in Valladolid, Spain.

1542: Bartolomé de las Casas writes that a mere 200 Taínos still live in Española. One scholar recently estimated that perhaps more than 3 million Taínos lived there when Columbus first arrived.

— compiled by Bill Bigelow

Sources include: Cecil Jane, The Journal of Columbus; *Benjamin Keen, ed.* The Life of the Admiral Christopher Columbus by His Son Ferdinand; *Hans Koning,* Columbus: His Enterprise; *Milton Meltzer,* Columbus and the World Around Him; *Samuel Eliot Morison,* Admiral of the Ocean Sea; *Kirkpatrick Sale,* Conquest of Paradise; *The Arab World and Islamic Resource and School Services.*

"OPEN YOUR HEARTS"
A Dominican Friar Speaks Out

ADAPTED FROM BARTOLOMÉ DE LAS CASAS

It was the Sunday before Christmas, 1511. The whole city of Santo Domingo would be in church that day, even Christopher Columbus's son, Admiral Diego Columbus. All the important people were invited by the Dominicans to come hear the sermon. Everyone agreed to come. But if they had known what the sermon was to be about, they would have been very angry and would have stayed home.

The Dominican Friar Antonio de Montesinos walked to the pulpit. He stood before them and looked out on the crowded church. "I am a voice crying in the desert!" he shouted. "What is wrong with you?" he called to the people. "You are blind, you are in danger of going to hell. Can't you see?" Then, his voice growing louder, he said: "I have come here to tell you, in the name of Christ, that it is time for you to open your hearts — all of you."

The people in the church were shocked. Some of them were afraid. What in the world was this friar talking about?

Friar Montesinos continued to speak to them angrily.

"Tell me, what right have you to kill the Indians? What have they ever done to you? And why do you make them slaves? You attack them and torture them. Why do you do this?

"Why can't you feed them and care for them? It is because you are so greedy for gold that you work them to death. You don't even teach them about God or let them go to church.

"Aren't the Indians people? Doesn't the Bible tell you to love them as much as you love yourselves? You are living in a dream! Don't you understand?"

Admiral Diego Columbus and the other rich Spaniards could not believe their ears. Some were too afraid to look up from the ground. Others were shaking, they were so angry. None of them believed what the priest had told them.

Friar Montesinos ended his sermon. He walked down the aisle with his head held high. He was not afraid. He left and went to the small straw house of the Dominicans.

When Friar Montesinos had left the church, all the people began talking to each other. "Who does he think he is?" one man shouted.

"He should be hung!" shouted another.

"No, we cannot hang a priest. But Admiral Columbus, you can order him to stop. Send him back to Spain. Send them all back."

The admiral looked at the man who had just spoken. "No," he said. "First, we must give him a chance to say he is sorry. He must take back what he has said. When he attacks us for using the Indians, he is really attacking the King. It is the King who tells us to use Indian workers. It is very serious to criticize the King. Let us go now to talk to Montesinos."

A group of men arrived at the house of the Dominican friars. They knocked on the door. When a porter answered, Admiral Columbus said, "We have come to see the Superior." Friar Pedro de Cordoba came alone to meet them.

"We have come to speak with Friar Montesinos. He has offended us and he has offended the King," said Diego Columbus.

"I see," replied Cordoba. "But if you have something to say, please tell me. For all the Dominicans agree with what Friar Montesinos said in his sermon today."

"Let us see Montesinos, he is the one we are angry with!" called out a tall, beaded man standing behind Columbus.

"I will tell you once again," said Friar Cordoba. "If you have something to say, please say it now. Say it to me."

"Father, we don't mean to be rude," said Columbus. "But because Friar Montesinos is the one who spoke the words today, we kindly ask to speak to him. We only wish to ask him some questions."

Seeing that the men's tone had changed, Cordoba agreed to go get Montesinos.

Montesinos seemed to be a little afraid when he returned with Friar Cordoba. They all sat down.

Columbus began: "Friar Montesinos, how dare you criticize us like that in church? The King himself gave us the Indians to use as workers. My father and his men spent years fighting the Indians after they attacked Christians. Your sermon was a scandal, an insult to our whole way of life." Columbus paused. He looked directly at Friar Montesinos. "I demand that you take back what you said today. And if you don't, we will take action against you."

Montesinos appeared calm. "What I said today

in my sermon was the result of much thought. It is what all the friars believe. Again I say to you: You are killing off the Indians. You treat them as if they were animals. But they are people, and it is up to the friars to save the souls of all people, Spaniard and Indian. I believe that in doing this, we are serving the King. Believe me, once the King knows what we friars are doing, he will thank us."

These words angered Columbus and the men. They had come to the Indies to get rich by finding gold. How could they find gold without the Indians? Who would work in the mines? Who would work in the fields?

Columbus spoke for the men. "Look, we are warning you. I demand that you preach another sermon next Sunday. And take back what you have said today. If you don't, we shall have you all sent back to Spain."

Now, it was Friar Cordoba's turn to speak. "Of course you can send us back to Spain. This can be easily done." It was true. The Dominicans had very little in the Indies. Besides their rough clothes, they owned nothing except a simple blanket. They slept on straw pads. Everything they owned could be fit into two trunks.

Admiral Columbus saw that his threats did not scare these Dominicans. "Please, Friar Cordoba, Friar Montesinos. Please preach another sermon next Sunday. People are very upset."

Friar Montesinos looked at Friar Cordoba. "Alright," he said. "I will preach another sermon next Sunday. I will do my best to make myself more clear."

Diego Columbus thanked the friars and the men left. They were happy and joked to themselves as they walked away from the Dominicans' house.

News spread quickly that next Sunday, Friar Montesinos would preach another sermon. People heard that Montesinos had promised to take back everything he had said. The church was crowded with people.

Friar Montesinos walked steadily to the pulpit. "I take my theme from Job 36," he said in a loud, strong voice. "From the beginning, I shall repeat my knowledge and my truth. I will show that what I said last Sunday, that made you so angry, is true."

People in the church looked at each other. They wanted to stop him, but he had already begun. Diego Columbus stared at him with anger.

"With my own eyes, I have seen Indians starving to death. With my own eyes, I have seen people who call themselves Christians whip an Indian to death. Dogs are treated better than Indians. Again, I tell you: You will go to hell if you do not stop. If you don't like what I say, then write to Spain. Do whatever you like. I will not stop saying what I know

The Spanish priest, Bartolomé de las Casas chronicled Spanish abuses of the native Taínos.

is true. It is the only way I know how to serve my God and my King."

Montesinos ended his sermon. Again, he left the church with his head held high.

"He lied to us," said one man. "He promised he would take back what he said last week."

"Yes, let's go back to the Dominicans and order them to preach another sermon," called out someone from the back.

Others became quiet as Diego Columbus spoke: "And what good would that do? He would continue to tell us we are going to hell. I'm tired of listening to that idiot! No, we must tell the King. He will order Montesinos to stop. The King has no wish to be poor like a Dominican friar." The others laughed. "And without the Indians, the King would get no gold. He would lose his power."

When the King received Diego Columbus's letter, he ordered the head of the Dominicans in Spain to come to him. "What is this man causing so much trouble for? You must stop him. And if you don't, I will."

You see how easy it is to fool a king....

— *adapted by Bill Bigelow from Bartolomé de las Casas,*
History of the Indies, *1542.*

Additional Reading:

Stopsky, Fred. Bartolome de las Casas: Champion of Indian Rights *(Lowell, MA: Discovery Enterprises, 1992)*

Bartolomé de las Casas. A Short Account of the Destruction of the Indies. *New York: Penguin, 1992 (pb. edition).*

THE TAÍNOS

I looked at the place where I was,
to remember it.
The island was all green and brown,
the flowers red and yellow,
the sky a deep and brilliant blue.
At my feet, the tip of something white
stuck from the sand.
I stooped, dug with my fingers,
and pried out a small, empty conch,
washed so gently by the sea
that not a single chip was missing.

— Michael Dorris,
from the children's novella "Morning Girl"

THE TAÍNOS
"Men of the Good"

BY JOSÉ BARREIRO

This article offers some descriptions of the first Caribbean people to encounter Columbus in 1492. Taíno is what these people called themselves; they belong to a larger family of related languages called Arawak.

The word Taíno meant "men of the good," and from most indications the Taínos were good. Living on the lush and hospitable islands over fifteen hundred years, the indigenous people of "La Taína" developed a culture where the human personality was gentle. Among the Taíno at the time of contact, by all accounts, generosity and kindness were dominant values.

The Taíno's culture has been designated as "primitive" by Western scholars, yet the Taínos strove to feed all the people, and maintained a spirituality that respected most of their main animal and food sources, as well as the natural forces like climate, season, and weather. The Taíno lived respectfully in a bountiful place and so their nature was bountiful.

The naked people Columbus first sighted lived in an island world of rainforests and tropical weather, and adventure and fishing legends at sea. Theirs was a land of generous abundance. They could build a dwelling from a single tree (the Royal Palm) and from several others (*gommier, ceiba*), a canoe that could carry more than one hundred people.

The Taínos lived in the shadows of a diverse forest so biologically remarkable as to be almost unimaginable to us. Indeed because what happened to their world in the last few centuries was so devastating, we may never again know how the land or the life of the land appeared in detail. What we do know is that their world would appear to us, as it did to the Spanish of the 15th century, as a tropical paradise.

The Taíno world, for the most part, had some of the appearance that modern imaginations ascribe to the South Pacific islands. The people lived in small, clean villages of neatly appointed thatch dwellings along rivers inland and on the coasts. They were a handsome people who had no need of clothing for

warmth. They liked to bathe often, which prompted a Spanish royal law forbidding the practice, "for we are informed it does them much harm," wrote Queen Isabella.

The Taíno were a sea-going people, and took pride in their courage on the high ocean as well as their skill in finding their way around their world. They visited one another constantly. Columbus was often astonished at finding lone Indian fishermen sailing in the open ocean as he made his way among the islands. Once, a canoe of Taíno men followed him from island to island until one of their relatives, held captive on Columbus's flagship, jumped over the side to be spirited away.

Among Taínos, the women and some of the men harvested corn, nuts, cassava, and other roots. They appear to have practiced a rotation method in their agriculture. Boys hunted fowl from flocks that "darkened the sun," according to Columbus, and the men forded rivers and braved ocean to hunt and fish for the abundant, tree-going *jutia*, the succulent *manati*, giant sea turtles and countless species of other fish, turtles and shellfish. Around every hut, Columbus wrote, there were flocks of tame ducks (*yaguasa*), which the people roasted and ate. Taínos along the coasts kept large circular corrals made of reeds which they filled with fish and turtles by the thousands. They were known to catch fish and turtles by way of a *remora* (suction fish) tied by the tail.

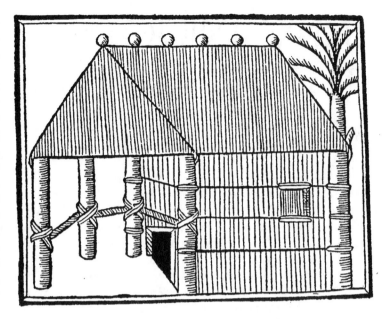

The Taíno world of 1492 was a thriving place. The Taíno islands supported large populations that had existed in an environment of Carib-Taíno conflict for, according to archeological evidence, perhaps fifteen hundred years, although the earliest human fossil in the region is dated at fifteen thousand years. Taínos and Caribs may have fought one another, but there is little evidence to support any notion that they tried to wipe each other out through warfare. A Carib war party arrived and attacked, was successful or beaten back, and the Taínos, from all accounts, returned to what they were doing before the attack.

Early descriptions of Taíno life at contact tell of large concentrations, strings of a hundred or more villages of five hundred to one thousand people. These concentrations of people in coastal areas and river deltas were apparently well-fed by a nature-harvesting and agricultural production system whose primary value was that all of the people had the right to eat. Everyone in the society had a food or other goods-producing task, even the highly esteemed *caciques* (community leaders) and *behiques* (medicine people), were often seen to plant, hunt, and fish along with their people. In the Taíno culture, as with most natural world cultures of the Americas, the concept was that the primary bounties of the earth, particularly those that humans eat, are to be produced in cooperation and shared.

Like all American indigenous peoples, the Taíno had an involved economic life. They could trade throughout the Caribbean and had systems of governance and beliefs that maintained harmony between human and natural environments. The Taínos enjoyed a peaceful way of life that modern anthropologists now call "ecosystemic." In the wake of recent scientific revelations about the cost of high-impact technologies upon the natural world, a culture such as the Taíno, that could feed several million people without permanently wearing down its surroundings, might command higher respect.

There was little or no quarreling observed among the Taínos by the Spaniards. The old caciques and their councils of elders were said to be well-behaved, had a deliberate way of speaking and great authority. The people either worked in the gardens (*conucos*) or fishing and hunting. They had ball games played in

bateyes, or courtyards, in front of the cacique's house. They held both ceremonial and social dances, called *areitos*, during which their creation stories and other cosmologies were recited.

Among the few Taíno-Arawak customs that have survived, the predominant ideas are that ancestors should be properly greeted by the living humans at certain times and that natural forces and the spirits behind each group of food and medicinal plants and useful animals should be appreciated in ceremony.

Excerpted from an article by José Barreiro, first published in "View from the Shore" American Indian Perspectives on the Quincentenary" (Northeast Indian Quarterly, Fall 1990). Barreiro is a member of the Taíno Nation of the Antilles.

IMAGINING THE TAÍNOS

BY BILL BIGELOW

Most students who have been exposed to the traditional Columbus-discovers-America tale have never heard the name, Taíno. Children's books almost always tell the encounter from Columbus's perspective: the people he meets are called Indians, the first island he bumps into, San Salvador. Children are thus inducted into a "let's look at the world as if we're all white Europeans" framework.

Scholarship on the Taínos, as well as on the Carib Indians of the region, is contradictory. Much is based on early archaeological research, which often accepted at face value written descriptions recorded by the Spanish colonists. The scholarly accounts fail to question the friendly Indian/unfriendly Indian dichotomy that arose as a convenient explanation for resistance to the Spanish invasion: if an Indian group acquiesced to colonists' demands they were labeled "friendly" Taínos; if they fought back, they must be "warlike," "ferocious," "unfriendly" Caribs. Unfortunately, many children's books and textbooks parrot these clichés. The goal of this writing assignment is to humanize the people Columbus described as kind, generous, and intelligent.

Suggested procedure:

1. I like to start by reading the piece by José Barreiro (see page 106), "The Taínos," aloud with the class, discussing it as we go. Some students will find this method slow, but it is more democratic as it lessens the chance that some students won't "get it." It's also crucial to the success of the writing assignment that follows that everyone begins from a base of real information. Otherwise students will construct pieces based on whatever stereotypes they happen to carry around about generic "Indians."

2. Before beginning the reading, you might alert students to the assignment ahead: to write a short story, a series of diary entries, a letter, or a dialogue from the point of view of Taínos on Guanahaní shortly after Columbus's arrival. As you read, students can highlight passages about Taíno culture that they might incorporate into their writing.

3. Some questions to raise and points to emphasize in the reading:
  •When you first studied about Columbus in grade school, what did you learn about the Taínos? If

you learned nothing or almost nothing, why not?

  •Do you think the Taíno were a "primitive" people? (Many Western thinkers imposed a false hierarchy of "least advanced" to "most advanced" on cultures. Thus, for example, the Taínos were dubbed "primitive," even though they could feed millions without destroying the environment, while Spaniards were considered "advanced," even though many starved rather than perform manual labor. Encourage students to reflect on how we think about so-called primitive and advanced cultures, and the criteria used to determine these categories.)

  •Is there anything in the reading that helps explain how the Taínos responded to the arrival of Columbus and his men?

  •What questions about the Taínos are you still left with after this reading?

4. The Writing. Ask students to imagine that they are Taínos and to record their reaction to the arrival of Columbus. They might write a series of diary entries, a short story, an autobiography, a dialogue, etc. Their papers might focus on one event or describe how life changed for the Taínos over a period of time. Students might decide to depict the first arrival of Columbus on Guanahaní (San Salvador) or to record events on Hispaniola during his second voyage. Encourage them to create particular individuals and to use dialogue. I don't like to prescribe length for an assignment, but I will tell students, "It's hard for me to imagine doing a good job in less than a couple of pages." You might offer excerpts from other student papers as writing prompts (see p. 110). The advantage of offering examples is that it provides some idea of what you're looking for, and can spark ideas; the disadvantage is that occasionally students adhere too closely to the model and it can fence in their imaginations. You might read the prompt aloud and then brainstorm with the class possible approaches to the assignment.

Encourage students to draw not only on their imaginations but also on information in their readings about the Taínos, Columbus's diary (see p. 96), and other research they may have done. Imagination is vital, but for many, perhaps most students, it's also filled with stereotypes. (Invariably, at least one student will have the Taínos wrapped in buffalo skins, emerging from their tipis to greet Columbus.) The aim of the assignment is to provoke students to imagine perspectives of the people who traditionally have been silenced. But the assignment can backfire if students assume the caricatured personas of tomahawk-chopping warriors and disregard the information in the reading.

Generally, I want students to read their pieces to each other. However, because this writing will cover the same essential contacts or confrontations, it doesn't lend itself to a whole-class read-around. With this assignment, I put students in small groups and ask them to read their papers to one another. Afterwards, I'll ask for several volunteers to share their work with the entire class.

Native fishing techniques used spears, nets, and weirs to catch many varieties of fish, crabs, and turtles.

THE GOLD PEOPLE

BY ANNA HEREFORD

I was gathering cassava root when I first saw it. My hands were red and swollen from harvesting all day. It was the first day we had harvested since last year. All the women and many of the men had baskets as full as mine. I was looking forward to the *areito* that night, so my mind thought of dancing as I picked. I looked down at my hands as the river's cool water washed over my palms. Movement from the water caught my attention. I assumed it was Taíno men returning from hunting the fish. A smile crept to my face as I looked up. But none of our canoes met my gaze. Instead, I stared at a very large canoe with a lot of cloth. It resembled nothing I had ever seen before.

I followed my first impulse and ran as far as I could away from the unfamiliar thing. As I ran on the small trail, my legs could hardly hold me up.

"Father, come quick. I have spotted something in the ocean," my voice was weak as fear spread throughout my body. My father was a *behique*. He healed all the wounds of my people. Once I stepped on a rock and it punctured my foot. I didn't tell my father until my puncture became infected. He healed it in a week by making me drink herb tea and soaking my foot with the root of a certain tree. He is the most intelligent man I know.

Many others ran to the beach with my father. I followed a ways behind them. I closed my eyes as the strange object drew nearer and nearer. My ears first told me that the large canoe had arrived. I heard a language different than my own. I saw strange men with skin as pale as the belly of a fish. They had an array of hair color. One had hair as black as night, while another's was as red as the sun.

I crept near the visitors as my fear vanished. They were showing my people treasures. I looked on with big eyes, wanting everything I saw.

One of the pale men pulled out a long, silver rectangular object with a point on the end. One of my people reached out and grabbed it. Blood dripped through his fingers as he drew back in pain. The white men looked at the red liquid trickling to the ground and laughed. I, along with many others was intrigued with this weapon. The visitors offered more people to grab the sharp object. Soon a dozen men had lost their battle with the silver weapon.

Our leader motioned for the pale people to follow us to our village. The man who seemed to lead the strange men grinned as they accepted the offer.

That night the *areito* was canceled. I was not too disappointed because the pale visitors traded beautiful treasures with us. One word I picked up from that night was "gold". Their leader seemed to want some gold badly. If only I knew what it was. The leader of the men slept in our hut that night. He had problems sleeping, but refused my father's tea. I wish to learn this strange language so I can speak with these interesting people. The whole village is excited about the arrival of our new friends. We hope that they will teach us about their land and we will teach them about ours.

The first day of the strange men had ended, and unfortunately there were many more days to come.

Anna Hereford wrote this piece as a 10th-grade student at Grant High School in Portland, Oregon.

TAÍNO RESISTANCE
Enrique's Uprising

BY ALVIN JOSEPHY, JR.

The Taíno leader, Caonabó, had been captured and shipped to Spain as a slave; he died en route. Caonabó's widow Anacaona was invited with 80 of her followers to a meeting with the Spanish governor, de Ovando. When they arrived and were led into a house, the house was set on fire and the Taíno people stabbed with bayonets and swords when they tried to escape. The Spaniards took Anacaona and executed her by hanging. A young boy , Guarocuya, the grandnephew of Anacaona and Caonabó, survived the fire, but he was given to Spanish missionaries to be raised. They gave him a new name, Enrique.

According to the Spanish law of encomienda, Taínos living on lands claimed by the Spanish owed their labor to that landlord. Although the rightful heir to his region, young Enrique became a slave to a cruel landlord named Valenzuela.

Theodore de Bry

Enrique did his best to comply with Valenzuela's tyrannical demands, suffering beatings and other abuse. But when Valenzuela raped his wife, Enrique reached the breaking point.

With a group of followers, he escaped to the Bahoruco Mountains. The enraged Spaniards called him the rebel Enrique, and his followers were condemned as insurgents. Armed only with spears, iron spikes, and bows and arrows, they fought with determination against the Spaniards and their more sophisticated weapons. Time and again, they resisted the Spaniards and made them retreat.

As word of Enrique's victories spread across the island, many Arawaks [Taínos] fled to his refuge and joined him. Acting according to the traditional rights and responsibilities of a paramount chief, Enrique assumed his proper role as protector of his people. He organized his followers, directed their tasks, and trained the military. Village chiefs assisted him. Women, children, and old people were sent to live in caves high in the mountains, where they raised chickens and tended vegetable plots to feed the Indian army. Scouts were posted on all the crags above the passes, and big boulders were rolled into place above the mountain paths.

Fighting defensively, Enrique instructed his men to kill Spaniards only in the course of a battle, and otherwise simply to deprive them of their arms. On one occasion, he even spared Valenzuela's life. It was said that Enrique never slept at night and himself patrolled the village until every dawn. For fourteen years, Enrique and his Arawak supporters fought the Spaniards to a standstill.

There was one Spaniard to whom Enrique would still talk — the priest las Casas. Las Casas, who would become known as the Protector of the Indians, met with Enrique in his mountain stronghold. Two months later, the two men appeared before the Spanish authorities and negotiated a truce. The Spaniards agreed to Enrique's terms: the guarantee of freedom for all the remaining Arawak people.

There were few of them left. Of all the millions who had inhabited the island in 1492, only handfuls survived. On Hispaniola, 4,000 Arawaks remained to follow Enrique to a settlement at the base of the Cibao Mountains. By 1542, fifty years after Columbus had first come upon them, the Arawak population was down to 200, and the Spaniards were replacing their labor with that of black slaves imported in chains from Africa.

Excerpted from the book 500 Nations: An Illustrated History of North American Indians *(New York: Knopf, 1994), produced to accompany a documentary video series of the same name.*

RETHINKING TERMS

BY PHILIP TAJITSU NASH AND EMILIENNE IRELAND

Think about the people in your hometown. Is there any adjective that describes them all? Are they, without exception, honest, wild, immoral, spiritual, ignorant, hostile, generous, brutal or noble?

Sure, you may be able to come up with a few generalizations. But it would make no sense to describe them as a group in terms of personality traits, moral values, or even physical appearance.

Now think about the words used to describe the events of 1492, and to refer to Europeans and Native Americans in general. You may find that these reveal hidden assumptions or biases.

People and Cultures

Many words used to describe peoples and cultures implicitly compare one group with another. What do we really mean by terms such as "primitive culture" or "simple society?" In what ways are communities "primitive" or "simple"? Do we just mean that their material technology is less complicated and less expensive to produce than that of modern-day industrial societies?

No human society is "primitive" or "simple." Every society is complex.

Traditional Native American life cannot be called "simple" or "primitive" in any way. A typical elder of the Wauja people in the Amazon rain forest, for example, has memorized hundreds of sacred songs and stories; plays several musical instruments; and knows the habits and habitats of hundreds of forest animals, birds, and insects, as well as the medicinal uses of local plants. He can guide his sons in building a two-story tall house using only axes, machetes, and materials from the forest. He is an expert agronomist. He speaks several languages fluently; knows precisely how he is related to several hundred of his closest kin; and has acquired sufficient wisdom to share his home peacefully with in-laws, cousins, children, and grandchildren. Female elders are comparably learned and accomplished.

Other phrases to watch out for include: Stone Age, trapped in time, prehistoric, timeless, and ancient. All imply that cultures and people never change, that they no longer exist, or that they are somehow inferior or backward. And words such as warlike, bloodthirsty, or treacherous do not ask whether a group resorted to war in self-defense.

There are also biases in geographic terms. The earth was all formed at one time, so why is one hemisphere called old and the other new? Why is one hemisphere called the Western Hemisphere? Or the Americas? How are these terms based on a European point of view?

Maps also reveal biases. For example, the Mercator Projection Map is useful for sailing, but distorts geography. It turns the top half of the world into two-thirds of the map — subtly but surely sending the message that the southern hemisphere is less important.

Popular descriptions of the events of 1492 are often one-sided. Seemingly neutral terms such as "encounter" and "discovery" are less painful to European Americans than the words some Native Americans would prefer: genocide, murder, rape, butchery, or conquest.

"Civilizing" or "Christianizing" a people presumes that their own society and religion are inferior. Calling the European conquerors "courageous" or "far-sighted" justifies their actions. Saying that European atrocities in the Western Hemisphere were "unavoidable" (or that the perpetrators of genocide were only "products of their time") dulls our sense of injustice regarding events both past and present.

Since Native Americans were around before Columbus, why do phrases such as "uninhabited land," "virgin land," and "unknown land" persist? Do terms such as "untamed land" and "unproductive land" imply that deforestation and agriculture are the only suitable ways to use land?

We need to be sensitive to how Native Americans refer to themselves. When appropriate, cultures and peoples are best defined as precisely as possible, using specific names such as Apache or Wauja.

Ask yourself how people refer to themselves, before describing them to someone else. Whose point of view is represented? Whose point of view is left out, minimized, or distorted?

Rethinking our terminology is essential to developing analytical minds. As we look at the events of 1492 and following, we must teach our children to respect all peoples, and to celebrate humanity rather than its destruction.

Phil Tajitsu Nash teaches Asian American Studies at the University of Maryland. He and Emilienne Ireland manage a company, Science Writers, that produces a variety of technical publications and information products. Both have done advocacy on behalf of the Wauja and other Native American peoples.

SECONDARY SCHOOL ISSUES

In school I learned of heroic discoveries
Made by liars and crooks. The courage
of millions of sweet and true people
Was not commemorated.

— Jimmie Durham,
from the poem "Columbus Day"

CEREMONY

BY LESLIE MARMON SILKO

I will tell you something about stories,
        [he said]
They aren't just entertainment.
Don't be fooled.
They are all we have, you see,
all we have to fight off
illness and death.

You don't have anything
if you don't have the stories.

Their evil is mighty
but it can't stand up to our stories.
So they try to destroy the stories
let the stories be confused or forgotten.
They would like that
They would be happy
Because we would be defenseless then.

He rubbed his belly.
I keep them here
[he said]
Here, put your hand on it
See, it is moving.
There is life here
for the people.

And in the belly of this story
the rituals and the ceremony
are still growing.

— from Ceremony *(New York: Penguin, 1977)*

Sitting Bull's prayer drum.

Silko is of Laguna Pueblo heritage and author of the book, **Ceremony,** *about a young Laguna Pueblo who returns to the reservation after being a prisoner of the Japanese during World War II.*

TALKING BACK TO COLUMBUS
Teaching for Justice and Hope

BY BILL BIGELOW

Of course, the writers of the books [that hide the truth or lie about Columbus] probably think it's harmless enough — what does it matter who discovered America, really, and besides it makes them feel good about America. But the thought that I have been lied to all my life about this, and who knows what else, really makes me angry.

Rebecca's written reaction to textbook accounts of Columbus's "discovery" hints that, in fact, the truth may not always set us free. Often it makes us angry — and that anger can all too easily lead to cynicism.

Over the years, I've tried to find ways to tell the truth about history so that students leave feeling more hopeful and powerful than when we began. I encourage students to "talk back" to the history and to the history writers. I prompt students to give voice to the social groups silenced in the traditional curriculum. I highlight historical episodes of struggle for social change and try to relate those movements to the present day. I provide opportunities for students to see themselves as activists for justice. And I ask students to draw on their own lives as a source of hope and wisdom about resistance to injustice. These are lofty goals and I'd be less than honest if I didn't admit that results are sometimes ambiguous.

Trying Out New Values

In *Annie John*, a novel by Jamaica Kincaid about a young black woman's coming of age on the Caribbean island of Antigua, Annie "talks back" to history by defacing her school book's chapter on Christopher Columbus. Annie dislikes Columbus, representing as he does the colonization of the West Indies and the initiation of the Atlantic slave trade. So in her textbook, under a picture of Columbus being transported in chains back to Spain during his third voyage, Annie writes in large letters: "The Great Man Can No Longer Just Get Up and Go."

It's probably not a good idea to encourage students to scribble critical commentary in the pages of history books like Annie did. But we can encourage them to write critiques of Columbus and his

worldview. In my U.S. history class, students read numerous excerpts from Native oratory and poetry which reveal a different way of viewing the living world than that of the European conquerors. Whether Shawnee — "Sell a country! Why not sell the air, the great sea, as well as the earth? Did not the Great Spirit make them all for the use of his children?" — or Lakota — "Every seed is awakened and so has all animal life. It is through this mysterious power that we too have our being and we therefore yield to our neighbors, even our animal neighbors, the same right as ourselves, to inhabit this land" — the first Americans share a common understanding of the web of life.

I ask students to step inside this worldview and talk back to the materialistic and exploitative values imported to the Americas by Columbus and those who followed. Though I never limit them to working from my suggestions, I provide quotes the students may respond to: "Gold is a wonderful thing! Whoever owns it is lord of all he wants. With gold it is even possible to open for souls the way to paradise," Columbus wrote in a letter to Isabella and Ferdinand in 1503. And another, from Governor William Bradford of Plymouth Plantation, who, in sharp contrast to the Indians, saw the American landscape as "a hideous and desolate wilderness full of wild beasts and wild men."

My student Kimberly Stubbs, then a sophomore, adopted the persona of a Plains Indian and wrote a stinging rebuttal to the kind of arrogance she saw in the Columbus quotation:

What is gold
when the buffalo's thunder
is stilled, the earth
no longer drummed by mud-hard hooves?...
What is gold
when grass turns brown
when cold, cold wind blows ice
through tents and houses
and there's no more buckskin
no fur to bring warmth

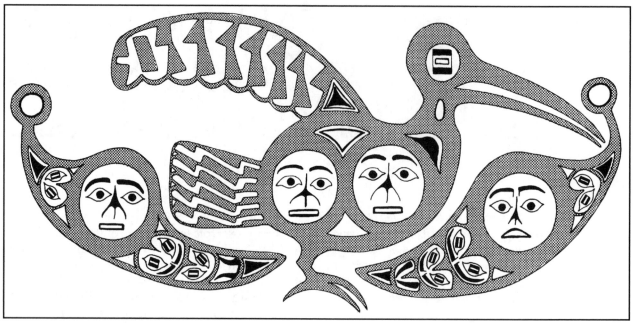

Traditional design from the Northwest Coast, representing the Raven.

no wood for fire,
for all the trees have died?
With gold it is even possible
to open for souls
the way to paradise,
but I say that way is death,
and gold the destroyer of life.

Kim's poem longs for life pursuits that don't "destroy life." While her piece does not provide a blueprint for social transformation, the talking-back assignment challenges and encourages students to give voice to a humane and environmentally respectful value system. I hope that once students have "tried on" new ways of understanding the world, they are more able to incorporate aspects of those worldviews that make sense to them.

Giving Voice to the Taínos

Students might be encouraged to complete their writing assignment from the standpoint of Christopher Columbus. Some students may want to shun Columbus, or anyone else, as mediator and simply let the Taínos speak for themselves.

In a long illustrated poem, "Christopher's Fall From Grace," Jefferson student Rachel Drown imagines the unequal dialogue between Columbus and Taínos. Through verse, the cultures speak to each other:

... No welcome can we give to you,
our souls you cannot steal.
You've taken all we have by force,
as your fate you try to seal.
We have no more gold, we have no more

pride,
We have no more carefree days.
Too many we love are dead or gone
and we fear there are more on the way.

Salutations lowly slaves,
I see you all look sad
You'll join your friends if you find no gold
or in any way make me mad.
I've taken your loved ones back to Spain,
to serve rich noble men.
I need more gold or I'll make slaves,
of all your kith and kin.

Unwelcome is the mortal man,
through heaven's pearly gates,
who lies and steals and kills his own,
with greed and lust and hate.
You cannot harm us anymore,
or use us for your gain.
And long after your memory fades,
our spirits will remain.
You became an evil man,
Amidst your lust for gold.
But all the wealth within the world,
won't save your tarnished soul.

Rachel's Taínos "resist" Columbus and crew by maintaining their humanity in the face of his kidnapping, slavery and extortion. The last drawing accompanying her poem portrays Taínos with their hands linked and thrust in the air — spiritually triumphant even in their defeat. (That this resistance of the soul is the only fight the Taínos offer probably indicates that I didn't do an adequate job teaching the varieties of Caribbean Indians' flesh-and-blood struggles.)

Students can also find hope by learning about other people who fought for what they thought was right. Our curriculum needs to feature movements for social justice — against slavery and imperialism, for workers' rights, for women's liberation — as well as individuals who joined and led these movements —Sojourner Truth, Frederick Douglass, John Brown, Eugene Debs, Margaret Sanger, Cesar Chavez. In that way, the link between injustice and people's capacity to resist becomes for students a "habit of the mind."

Giving Voice to Resistance

From the beginning of the European conquest, Native Americans stood up for themselves in myriad ways. On Monday, October 15, 1492, just three days after his arrival on Guanahaní, Columbus writes in his journal that some of the people he had earlier kidnapped were attempting to mislead him in order to escape: "... all that [my captives] said was a ruse in order to get away." Sure enough, that same day, two of the Indians he'd kidnapped threw themselves overboard and escaped with the help of Indians in canoes. Columbus's men searched for the escapees on a nearby island but they "all ran off like chickens," Columbus writes.

But Indians didn't just run away. As the Spaniards began to reveal the exploitation and brutality inherent in *La Empresa* — the Enterprise — the Indians also attacked. The men Columbus left behind at La Navidad on Hispaniola after his first voyage formed "a gang that roved the island in search of more gold and women." Later reports indicated that each of the Spaniards had taken four or five Indian women as concubines. The Indian *cacique* (leader), Caonabó, led a mission against members of the gang, killed them and "promptly descended on Navidad with a strong force to wipe out the source of trouble." Caonabó's raiders attacked Spaniards in their camps, killing some and chasing others into the sea where they were drowned. "The others wandering about the interior were killed off by the Indians whom they had robbed or otherwise wronged."

Even in death, the Indians refused to bow to the will of the conquerors. In the first volume of his trilogy, *Memory of Fire*, Eduardo Galeano reconstructs the defiant conduct of Hatuey, an Indian cacique in the Guahaba region of Hispaniola, after his capture by the Spaniards:

They tie him to a stake.
Before lighting the fire that will reduce him to charcoal and ash, the priest promises him glory and eternal rest if he agrees to be baptized. Hatuey asks: "Are there

A Cree tribal member has seen thousands of acres of traditional land flooded by Hydro Quebec's massive plans to re-route rivers to furnish electric power to Canadian and U.S. industries.

Christians in that heaven?"

"Yes."

Hatuey chooses hell, and the firewood begins to crackle.

These and dozens of other instances of indigenous resistance can be shared with students. The purpose is never to glorify violence, but to underscore people's capacity to stand up for their rights even against tremendous odds.

Students should also realize that not all Spaniards participated in the orgy of killing and plunder. I use the story of the Dominican friar, Antonio de Montesinos, who on the Sunday before Christmas in 1511 delivered the first sermon in the Americas attacking the enslavement and murder of Indians (see p. 103). Montesinos' congregation that day included all the royal officials of Santo Domingo, including the Admiral Diego Columbus, son of Christopher Columbus. Montesinos scolded them, saying that their conscience was "sterile like the desert" and warned them the voice of Christ says "that you are living in deadly sin for the atrocities you tyrannically impose on these innocent people [the Indians.] Tell me, what right have you to enslave them?"

While I hope students will draw inspiration from these church people's courage and tenacity, I also want them to approach the ecclesiastic resistance critically. Although Montesinos' sermons were brave and angry, they also contained an attitude of we-know-what's-best-for-the-Indians.

To the Present

When possible, I try to bring struggles for justice up to the present, so as not to leave resistance back in history, lying there like a corpse. A few years ago, my teaching partner in a literature and history class, Linda Christensen, and I decided to acquaint students with the fight for native fishing rights on the Columbia River. David SoHappy and 12 other Native Americans had recently been arrested for poaching salmon, even though a treaty signed in 1855 grants Indians perpetual rights to fish at all the "usual and accustomed places" — as Native peoples along the Columbia had been doing for the last 12,000 years or more.

We read Craig Lesley's *Winterkill*, a novel about a Nez Perce and his son, and articles about David SoHappy's struggle. We also role-played the controversy over the building of the Dalles Dam in 1957, a dam which violated native treaty rights by drowning Celilo Falls, a sacred fishing ground and trading center. We invited a representative from the Columbia River Defense Committee to talk to the class and also took a field trip to the museum at the Dalles Dam. There we heard a talk from the Army Corps of Engineers (builders of the dam), and hiked along the banks of the river, where 3,000 year old native pictographs overlook the water below and Indians still fish from platforms fastened to the cliffs.

The museum is a Corps of Engineers house of propaganda. Native people are portrayed as relics from a distant past, associated solely with archaeological digs. The exhibit texts' passive and muddy prose hides any human responsibility for the sabotage of river Indians' lives. The museumspeak acknowledges that changes occurred, but masks the choices preceding these changes, who made them, and why. Linda and I encouraged students to take notes on the exhibits and through poetry and essay to write about the day.

Rebecca wrote in part:

... You learn how a lifestyle
can be bought and sold
You learn you can picnic
where ancestors of a culture
were once buried
And a white man's greed
means more than a red man's
survival ....
You learn to sit back
and let progress progress.

And Matthew wrote:

... I could hear the churning and growling
from deep inside the cold, windowless,
cement walls
and from the depths of the water
I could almost hear the chanting and
crying of Celilos
as they watched their fishing grounds
become as dead as their forefathers.

Linda and I were proud parents of what had been some powerful learning experiences for students. But in our class discussion to evaluate the study, Nikki said, "Why is it that we just kept talking *about* Indians, but we didn't actually get to meet any Indians? It couldn't be that hard to get on the phone and call Chief Johnny Jackson [of the Celilos] and see if he would come in to speak."

It wasn't the most gentle way to bring it up, but Nikki was right. Inadvertently, we had replicated the textbook and museum discourse that talks about native peoples in the third person — and in the process silences them and dumps them somewhere in the past. Without intending it, we reinforced the portrayal of Indian as Other, one of the very notions we so insistently criticized.

In years past, American Indian Movement repre-

A Chippewa tribal member defends his legal fishing rights due under lasting federal treaties, despite local opposition by anti-Native groups.

Andrew Lichtenstein/Impact Visuals

sentatives and members of local native organizations had spoken in my classes, but I underestimated the importance of this personal contact for students. The significance of the omission went beyond the error of reinforcing the Us and Them myth. In the face of such overwhelming and continuing injustice, students needed to meet people face to face who were working for change. Merely reading about these people and movements unnecessarily distanced students from the hope that comes from hearing actual voices say, "I believe we can make a difference."

Students as Activists

That year, Linda and I asked students to create a project that would reach beyond the classroom walls to educate others in the school or larger community. Unless we offered students a chance to act on their new learning, our teaching would unintentionally yet effectively tell students that their role is merely to uncover injustice, not to do anything about it.

Students could choose the form of their projects. The only requirement was that each individual or group make a presentation outside the classroom. They took us at our word. One group of musicians produced a raucous rock video about the damming of the Columbia River at The Dalles Dam. Another group choreographed and performed a dance for other classes, at the same time bitter and humorous,

on Columbus's "discovery" and search for gold. As some students danced/acted, one recited quotes from Columbus. Several students interviewed local Northwest Indian tribal leaders about their struggle for fishing rights, and produced a videotape, subsequently broadcast over the school's closed-circuit TV news show.

One young woman, Nicole Smith-Leary, wrote and illustrated a children's book, *Chris.* In Nicole's story, a young boy named Christopher moves from his old Spain Street neighborhood to a new house on Salvadora Street. He's miserable and misses his old friends, Ferdie and Isie. While wandering the new neighborhood he spots a colorful playhouse and declares, "I claim this clubhouse in the name of me, and my best friends Ferdie and Isie." The rightful owners of the clubhouse soon return and confront Christopher, who insists that the structure is now his because he "discovered" it.

"How can you come here and discover something that we built and really care about?" the boys demand.

The story ends happily when they agree to let Christopher share the clubhouse if he helps with the upkeep—a metaphorical twist that would have been nice 500 years earlier.

Nicole read her story in a number of classes at a local elementary school. She opened each session by asking if anyone had something to write with. When an unsuspecting youngster volunteered a pencil, Nicole thanked the student, then pocketed it. This elementary school version of purse-stealing (see p. 17) gave Nicole a handy introduction to the theft-posing-as-discovery lesson in her short story.

Like Rebecca and many other students, Nicole was angry she had been lied to about Columbus and the genocide of indigenous people in the Caribbean. However, the final project assignment encouraged her to channel that anger in an activist direction. She became a teacher, offering the youngsters a framework in which to locate and question the romanticized textbook patter about "exploration" and "discovery." But as she taught she also learned — learned that the best way to address injustice is to work for change.

Because Nicole's book functioned as such a wonderful model, I've encouraged students in subsequent years to use this form to talk back to history. For those who choose the metaphorical path blazed by Nicole, their stories assert that yes, people can share and cooperate. They imply that there are alternative models of social organization to the one based on exploitation and violence practiced by Columbus and the colonialists who came after.

In "Chris and the Cherry Tree," Stephanie Clay sees justice coming only from collective resistance. Every week, Christopher's mother asks him to pick cherries so she can make cherry pie. Lazy Christopher forces several little neighborhood boys to pick cherries for him.

"Fill this bag up with cherries or I will take your picnic food and lunch money," he threatens.

In a playful, but also serious way, Stephanie captures the extortion central to Columbus's Enterprise: "Christopher reached for a peanut butter and jelly sandwich and ate it to let the boys know he meant business." The exploitation continues until one afternoon Christopher returns to find his little workers missing. Suddenly, the boys jump out of the tree and pelt Christopher with cherries. Christopher runs home to his mother, never to bother the boys again. (In his *History of the Indies*, Spanish priest Bartolomé de las Casas describes Taínos, forced to work in the Spaniards' mines, picking up the only weapons they had, stones, to throw at heavily armed soldiers.)

Hearing Silent Voices

Nicole's and Stephanie's stories denounce injustice but they also imagine alternatives: through discussion, through sharing, and yes, through resistance, we can live better. It's more than just wishing history had come out differently, though it certainly is that as well. History is not destiny, their stories assert. And through envisioning ourselves as subjects of a better world, we help play a small part in bringing it about.

In a discussion about the U.S. media at the height of the Gulf War, my student Sekou Crawford said, "It's just like with Columbus. The textbooks all told the story from his point of view, from the winners' point of view. They called it a discovery instead of an invasion. The only story we get now is from the bombers' point of view. We hardly hear anything from the victims."

Sekou's point couldn't be denied: nightly newscasts were dominated by U.S. military spokespeople and images from "our" side.

Sekou had begun to "hear" the silence and linked the wartime muzzling of the bomb victims to the absence of an indigenous perspective in most teachings of Columbus. Through our critical reading of textbooks and children's books, beginning with Columbus, I introduce students to the idea that language takes sides. They see how books on Columbus and the "discovery" highlight certain ways of understanding reality and silence other perspectives. Thus, a number of students decide to give voice to what they imagine to be Native American perspectives in their children's books.

Tina Thomas wrote "The Untold Story" (see p. 42) recounting the tale of discovery from the point of view of the "discovered." The narrative doesn't sail breezily along with Columbus and crew. "These people [the Europeans] were not like us. Their skin was pink, their hair the color of sand, and their eyes the color of the open sea. They wore strange items that covered their bodies, even though it was very hot." Eventually, Columbus takes slaves and kills many others. Unlike the traditional stories, Tina refuses to end her tale happily ever after: "We have little to show our children as proof of what happened to the Taínos. But we have our stories, told from generation to generation."

Listening for "untold stories" begins with the Columbus tale, but is more than just a quest for historical accuracy. For students, learning to recognize that those in power privilege the voices of the powerful over the powerless is a basic skill. In most textbooks, in most movies, on most TV sets, the real life struggles and accomplishments of the majority of people are as absent as the Taínos are from Columbus books. Working-class children, children of color, young women, all can begin to reclaim their own histories once they begin to look for what is missing as well as for what is there.

"Legacy of Defiance"

Finally, I want students to look at their own lives, so as to locate a personal "legacy of defiance" from which to draw hope — and wisdom. Linda and

A grandmother defies a roadblock to take food supplies to Native activists.

I ask students to think of times in their lives when they stood up for what they felt was right. It might be a time they physically confronted a perpetrator of injustice, or simply a time they "talked back" to someone in authority. To help prompt students' memories of resistance, we give examples from each of our lives — times we stood up to overbearing administrators, challenged friends who were treating someone unfairly, or demonstrated against unjust laws or policies.

After brainstorming and prodding each other's memories, students choose an incident and write a story about it. In our discussion circle the next day, students read their stories to the group, piecing together a patchwork quilt of caring and determination. As a kindergartner, Marnie implored her mother to remove her from a school where the teachers frequently beat students. Aashish joined a team protest to defy a rule requiring a minimum height for soccer players that discriminated against East Indians. Amanda challenged a friend who called a gay student a "fag." Felicia refused her boyfriend's demand to prove her love by having his baby — "I

walked up in his face and told him that I was tired of him running the relationship." Sara angrily confronted a group of girls who taunted their Mexican classmates with racist comments — "Yes, I'm proud of being a damn spic, as you white people say it. But you have no right telling us that. We have rights just like everybody else."

One of our aims is for students to remind each other that, "Yeah, I'm the kind of person who stands up for myself, who believes in doing the right thing." During the read-arounds, there is often a palpable aura of dignity and solidarity that settles over the classroom. Our hope is to nurture the beginnings of this community of justice and courage. But we also see the read-arounds as building a "collective text" of student experience to be probed for deeper social meaning. As we saw from the Dominicans' experience on Hispaniola, righteous defiance is important but ultimately insufficient to achieve justice. We celebrate resistance, but we should also evaluate it.

Linda and I ask students to take notes on each other's story, to listen for:

1. What conditions allowed us to stand up for ourselves or others?

2. Was the resistance effective in rooting out the causes of injustice?

3. How were we changed by our acts of defiance? and

4. What other patterns did we notice as we listened to the papers?

After our read-around, in which students call on each other to praise and comment on the stories, we ask them to write for a few minutes on the questions as preparation for discussion.

Some people, like Maryanne, notice that at times people fail to look for allies: "It was interesting to me that in most of these incidents people stood alone with the exception of Sonia." Kurzel agreed: "It seems to me that most of the class stood alone and against people they knew, like Chrissy and her uncle, Millshane and her aunt, Rita and her teacher, me and my teacher. In some cases they should have stood as a people instead of their self, and as far as results nothing really happened." And Jeff noticed that "there were some cases where people tried to use anger, but could of done something else instead of using cuss words and their fist."

Protesting Columbus Day celebrations.

Kirk Condyles/Impact Visuals

Celebration of Resistance

Students' celebration of resistance is often tempered with the realization that the way we stand up for ourselves can be needlessly individualistic or violent. On the other hand, when I told one class that it didn't appear that students' physical fights did much good and that talking might have gotten them further, Kevin seemed to speak for the majority, saying, "Nah, that talking stuff don't work anymore."

While most students begin to sense the limitations and contradictions of their actions, they almost always come away with a greater appreciation of their capacities to make a difference — and with more respect for each other. Heather commented that "standing up showed these people they have power over their lives and power to protect themselves." Scott wrote that hearing people's stories "showed us that we can achieve things if we stand up for our-

selves. We all felt better about ourselves." Keely noticed that even though people often stood alone, the experience was much more satisfying when they fought for change together: "I think people enjoy doing something together rather than alone. It seems in today's world people would rather accomplish some feat on their own. So they're the one on top. But I really believe when something is successful, it's better to have someone to celebrate with. When you do something alone it's like you are doing it for yourself, but when other people are involved, you did it for each other."

But Christie understood the issue differently and underscored one's individual responsibility to confront wrongdoing: "I got out of this assignment that you have to be the one who stop the pain. If you don't say anything about your feelings people will always run over them."

The Columbus myth teaches children to accept racism as normal, to believe that powerful, rich, white, Christian countries have the right to dominate people of color in poor countries. It encourages people to listen for the perspectives of the winners, the social elites, and inures them to the historical and literary silences of everybody else. And it's a male myth of conquest: leave women and community behind; encounter shortsighted or naive people; convert, trick or overpower them — just pursue your dream of wealth and fame.

No curricular task can be more important than encouraging students to critique this powerful social myth. In numerous ways, we can invite students to "talk back" to Columbus and all he symbolizes, ever vigilant to guard against anger becoming despair. Our overriding concern must be to engage young people in activities that reveal their power to build a society of equality and justice.

Bill Bigelow (bbpdx@aol.com) teaches at Franklin High School in Portland, Oregon, and is an editor of Rethinking Schools.

COLUMBUS DAY

BY JIMMIE DURHAM

In school I was taught the names
Columbus, Cortez, and Pizzaro and
A dozen other filthy murderers.
A bloodline all the way to General Miles,
Daniel Boone and General Eisenhower.

No one mentioned the names
Of even a few of the victims.
But don't you remember Chaske, whose spine
Was crushed so quickly by Mr. Pizzaro's boot?
What words did he cry into the dust?

What was the familiar name
Of that young girl who danced so gracefully
That everyone in the village sang with her —
Before Cortez' sword hacked off her arms
As she protested the burning of her sweetheart?

That young man's name was Many Deeds,
And he had been a leader of a band of fighters
Called the Redstick Hummingbirds, who slowed
The march of Cortez' army with only a few
Spears and stones which now lay still
In the mountains and remember.

Greenrock Woman was the name
Of that old lady who walked right up
And spat in Columbus' face. We
Must remember that, and remember
Laughing Otter the Taíno who tried to stop
Columbus and was taken away as a slave.
We never saw him again.

In school I learned of heroic discoveries
Made by liars and crooks. The courage
Of millions of sweet and true people
Was not commemorated.

Let us then declare a holiday
For ourselves, and make a parade that begins
With Columbus' victims and continues
Even to our grandchildren who will be named
In their honor.

Because isn't it true that even the summer
Grass here in this land whispers those names,
And every creek has accepted the responsibility
Of singing those names? And nothing can stop
The wind from howling those names around
The corners of the school.

Why else would the birds sing
So much sweeter here than in other lands?

Durham is a Cherokee artist, poet, and native-rights activist.
"Columbus Day" is from a book of poems by the same name
(Minneapolis: West End Press, 1983).

BROKEN SPEARS
LIE IN THE ROADS
by an Aztec poet

Broken spears lie in the roads;

we have torn our hair in our grief.

The houses are roofless now, and their walls

are red with blood.

Worms are swarming in the streets and plazas,

and the walls are spattered with gore.

The water has turned red, as if it were dyed,

and when we drink of it,

it has the taste of brine.

We have pounded our hands in despair

          against the adobe walls,

for our inheritance, our city, is lost and dead.

The shields of our warriors were its defense,

but they could not save it.

We have chewed dry twigs and salt grasses;

we have filled our mouths with dust

          and bits of adobe;

we have eaten lizards, rats and worms....

This song of sorrow was written by an Aztec chronicler describing the conquest of Tenochtitlán, the great capital city of the Aztecs located on a low-lying island (where Mexico City stands today). The city had at least a quarter of a million inhabitants, with great causeways across the surrounding lake, aqueducts to bring in drinking water, canals, drawbridges, temples, towers, flat-topped pyramids, and a great central marketplace.

The Spaniards led by Hernando Cortez entered the city in November 1519 looking for gold; they remarked that they had never seen a place so well regulated and arranged. In August, 1521, they sacked the city, leaving it in ruins.

The poem is from a dramatic and very readable illustrated history, in brief stories, about the arrival of the conquistadors, direct from native Aztec documents, The Broken Spears: The Aztec Account of the Conquest of Mexico, *edited by Miguel Leon-Portilla (Boston: Beacon Press, 1990, pb. edition). Illustrations by Alberto Beltran.*

BLACK INDIANS & RESISTANCE

BY WILLIAM LOREN KATZ

An escaped slave in Surinam is captured and punished.

William Blake

On Christmas Day in 1522, Europeans in the Americas first learned that slavery did not always lead to easy wealth. On that day, African and Indian slaves on a plantation owned by Diego Columbus rose and murdered their masters and overseers. Nearby Native Americans quickly joined the rebels. The beautiful island of Santo Domingo shook with the first recorded slave rebellion in the Americas.

The conspiracy had spread across the sprawling sugar plantations of the island in the weeks before Christmas. Patiently, the plotters waited until Christmas Day when the planters and their families would be bloated with food, soaked with liquor, and too weak or sleepy to offer much resistance. Then they struck, plunging into the night to kill whites and find freedom.

For two days, the rebels met with little opposition, but on the third day, Spanish troops caught up with them in an open field and opened fire. The fugitives broke for the woods. Unfamiliar with the treacherous terrain, the Spaniards were unwilling to pursue.

Governor Diego Columbus decided on a new strategy. The governor hired Native Americans for the dangerous task of tracking the fugitives. A hunt began. Although the exact outcome is unclear, this first uprising was a landmark event in the fresh history of European, African, and Indian relations in the Americas.

Masters and slaves both learned some important lessons from this first bloody confrontation. Enslaving Indians and Africans was not going to be free of pain. Masters in a slave land could not sleep easily at night. While they concluded it was absolutely necessary to remain armed, they also learned it was expedient to use one race to fight the other. Racial division would be a tool employed by the Europeans. A French colonial dispatch later in the century put the matter simply: "The law is hard, but it is both wise and necessary in a land of 15 slaves to one white. Between the races we cannot dig too deep a gulf."

But another American tradition also took root. The men and women enslaved in the New World began a pattern of resistance. The first people enslaved were the first to flee. They were the first to rebel. They were the first to announce that chains were meant to be broken.

The spirit of rebellion spread like a wildfire. In the next ten years, revolts spread to Colombia, Panama, Cuba, Puerto Rico, and Mexico. In 1527, a major insurrection threatened Spanish headquarters at Mexico City. Viceroy Antonio de Mendoza reported that Africans "had chosen a King ... and that the Indians were also with them." Terrified Mexican officials agreed to halt any further importations of Africans. Slave resistance had temporarily halted the African slave trade.

By the 1570s, the flames of revolt were burning brightly in Mexico. One in every ten slaves was living a free life in hiding.

It was in Mexico that Europeans made their strongest effort to keep Africans apart from Native Americans. As early as 1523, Hernando Cortés was given a Royal Order to keep Indians in their villages, apart from Africans at all costs. One Royal Order forbade "trade, commerce, or communication" between the two dark peoples. But racial mixing was so common in Mexico that it became hard to tell by skin color who was free and who was slave. "One lived in constant fear," wrote a Spanish colonist.

Maroon Settlements

From the time of Columbus, the gravest threat to European domination of the Western Hemisphere came from outlaw communities of former slaves. These *maroon* colonies, as they were called, were considered a knife poised at the throat of the slave system.

Men and women who lived in them, though, saw their settlements as the fulfillment of an American dream — a sheltered home in freedom. The maroon communities were places for families to educate their young, to develop agriculture and trade, to practice religion and justice based on their own traditions, not those of slave masters.

Some colonies were begun by a single African or Indian; others were the result of many slaves fleeing together. The history of the Saramaka people of Surinam in South America started around 1685 when African and native slaves escaped and together formed a maroon society. For eight generations, Dutch armed forces tried to crush their community, but today it is still alive, with 20,000 members.

From the first day, maroon colonies faced enormous problems. They had to quickly find a safe location, plan a defense, and feed and clothe their people. Women were usually in short supply, and many maroon raids sought to free African or Indian women in slavery, for wives. Families meant that communities would be stable and desire peace, and that their soldiers would fight harder to defend loved ones and children.

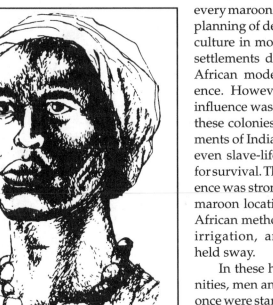

"Nanny," an 18th-century Jamaican maroon hero.

Some maroons stayed near large cities, living as bandits. They raided local plantations, merchants, and even Indians and slaves. These communities were unstable, often with few women and no children, and usually disappeared into the violence they helped create. Although some earned a reputation for daring raids on rich Europeans, most were feared by people of every race.

Fear of attack haunted every maroon settlement. The planning of defense and agriculture in most Black Indian settlements drew largely on African models and experience. However, no type of influence was discarded, and these colonies combined elements of Indian, African, and even slave-life heritage vital for survival. The African influence was strongest in tropical maroon locations, and there, African methods of planting, irrigation, and harvesting held sway.

In these hidden communities, men and women, who once were starved and beaten by masters, grew strong and vigorous. So far from home, Africans in particular made special efforts to preserve their ancestral ways and pass them on to their children.

To the surprise of Europeans, many maroon colonies became successful, independent farming communities. In the 18th century, Captain John Stedman, leading Dutch troops against maroons in the Guianas, wrote that maroon foods were superior to European products and in great supply. Men and women in maroon settlements were often described as healthy, tall and muscular, a tribute to their diets and to their freedom.

For some colonies, trade became a vital part of economic life. Black Indians in Venezuela in 1728, for example, ran a successful shipping operation. Led by a man named Juan Andresote, they carried cacao from Spanish merchants to Dutch merchants about 150 miles away. But Philip V of Spain awarded friends a monopoly of this trade, and in 1732, Spain sent out 250 soldiers, including 150 men conscripted from Indians and African slaves, to challenge the dark businessmen of Andresote.

Outside the town of Cabria, Andresote changed from shipping expert to guerrilla warrior. He maneuvered his army into battle with skill, and the slave and native soldiers quickly deserted the European command. Andresote's sharpshooters' musket fire then brought down all but 44 European soldiers. But Spain sent another 1500 troops after Andresote, and he had to flee to save his life.

Although colonial law often threw whites in jail for trading with outlawed maroon communities, some Europeans clearly saw a profit in doing business with their Black Indian neighbors.

In a military campaign against the maroons, Captain John Stedman told how his troops, which included Europeans and Indians, destroyed "the most beautiful field of ripe rice" and left a village of one hundred homes "in smoking ruins." Against these well-armed soldiers, maroons had to devise creative strategies.

In one battle, Stedman's men all suffered wounds from maroon musket fire, but later, upon examining their wounds, they found pebbles, coat buttons, and pieces of silver coins embedded in their flesh. These maroons had no bullets to defend themselves.

That night, Stedman's troops found themselves in the midst of a shouting match with their maroon foes. All night, voices from the woods hurled curses and ridicule at the invaders, and the Europeans shouted back. The next morning, Stedman's troops discovered that, under cover of darkness, the maroons had moved out all their women, children, and elderly, their rice, yams, and other possessions.

William Loren Katz is author of the book Black Indians *(New York: Atheneum Books for Young Readers, 1991), which documents the history of close relations between Africans and native peoples in the Americas. This excerpt is adapted by the author.*

The Republic of Palmares

For almost a century, a maroon colony called the Republic of Palmares, in northeastern Brazil, stood as the greatest challenge to European rule in Latin America.

It began around 1600 with a few runaway slaves and friendly Indians. In 1640, a Dutch citizen named Lintz reported 11,000 people living in Palmares's three villages. The Dutch West India Company decided to put Palmares through "fire and sword." Unsuccessful, they tried again a few years later, and again failed.

By then Palmares was half a mile long, with streets six feet wide. It had hundreds of homes, churches, and shops. Its well-kept lands produced cereals and other crops irrigated African-style with streams. It boasted courts that carried out justice for its thousands of citizens, and was ruled over by King Ganga-Zumba. (Ganga-Zumba combined an Angolan African word for "great" with a Tupi Indian word for "ruler.") Christianity was commonly practiced, including elaborate marriage and baptism ceremonies that drew large crowds.

In 1657, life in Palmares was still relatively peaceful. But the new rulers of Brazil, the Portuguese, decided it must be destroyed. A foreign expedition was launched every 15 months against the Republic of Palmares; each was beaten back with heavy losses on both sides. Palmares, with its determined armed forces, and three huge surrounding walls, cost many a foreign commander or governor his post or his life. Men in splendid uniforms turned and fled back to Rio de Janeiro or Lisbon, relieved to abandon a war they could not win.

Finally, in 1694, the invaders brought in an army of Brazilian Indians called "Paulistas" to lead a massive assault on the Republic of Palmares. Some 6,000 Paulistas, supported by Portuguese soldiers and weapons, laid siege to Palmares for 42 days. Finally it was overrun, with hundreds dying in hand-to-hand combat. Many others, including some of the bravest warriors of Palmares, according to a legend, hurled themselves over a cliff rather than surrender.

The ruler, King Zambi, wounded in the struggle, was captured and beheaded by the enemy. His head was displayed, said the European victors, "to kill the legend of his immortality."

But death does not kill legends. For almost a century the Republic of Palmares had shone as the brightest star of freedom in Latin America. It had united many peoples under an African form of government and culture. For generations, it had met and turned back European invaders and their hired mercenaries. Each time, it had returned to planting and harvesting abundant crops.

The meaning of Palmares and its legendary rulers was that dark people — Africans and Indians — in the Western Hemisphere meant to be free. This idea terrified Europeans more than the powerful armies and defenses of Palmares.

—William Loren Katz

INDIAN SINGING
IN 20TH-CENTURY AMERICA
by Gail Tremblay

We wake; we wake the day,

the light rising in us like sun —

our breath a prayer brushing

against the feathers in our hands.

We stumble out into streets;

patterns of wires invented by strangers

are strung between eye and sky,

and we dance in two worlds,

inevitable as seasons in one,

exotic curiosities in the other

which rushes headlong down highways,

watches us from car windows, explains

us to its children in words

that no one could ever make

sense of. The image obscures

the vision, and we wonder

whether anyone will ever hear

our own names for the things

we do. Light dances in the body,

surrounds all living things —

even the stones sing

although their songs are infinitely

lower than the ones we learn

from trees. No human voice lasts

long enough to make such music sound.

Earth breath eddies between factories

and office buildings, caresses the surface

of our skin; we go to jobs, the boss

always watching the clock to see

that we're on time. He tries to shut

out magic and hopes we'll make

mistakes or disappear. We work

fast and steady and remember

each breath alters the composition

of the air. Change moves relentless,

the pattern unfolding despite their planning —

we're always there — singing round dance

songs, remembering what supports

our life — impossible to ignore.

From Indian Singing in 20th Century America
(Corvallis, OR: Calyx Books, 1990).

Gail Tremblay (Onondaga and Micmac) is a visual artist
and poet who teaches at The Evergreen State College in
Olympia, Washington.

COWBOYS AND INDIANS
on the Playground

BY RAY GONZALEZ

When I was in elementary school in El Paso in the fifties and sixties, we studied American historical icons like Davy Crockett, Abraham Lincoln, and Christopher Columbus. The heroic importance of historical characters like Crockett and Lincoln was obvious to a daydreaming boy like myself. I always wanted to be a hero and created my own characters in the strange little stories I wrote in my spiral-bound notebook.

Columbus was something else, though. It was harder for me to understand what my history and social studies teachers were saying when they told my classmates and me that Columbus sailed in three ships and discovered where we lived. I didn't understand how people in the 15th century couldn't know the United States was here.

In the 5th grade, I added Columbus to my list of heroes, and even made up my own stories of exploration where my friends and I sailed down the Río Grande in wooden rafts we built in my backyard, bound for those narrow, sandy islands that stuck out in the middle of the dry river. We never actually did anything like that, but when the whole concept of exploration and discovery finally sunk in, I knew heroes like Crockett and Lincoln could not have performed their mighty deeds without Columbus coming along to get the whole thing started. This guy with his *Niña*, *Pinta*, and *Santa María* was our true leader and he must have been a brave man taking on so many red-skinned Indians.

I can still see those colorful illustrations in my history textbook, the bearded and armored Spaniards taking on the dark-painted, half-naked hordes of savages. My friends and I didn't play cowboys and Indians for nothing. We knew who the good guys were, even though a cowboy hat and a shiny gun and holster were more fun than weird armored helmets and long swords. I got stuck being one of the Indians because, when sides were drawn on the playground, the few Chicanos who went to Putnam Elementary were told they were the Indians. I rarely got to be one of the good guys.

I did a report on Columbus's three ships and got an A+ on it. I was a good artist and spent a great deal of time drawing the intricate sails on the ships. I knew everything about them, and my 5th-grade teacher was pleased. That A+ told me I was an explorer, and I knew the history of my country. I understood all about good and evil, how the story of us all was clearly written and told in the textbooks I loved to take home and read. No one had to force me to do homework.

My fascination with explorers pushed me to read more and find those books in the library that told me the Mexicans who killed Davy Crockett at the Alamo were blood-thirsty, dumb peasants, that our proud forefathers settled the west because those same tribes of people who resisted Columbus were keeping cities like El Paso from being established.

When I was forced to play Indian at school, I resigned myself to it, though I felt shamed and hoped that not too many of my teachers would see me on the playground and wonder why this student, who was so good at re-creating the voyage of Columbus, was whooping and hollering on the monkey bars. At times, I was afraid they would not let me do another report on the good guys because I was some kind of traitor on the playground. The other boys had the wooden pistols and the cowboy hats. I had nothing except my hand over my mouth, hollering and jumping like an Indian, waiting for the tougher kids to

> When the whole concept of exploration and discovery finally sunk in, I knew heroes like Crockett and Lincoln could not have performed their mighty deeds without Columbus coming along to get the whole thing started.

run around the swing set and shoot me.

By the time the bell rang to go to class, all the Indians had to roll in the dirt and play dead. If you got up, the cowboys would kick you or throw dirt at you. As the Indians, guys like Carlos Uranga, Sammy Madrid, and myself were always the last ones to walk into class. The cowboys got to go in first. That is the way it was, and my fascination with Columbus and his three ships took on a secret role in my world of heroes because I had to be an Indian on the playground. My A+ didn't mean anything outside the classroom.

My later years in high school were often marked by extreme incidents of racism against me and the few Chicanos who went to Coronado High School. I got used to being called "dumb Mexican," hearing the jokes about "wetbacks," being left out of projects with other students, being assaulted for being so quiet and "greasy." The racism influenced the beginning of my life of silence, where my heroes had been replaced with a desire to write and create my own worlds.

As an avid reader, I began to discover the truth behind the myths of Crockett and Columbus. Yet, the story of genocide against native people has taken me a lifetime to come to terms with and try to understand. I have yet to truly study and comprehend the impact of Hernán Cortés burning the Aztec civilization and Mexico City to the ground, fusing it into my own mestizo family lines that have a great deal to do with how Chicanos and other Hispanics should look at these last 500 years.

Growing up in Texas made me aware of the long, bloody history of oppression against Mexican Americans. Moving to San Antonio recently, and going to the Alamo for the first time, brought it all home. That Texan icon is not my own and will never be the icon of many people I know, but the fact the little mission still stands in the middle of busy, downtown San Antonio has something to do with playing Indian in school and with the celebration of the anniversary of those three ships coming west.

Those of us who became writers because that inner silence burst upon our spirit, started writing for many undiscovered reasons. One of them has to be the childhood influence of being stuck on those monkey bars, yelling like the wild animals we were told we were. Even our skin was the right color to match our savage psyche, the appropriate madness to resist the deeds of Columbus or Cortés.

As a writer, I have been influenced by my shame in playing an Indian when I was a boy. To write and create is to rise above that playground level and get to class on time without having to wipe the dirt off my mouth. I have also been influenced by Steve Kinnard, Bruce Burns, John Dodson, and all the good guys who got to beat up on me, then take off their cowboy hats, and go into class without being counted tardy. My writing is also haunted by the 5th-grade report I did on the *Niña, Pinta*, and *Santa María*.

I still want to sail to unknown lands and discover something, draw as innocently and precisely as I did in 5th grade, but that A+ paper dissolved into the earth a long time ago. Perhaps, I only deserved a C, because I couldn't tell the true story of the conquest and genocide of the American continent.

I wish I had copies of every textbook I was handed in my elementary school years. One of my favorite tasks on the first day of school was writing my name in neat, large script on the inside cover. It meant a brand new year and fresh challenges for an intelligent kid who knew that book was his and that he could devour it in no time. I can imagine a close study of those books would say a great deal about textbook adoption policies in the state of Texas in the fifties and sixties, policies that have not changed a great deal in thirty years.

Where is the historical truth? Why couldn't a boy like me have the right to be taught the truth?

Ray Gonzalez is a Chicano writer, author of several books of poetry and editor of numerous anthologies. This excerpt is from an article which appeared first in Blue Mesa Review *(Spring 1992) and was included in his anthology,* Without Discovery: A Native Response to Columbus, *Ray Gonzalez, editor (Seattle: Broken Moon Press, 1992).*

Susan Lina Ruggles

HUMAN BEINGS ARE NOT MASCOTS

BY BARBARA MUNSON

"Indian" logos and nicknames create, support, and maintain stereotypes of a race of people. When such cultural abuse is supported by one or many of society's institutions, it constitutes institutional racism.

These logos — along with other abuses and stereotypes — separate, marginalize, confuse, intimidate and harm Native American children and create barriers to their learning throughout their school experience. Additionally, the logos teach non-Indian children that it's all right to participate in culturally abusive behavior.

As long as such logos remain, both Native American and non-Indian children are learning to tolerate racism in our schools. The following are some common questions and statements that I have encountered in trying to educate others about the "Indian" logo issue.

"We have always been proud of our 'Indians'"

People are proud of their school athletic teams even in communities where the team's name and symbolism does not stereotype a race of people. In developing athletic traditions, schools have borrowed from Native American cultures the sacred objects, ceremonial traditions, and components of traditional dress that were most obvious — without understanding their deep meaning or appropriate use. Such school traditions are replete with inaccurate depictions of Indian people, and promote and maintain stereotypes. Schools have taken the trappings of Native cultures onto the playing field where young people have played at being "Indian." Over time, and with practice, generations of children have come to believe that the pretended "Indian" identity

is more than what it is.

"We are honoring Indians; you should feel honored."

Native people are saying that they don't feel honored by this symbolism. We experience it as no less than a mockery of our cultures. We see objects sacred to us — such as the drum, eagle feathers, face painting and traditional dress — being used, not in sacred ceremony, or in any cultural setting, but in another culture's game.

Why must some schools insist on using symbols of a race of people? Other schools are happy with their logos which offend no human being. Why do some schools insist on categorizing Indian people along with animals and objects?

"Why is the term 'Indian' as a mascot name offensive?"

The term "Indian" was given to indigenous people on this continent by an explorer who was looking for India, a man who was lost and who subsequently exploited the indigenous people. "Indian" is not the name we prefer to be called. We are known by the names of our Nations — Oneida (On^yote I a"ka), Hochunk, Stockbridge-Munsee, Menominee (Omaeqnomenew), Chippewa (Anishanabe), Potawatomi, etc.

"Why is an attractive depiction of an Indian warrior just as offensive as an ugly caricature?"

Both depictions are stereotypes. Both firmly place Indian people in the past. The logos keep us marginalized. Depictions of mighty warriors of the past emphasize a tragic part of our history; they ignore the strength and beauty of our cultures during times of peace. Many Indian cultures view life as a spiritual journey filled with lessons to be learned from every experience and from every living being. Many cultures put high value on peace, right action, and sharing.

Indian men are not limited to the role of warrior; in many of our cultures a good man is learned, gentle, patient, wise and deeply spiritual. The depictions of Indian "braves," "warriors," and "chiefs" also ignore the roles of women and children. Although there are patrilineal Native cultures, many Indian nations are both matrilineal and child centered.

"We never intended the logo to cause harm."

That no harm was intended when the logos were adopted, may be true. But we Indian people are saying that the logos are harmful to our cultures, and especially to our children, in the present. When someone says you are hurting them by your action, if you persist, then the harm becomes intentional.

"Aren't you proud of your warriors?"

Yes, we are proud of the warriors who fought to protect our cultures and preserve our lands. We don't want them demeaned by being "honored" in a sports activity on a playing field.

"This is not an important issue."

If it is not important, then why are school boards willing to tie up their time and risk potential law suits rather than simply change the logos?

I, as an Indian person, have never said it is unimportant. Most Indian adults have lived through the pain of prejudice and harassment in schools when they were growing up, and they don't want their children to experience more of the same. This issue speaks to our children being able to form a positive Indian identity and to develop appropriate levels of self-esteem.

In addition, it has legal ramifications in regard to pupil harassment and equal access to education. If it's not important to people of differing ethnic and racial backgrounds within the community, then change the logos. They are hurting the community's Native American population.

"What if we drop derogatory comments and clip art, and adopt pieces of 'real' Indian ceremony, like pow-wows and sacred songs?"

Though well-intended, these solutions are culturally naive. To make a parody of such ceremonial gatherings for the purpose of cheering on the team at homecoming would multiply exponentially the offensiveness. Bringing Native religions onto the playing field through songs of tribute to the "Great Spirit" or Mother Earth would increase the mockery of Native religions even more than the current use of drums and feathers.

"This logo issue is just about political correctness."

Using the term "political correctness" to describe the attempts of concerned Native American parents, educators, and leaders to remove stereotypes from the public schools trivializes a survival issue. A history of systematic genocide has decimated over 95% of the indigenous population of the Americas. Today, the average life expectancy of Native American males in some communities is age 45. The teen suicide rate among Native people is several times higher than the national average. Stereotypes, ignorance, silent inaction and even naive innocence damage and destroy individual lives and whole cultures. Racism kills.

"Why don't community members understand the need to change? Isn't it a simple matter of respect?"

On one level, yes. But respecting a culture different from the one you were raised in requires some effort. Even if a person lives in a different culture — insight and understanding of that culture will require interaction, listening, observing, and a willingness to learn.

The Native American population, in most school districts displaying "Indian" logos, is proportionally very small. When one of us confronts the logo issue, that person, his or her children and other family members, and anyone else in the district who is Native American become targets of insults and threats; we are shunned and further marginalized. We appreciate the courage, support, and sometimes the sacrifice, of all who stand with us by speaking out against the continued use of "Indian" logos.

When you advocate for the removal of these logos, you are strengthening the spirit of tolerance and justice in your community; you are modeling for all our children: thoughtfulness, courage and respect for self and others.

Barbara Munson (Oneida) is active in educating school and community groups about the insensitivity in using stereotypes as school mascots and logos. This is excerpted from an article which can be found at www.nativeweb.org.

LOONEY TOONS AND PETER PAN
Unlearning Racist Stereotypes

BY LINDA CHRISTENSEN

Children don't pop out of the womb drawing Native Americans with feathers and hook noses and coloring them red, but when most students draw or write down their images of Native Americans, their depictions are shockingly similar. They learn these stereotypes from children's books and Saturday cartoons as well as from feature-length videos and movies. They also learn that women are passive, men are strong, fat people are stupid, servants happily devote their lives to the rich, and people of color are either absent or evil.

When I teach Native American history and literature in my high school English and History classes, I want to explode stereotypes of Native Americans as well as teach my students a history that puts a face to the nameless Indians of the Northwest: Nez Perce, Klamath, Yakama, Klickitat, Makahs, Quinaults. I want to shake from their memories the picture of paper-doll cut-out Indians who hid in the forest waiting to kill the brave men and women who crossed the Oregon Trail. I want the literature of Sherman Alexie, Wendy Rose, Gail Tremblay, and James Welch to reach beyond nature poetry and creation myths. I want students to tremble before Alexie's and Rose's anger, laugh at Alexie's humor, understand the enormous loss Welch's historical novel *Fools Crow* portrays.

Exposing the Myths: How to Read Cartoons

But I start the journey by asking students to list or draw their images of Native Americans. As they report out their findings, their pictures match the stereotypes of Chief Wahoo (mascot of the Cleveland Indian baseball team) and other Indian mascots as well as those in Disney's *Peter Pan*. "Where did you get these pictures?" I ask. Some students today are more knowledgeable about racism and many

Illustration in **Peter Pan.**

Mercé Llimona/Ediciones Destino

understand these are stereotypes, but they don't know the origins of their memories.

To help uncover and dismantle those old images, my students watch and critique some Looney Toons cartoons that feature Native Americans as well as a clip from *Peter Pan.* I ask students to keep a list detailing what the "Indians" look like, what they say, how they are portrayed in the cartoons and film. I cue up the *Peter Pan* video to the section where the children head off on their own through the forest and meet the "Injuns." After viewing the clip and listing details, students write about the generalizations young children might take away from these tales.

Mira, a senior, attacked the racism in these Saturday morning rituals. Because of her familiarity with Native American cultures, her analysis was more developed:

Indians in Looney Toons are also depicted as inferior human beings. These characters are stereotypical to the greatest degree, carrying tomahawks, painting their faces, and sending smoke signals as their only means of communication. They live in tipis and their language reminds the viewer of Neanderthals. We begin to imagine Indians as savages with bows and arrows and long black braids. There's no room in our minds for knowledge of the differences between tribes, like the Cherokee alphabet or Celilo salmon fishing.

But unveiling the racist stereotypes isn't enough. I also want students to question why they exist, why it was OK to portray a people in this way, to ask "Who benefits from this portrayal and who suffers?"

Linda Christensen (lchrist@aol.com) teaches in Portland, Oregon, and is an editor of Rethinking Schools.

BONES OF CONTENTION

BY TONY HILLERMAN

Through the doorway which led from her receptionist-secretary's office into her own, Catherine Morris Perry instantly noticed the box on her desk.

"Where'd that come from?" Catherine said.

"Federal Express," Markie said. "I signed for it."

Catherine Morris Perry pulled open the top flaps. Under them was a copy of the *Washington Post*, folded to expose the story that had quoted her. Part of it was circled in black.

MUSEUM OFFERS COMPROMISE
IN OLD BONE CONTROVERSY

The headline irritated Catherine. There had been no compromise. She had simply stated the museum's policy. If an Indian tribe wanted ancestral bones returned, it had only to ask for them and provide some acceptable proof that the bones in question had indeed been taken from a burial ground of the tribe. The entire argument was ridiculous and demeaning. In fact, even dealing with that Highhawk man was demeaning. Him and his Paho Society. A museum underling and an organization which, as far as anybody knew, existed only in his imagination. And only to create trouble. She glanced at the circled paragraph.

"Mrs. Catherine Perry, an attorney for the museum and its spokesperson on this issue, said the demand by the Paho Society for the reburial of the museum's entire collection of more than 18,000 Native American skeletons was 'simply not possible in light of the museum's purpose.'

"She said the museum is a research institution as well as a gallery for public display, and that the museum's collection of ancient human bones is a potentially important source of anthropological information. She said that Mr. Highhawk's suggestion that the museum make plaster casts of the skeletons and rebury the originals was not practical 'both because of research needs and because the public has the right to expect authenticity and not be shown mere reproductions.'"

The clause "the right to expect authenticity" was underlined. Catherine Morris Perry frowned at it, sensing criticism. She picked up the newspaper. Under it, atop a sheet of brown wrapping paper, lay an envelope. Her name had been written neatly on it. She opened it and pulled out a single sheet of typing paper. While she read, her idle hand was pulling away the layer of wrapping paper which had separated the envelope from the contents of the box.

Dear Mrs. Perry:

You won't bury the bones of our ancestors because you say the public has the right to expect authenticity in the museum when it comes to look at skeletons. Therefore I am sending you a couple of authentic skeletons of ancestors. I went to the cemetery in the woods behind the Episcopal Church of Saint Luke. I used authentic anthropological methods to locate the burials of authentic white Anglo types —

Mrs. Morris Perry's fingers were under the wrapping paper now, feeling dirt, feeling smooth, cold surfaces.

"Mrs. Bailey!" she said. "Mrs. Bailey!" But her eyes moved to the end of the letter. It was signed "Henry Highhawk of the Bitter Water People."

"What?" Mrs. Bailey shouted. "What is it?"

—and to make sure they would be perfectly authentic, I chose two whose identities you can personally confirm yourself. I ask that you accept these two skeletons for authentic display to your clients and release the bones of two of my ancestors so that they may be returned to their rightful place in Mother Earth. The names of these two authentic —

Mrs. Bailey was standing beside her now. "Honey," she said. "What's wrong?" Mrs. Bailey paused. "There's bones in that box," she said. "All dirty, too."

Mrs. Morris Perry put the letter on the desk and looked into the box. From underneath a clutter of what seemed to be arm and leg bones a single empty eye socket stared back at her. She noticed that Mrs. Bailey had picked up the letter. She noticed dirt. Damp ugly little clods had scattered on the polished desk top.

"My God," Mrs. Bailey said. "John Neldine Burgoyne. Jane Burgoyne. Weren't those — Aren't these your grandparents?"

From the novel Talking God, *by Tony Hillerman (New York: HarperCollins, 1989).*

THREE THOUSAND DOLLAR DEATH SONG

BY WENDY ROSE

Nineteen American Indian Skeletons
from Nevada ... valued at $3000...
— Museum invoice, 1975

Is it in cold hard cash? the kind
that dusts the insides of men's pockets
lying silver-polished surface along the cloth.
Or in bills? papering the wallets of they
who threaten the night with dark words. Or
checks? paper promises weighing the same
as words spoken once on the other side
of the grown grass and dammed rivers
of history. However it goes, it goes
Through my body it goes
assessing each nerve, running its edges
along my arteries, planning ahead
for whose hands will rip me
into pieces of dusty red paper,
whose hands will smooth or smatter me
into traces of rubble. Invoiced now,
it's official how our bones are valued
that stretch out pointing to sunrise
or are flexed into one last foetal bend,
that are removed and tossed about,
catalogued, numbered with black ink
on newly-white foreheads.
As we were formed to the white soldier's voice,
so we explode under white students' hands.
Death is a long trail of days
in our fleshless prison.

From this distant point we watch our bones
auctioned with our careful beadwork.
our quilled medicine bundles, even the bridles
of our shot-down horses. You: who have
priced us, you who have removed us: at what cost?
What price the pits where our bones share
a single bit of memory, how one century
turns our dead into specimens, our history
into dust, our survivors into clowns.

Our memory might be catching, you know;
picture the mortars, the arrowheads, the labrets
shaking off their labels like bears
suddenly awake to find the seasons have ended
while they slept. Watch them touch each other,
measure reality, march out the museum door!
Watch as they lift their faces
and smell about for us; watch our bones rise
to meet them and mount the horses once again!
The cost, then, will be paid
for our sweetgrass-smelling having-been
in clam shell beads and steatite,
dentalia and woodpecker scalp, turquoise
and copper, blood and oil, coal
and uranium, children, a universe
of stolen things.

— *From* That's What She Said: Contemporary Poetry
and Fiction by Native American Women, *ed. Rayna
Green (Indian University Press, 1984).*

*Wendy Rose is a poet, writer, and anthropologist of Hopi and
Miwok heritage.*

CANADA APOLOGIZES TO ITS NATIVE PEOPLE

BY ASSOCIATED PRESS (FINANCIAL TIMES)

In an unprecedented gesture of reconciliation to Canada's native peoples, the government apologized Wednesday for past acts of oppression, including decades of abuse at federally funded boarding schools.

The apology — sought for years by native leaders — was part of a sweeping federal initiative to improve strained relations with Indian and Inuit communities. More explicitly than ever before, the government expressed regret at past treatment of aboriginals and pledged to support native self-government.

The statement of reconciliation was read aloud by Indian Affairs Minister Jane Stewart and then presented in the form of scrolls to five senior native leaders at a ceremony on Parliament Hill in Ottawa.

"Sadly, our history with respect to the treatment of aboriginal people is not something in which we can take pride," Stewart said. "We must ensure that the mistakes, which marked our past relationship, are not repeated."

These include a network of boarding schools established across Canada with the goal of severing native youths from their own culture and assimilating them in white society. More than 80 of the church-run, government-funded schools operated for nearly a century, beginning in the 1880s.

Hundreds of former pupils have told investigators of rapes, beatings, suicides, suspicious deaths and humiliating punishments at the schools.

"To those individuals who experienced the tragedy of sexual and physical abuse ... and who have carried this burden believing that in some way they must be responsible, we wish to emphasize that what you experienced was not your fault and should never have happened," Stewart said.

The government pledged $245 million to fund counseling and treatment programs for victims of abuse at the schools.

Stewart also promised additional funds to improve life on reservations, including programs for health care, youth employment and career development.

The government's statement was the long-awaited response to a 1996 report by a royal commission on aboriginal peoples that called for hundreds of federal policy changes and recommended the government increase its annual spending on native peoples to $1.3 billion by 2000.

The commission said a major change in government attitude was needed to avoid a worsening of current problems, which include a 25% native jobless rate, Indian street gangs, pervasive substance abuse, family violence, high rates of teenage suicide and poverty.

Canada's aboriginal population is about 810,000, including Indians, 38,000 Inuits (formerly known as Eskimos) and 139,000 Métis — people of mixed Indian and white ancestry.

The government initiative was hailed by the head of the national assembly of Indian chiefs as a "historic opportunity."

"This gathering celebrates the beginning of a new era," said Phil Fontaine, grand chief of the Assembly of First Nations. "For the first time, the government has accepted us as full partners."

But Fontaine cautioned more work remained to build self-reliant native communities. Other native leaders criticized the initiative for not going far enough or for being too vague on financial commitments.

Gerald Morin, president of the Métis National Council, said the initiative "offers very little" to the Métis, especially because it still excludes them from filing land claims that could lead to self-government.

From the Milwaukee Journal Sentinel, *Jan. 8, 1998.*

WHAT'S IN AN APOLOGY?

For a government to apologize for past actions is rare and controversial. The issue presents an opportunity to motivate students to research, debate, think critically, and take social action. Using the adjacent article on Canada's apology to its native peoples, consider the following:

• Explore with your students what an apology is. Talk about how we know if an apology is sincere and meaningful. Have them give examples from their own lives. Have students define "reparations" and contrast it to an "apology." What does it mean if I apologize for stealing my brother's comic book, but I don't give it back?

• Have students research other cases where governments have apologized for past actions—e.g., the Japanese apology to Korea, Germany's apology to Jews, or the U.S. government's apology for the internment of Japanese-Americans during WW II. To what extent is the oppression of those involved ongoing?

• Have students search periodicals and the Internet for articles on whether the United States should apologize for the enslavement of Africans.

• Many people say that a person need not apologize for actions of his or her ancestors, nor make amends for past wrongs. Pose this hypothetical situation: If my dad killed your dad and took over his house and moved in my entire family, would it be fair for me to apologize, but continue to live in your house? How does this compare to the situation with Native Americans?

• Pose these and other questions to the students: Should the United States apologize for its treatment of Native Americans? Why or why not? What would make such an apology meaningful? Is it sufficient to apologize? Or is some other action required? What would be the text of such an apology? What actions should accompany an apology?

• The above questions and controversies could be examined through student interviews with parents and community people, student debates, a student meeting discussing a proposed resolution on the issue, essay writing, drawings, and letter writing and petitioning to elected officials.

— *Bob Peterson*

National Guard troops surround a site (a vacant religious mission building) taken over by Menominee people on New Year's Day, 1975.

Rethinking Schools Collections

Elizabeth Peratrovich Day

In 1994, the Southeast Alaska Regional Hospital Coop voted to give their employees Elizabeth Peratrovich Day — February 16 — as a holiday, instead of Columbus Day.

Why? Who was Elizabeth Peratrovich (1911-1958)? She was a native Alaskan, a member of the Tlingit Nation, who campaigned and spoke eloquently for native civil rights in the 1940s. During World War II, Alaska came into prominence as a key military center. Many Alaskan native men served in the Armed Forces. But in Alaska, native women were not allowed into USO clubs because of their race. They were not even allowed to be seen with soldiers on the streets of towns — even if the men were native men, possibly even their brothers.

Likewise, natives were forced to sit in segregated sections of movie theaters, and were discriminated against in housing and employment. In Alaskan towns like Juneau, many businesses had signs that said, "No Natives Allowed," "We Cater to White Trade Only," or "No Dogs, No Natives." Native children were excluded from public schools.

In the early 1940s, Elizabeth Peratrovich was president of the Alaska Native Sisterhood (ANS), and her husband, Roy, was president of the Alaska Native Brotherhood (ANB) — two native political organizations.

In 1945, an anti-discrimination bill was put before the state legislature. On a cold, bleak Alaskan February afternoon, the gallery was packed by native-rights supporters mobilized by ANS and ANB. The bill easily passed the House, and was sent to the State Senate, where it was opposed by many, led by Allen Shattuck.

Shattuck proclaimed in heated debate, "Far from being brought together ... the races should be kept farther apart. Who are these people, barely out of savagery, who want to associate with whites with 5,000 years of recorded civilization behind us?"

Others spoke in favor. Then, Elizabeth Peratrovich rose and asked to speak. She came forward and took her place at the podium before the all-male legislators.

"I would not have expected," she said in a quiet, steady voice, "that I, who am 'barely out of savagery,' would have to remind gentlemen with '5,000 years of recorded civilization behind them' of our Bill of Rights.

"When my husband and I came to Juneau and sought a home in a nice neighborhood, where our children could play happily with our neighbor children, we found such a house and had arranged to lease it. When the owners learned that we were Indians, they said 'no.' Would we be compelled to live in the slums?" (Juneau had restrictions on where natives could live; one downtrodden place, Robert's Row, was a series of shelters under one roof that was no more than man-sized kennels.)

When her opponent, Allen Shattuck, rose to ask if she thought the proposed bill would eliminate discrimination, she queried back, "Do your laws against larceny and even murder prevent those crimes? No law will eliminate crimes, but at least you as legislators can assert to the world that you recognize the evil of the present situation and speak your intent to help us overcome discrimination."

There was a wild burst of applause from the gallery and the Senate floor. Shattuck sat down in defeat. The opposition had been silenced by the testimony and strong will of this Tlingit woman. The bill passed 11 to 5, on February 8, 1945.

And today, Elizabeth Peratrovich Day is celebrated across Alaska as the birthday of a hero worthy of honoring.

Adapted from A Recollection of Civil Rights Leader Elizabeth Peratrovich, *compiled by the Central Council of Tlingit and Haida Indian Tribes of Alaska, 1991.*

Native Alaskans were excluded from many public places, until the 1945 landmark civil rights legislation was passed.

SECONDARY SCHOOL ISSUES

Teaching Ideas

Spain, Columbus, and Taínos
Historical Timeline (p. 99)

In preparing this timeline, we found it easy to find information about Christopher Columbus but more difficult to learn about the Taínos. How would you explain this? How do you think the Columbus expedition to the Americas was related to the war against the Moors, the expulsion of the Jews, and the Spanish Inquisition? (This might be a good topic for student research.)

What might Columbus have thought as he approached Guanahaní? What thoughts might his crew have had? What might the Taínos have thought as they watched Columbus and his men come onto their island? Is there any evidence to suggest that the Taínos thought Columbus was a god? Why has this myth become so widespread? (Students could write a set of interior monologues, contrasting the thoughts of Spaniards and Taínos.)

What appears to be the objective of Columbus's first voyage? On January 13, Columbus encounters what he decides is resistance. Why does he presume that these people are Caribs and not Taínos? How does Columbus justify taking slaves? What prevented the Taínos from mounting an effective resistance to Columbus's invasion?

Write the thoughts of Columbus's Taíno kidnap victims as they arrive in Spain.

Write Caonabó's interior monologue as he is led in chains onto a ship bound for Spain. Recall that he led the first resistance to the Spanish on Hayti.

Write an appropriate epitaph for Columbus.

Have students do more research and continue the timeline. Have them choose events on the timeline to research more thoroughly. Are there particular "choice points" suggested in the timeline where people's decisions could have resulted in different historical outcomes?

Also see "Talking Back to Columbus" (p. 115) for other teaching ideas.

"Open Your Hearts"
Adapted from las Casas (p. 103)

According to Antonio de Montesinos, what is wrong with Spanish rule in the Indies? What does Montesinos think about Native people? Does he believe Native people should rule themselves? How did Montesinos want the Spaniards on the island to change? Did he want them to get out of the Indies? Why are Columbus and the others so upset? Why don't they just ignore Montesinos? What did Montesinos risk?

Write the thoughts of Montesinos preparing for his second sermon. And/or ask students to improvise a discussion between Montesinos and Father Cordoba.

Write the reaction of a Taíno cacique to Montesinos. Does he approve of everything Montesinos says and does?

Encourage students to research Spaniards like Bartolomé de las Casas, author of the book that this excerpt is adapted from, who fought for Native rights in the Americas.

Ceremony
Poem by Leslie Marmon Silko (p. 114)

Read "Ceremony" aloud. Who is the "they" who tries to destroy the stories? Why would "they" want those stories destroyed? Whose evil is mighty? Why can't it overpower the strength of the stories?

Have students bring in stories from their lives — ones that teach, that amuse, that remember. Seat students in a circle, maybe even on the floor, and share these as a group. Afterward talk about the roles stories play in our families and in our cultures.

Columbus Day
Poem by Jimmie Durham (p. 123)

Read the poem aloud. Ask students to visualize the descriptions.

How does the poem make you feel? Why? Is Durham angry, sad, hopeful? Why do you think he wrote the poem? What else has been left out of the school curriculum that should be there?

Use Durham's poem as a prompt for students to write. Begin: "In school I was taught..." and begin a second verse: "No one mentioned..."

Choose someone referred to by Jimmie Durham — Chaske, Many Deeds — and write a poem from one of their perspectives. Or write a poem about people from another group that has traditionally been silenced in the curriculum.

Human Beings Are Not Mascots

Article by Barbara Munson (p. 131)

Watch the excellent film, *In Whose Honor?*, about activist Charlene Teters, who organizes against the use of Native American sports mascots (see listing in Resources, p. 182.)

Students could research your school district's use of and policy toward mascots and team names. Depending on what they discover they could write letters to administrators, school board members, or local papers about the issue. They might write a skit to perform for other classes or at an assembly, or arrange a showing of *In Whose Honor?*

Contact Native Americans active on this issue to address students.

In the early 1990s, the Portland *Oregonian* banned the use of race-based team names (e.g., the Atlanta Braves, the Cleveland Indians, etc.) in the paper's sports section. Have students contact newspapers in your area to learn their policies — or to challenge them.

Students might copy and distribute this article to other students, teachers, and parents or for publication in local papers or newsletters.

Bones of Contention

Story by Tony Hillerman (p. 134)

Why does Perry have such contempt for Henry Highhawk and the Paho Society? What can you tell about Perry's attitude toward native people? What motivated Highhawk's demands? Were they unreasonable? What do you think of Highhawk's action? How do you think Perry felt when she realized her grandparents' bones had been dug up? What should Perry do now?

Stage a debate between Highhawk and Perry.

Write a brief reaction from Perry's point of view. Or write Mrs. Bailey's reactions. Write Henry Highhawk's thoughts leading to his digging up Perry's grandparents' bones. Ask students to read these aloud.

You are an editorial writer for a local white-owned newspaper. Write an editorial attacking or defending Highhawk's actions. Complete the same assignment from the point of view of a writer for a paper that serves the Bitter Water people.

Investigate the policies of local museums about the remains of native people. Contact local native organizations to learn if they are satisfied that archaeologists respect their ancestors and sacred sites. Have students research national debates about the remains of native people. They might, for example, search for articles on the "Kennewick Man" debate. What are the policies of the Smithsonian Institution and other major museums?

Three Thousand Dollar Death Song

Poem by Wendy Rose (p. 135)

Why is she angry? Who does she blame?

Think of a time when something you really cared about was stolen. Quickwrite: Where did you get this object? Why was it meaningful to you? How did it feel to lose it? How did you feel about the person/persons who stole it? From these notes write about the incident as if you were telling a friend. Ask students to read their completed stories. Using the following questions as a guide, have them take notes as they listen: Whether or not we knew the person(s), how did we feel about them? Who did we blame? What did we do about the thefts?

Talk about: How does this help us understand the writer of the poem? of the Native American experience in general? In what ways were our experiences different?

Write a "talking back" poem modeled after Wendy Rose's. You might choose a quote to respond to, as she did. Notice the structure of her poem, how she remembers, invents details, poses questions.

Elizabeth Peratrovich Day

Article on Tlingit Civil Rights Leader (p. 138)

Read aloud the story of Elizabeth Peratrovich. Ask students to react to the story: What surprised them? What interested them?

In the story, the Southeast Alaska Regional Hospital Coop decided that Elizabeth Peratrovich's life was more worthy of celebration than Columbus's life. Divide your class into small groups. Tell them that their task will be to propose an alternative to Columbus Day that commemorates a "local hero" or an event that exemplifies values worth emulating. Students might interview other teachers, parents or community members to collect a list of possibilities. Or the class might first brainstorm possibilities drawn from your curriculum or from their own knowledge. Have students specify the values that a particular individual or event exemplifies.

For example, Elizabeth Peratrovich Day especially celebrates equality, anti-racism, and determination. Another example: a "1934 Longshore Strike Day" in Portland, Oregon, would highlight values of solidarity between workers of different industries, employed and unemployed, and farmers and workers; determination; self-sacrifice; and resistance.

Students should write up their suggested holidays as formal proposals, including how schools and communities might honor the individuals or events. They might present these to other community organizations, school board, or city council.

CONTEMPORARY STRUGGLES

What law have I broken?
Is it wicked because I am Sioux?
Because I was born
where my father lived?
Because I would die
for my people and
my country...?

Young men, help me,
do help me!
I love my country so;
that is why
I am
fighting.

— Sitting Bull

STRUGGLES AROUND THE HEMISPHERE

This is a brief snapshot of just a few examples of contemporary struggles of indigenous peoples in the Americas. The situations are constantly changing, so we've listed some websites for useful updates.

Belize

The Mopan and Ke-kchi Maya peoples fight for legal protection for ancestral lands; the government has opened 500,000 acres to logging by Malaysian and other interests.

Brazil/Venezuela

The Yanomami have seen their rainforest preserve illegally invaded by 3,000 wildcat gold and diamond miners, bringing disease and destruction. Over 1,300 Yanomami have contracted malaria, TB, influenza, and pneumonia; many have died.

British Columbia

The Nisga'a are among a number of First Nations working to reclaim ancient treaty rights, in a controversial 6-step negotiation process; tribes may receive cash, land, logging and other rights in return for giving up all future claims.

California

A coalition of Colorado River tribes have been fighting a low-level radioactive waste dump at Ward Valley that would desecrate sacred lands and potentially contaminate the Colorado River.

Canada

A tribunal is gathering testimony of sexual and other abuse suffered by native children who attended residential boarding schools.

Colombia

The U'wa people of the Andean cloud-forests fight attempts by Occidental Petroleum ("Oxy") to exploit oil-fields in the U'wa homeland at the headwaters of the Orinoco River basin. The project could be devastating to the ecosystem.

Florida

A Seminole community, trying to maintain its way of life, is now fighting a 22-story-high garbage dump to be located one-half mile from their lands.

Global

Native groups spearhead efforts to stop projects by bio-technology corporations to patent (as "inventors") the bloodline information (genetic codes) of indigenous peoples for profit. If used to develop new medicines or bio-engineering techniques, these would be owned exclusively by the multinational companies, who stand to profit enormously.

Global

Despite opposition by national governments, efforts continue to convince the United Nations to adopt a statement of indigenous peoples' rights to their land, resources, and sovereignty within the nation states that surround them.

Maine

The Penobscot Nation fights the dumping by paper mills of an estimated 40 million gallons of dioxin-laden water into Maine rivers each year. Dioxin is a very toxic chemical.

Mexico

In Chiapas, Mexico's southernmost state, the Zapatista rebellion, begun January 1994, continues to challenge conventional models of economic "development" and the lack of indigenous rights. Indigenous people have been the target of vicious attacks intended to suppress the democratic movement, including the massacre of 45 unarmed civilians in December 1997.

Montana

Gros Ventre and Assiniboine tribes in the Little Rocky Mountains oppose expansions of massive gold mines that use a cyanide-leaching process, destroying sacred mountains and contaminating waters.

Nevada

The Western Shoshone, the most bombed nation on earth, is fighting federal efforts to establish the country's main nuclear-waste dump at Yucca Mountain, a sacred site on land guaranteed to the Shoshone in the 1863 Treaty of Ruby Valley.

Nicaragua

The Miskito and Sumo Indians fight legal battles to stop logging concessions granted to a Korean logging company.

Ontario

The 300 people of the Grassy Narrows Reserve have faced clearcutting, hydro-dam projects, and mercury contamination. Now the Canadian Atomic Energy Council plans to site a high-level nuclear waste dump on their land.

Quebec

Mic'mac traditionalists blockade a provincial road on the Gaspé peninsula; the Quebec Government threatens to send in police forces to open the road. The Mic'macs are claiming rights to a greater share of logging on Crown lands.

United States

Around 2.1 billion dollars in funds held by the BIA in trust accounts are missing, due to the BIA's poor management. Native tribes have demanded a full accounting.

Wisconsin

A coalition, with Chippewa and Menominee tribes, opposes efforts by the Canadian company Rio Algom Ltd. to open a new zinc-copper mine, endangering nearby rivers with heavy metals—until it can be shown that any other similar mining operation has remained pollution-free, as the company promises this site will be.

For Additional Information:

Ejército Zapatista de Liberación Nacional (www.ezln.org). Provides information on the Zapatista movement in Chiapas.

ETC Group (www.etcgroup.org). Info and links combating the exclusive patenting of indigenous people's genetic information by biotechnology corporations.

First Nations/First Peoples Issues (www.dickshovel.com). An outspoken site for all interested in the American Indian Movement, Wounded Knee, and political issues in the U.S.

Global Exchange (www.globalexchange.org). Monitors human rights issues in Mexico, recent report of Chiapas situation.

Global Response (www.globalresponse.org). Newsletters for classrooms and school clubs on environmental struggles by indigenous peoples.

South and Meso American Indian Rights Center (http://saiic.nativeweb.org). A respected center for action alerts, a quarterly journal, and links to indigenous/environmental struggles in Latin America.

— compiled by Philip Martin

James Watts/Indian Law Resource Center

A large-scale gold mine in the Little Rocky Mountains of Montana.

TREATY RIGHTS
An Overview

BY PHILIP MARTIN

The white man made us many promises, but he kept only one. He promised to take our land and he took it.
— *Mahpiya Luta (Red Cloud), 1882*

A "treaty" is an agreement between two nations. It is a signed document and by international law is binding. In other words, one nation can not wake up one day and say, "I don't like that old treaty I signed." The only way to modify a treaty is to get both parties together again. If all agree, a new treaty can be signed to replace the old one.

From the beginnings of its history, the United States dealt with Native tribes as independent nations. The U.S. signed many treaties — by one count, 900 were negotiated, 600 signed, and almost 400 were ratified by Congress. They were to be permanent, everlasting agreements for "as long as the grass shall grow and the rivers shall run."

At first, the U.S. accepted that Indian peoples had original rights to their lands. For instance, in the famous Northwest Ordinance of 1787, the U.S. Congress stated that, in dealing with Native nations, "utmost good faith shall always be observed towards the Indians; their land and property shall never be taken from them without their consent."

From 1778 (with the Delaware Nation) to 1868 (with the Nez Perce Nation), the U.S. signed 374 treaties with Indian tribes. On March 3, 1871, Congress suddenly decided that it would sign no more "treaties" with Indian nations. After that, the U.S. negotiated what it called "agreements" — whenever a tribe had something the U.S. wanted. But the older treaties remained in effect.

Currently, the U.S. claims overall jurisdiction — or control — over Indian tribes, as a "dominant" nation over "subordinate" nations. The U.S. says the relationship is like "father and son." But Native tribes insist that the Native/U.S. relationship is legally one between equals, as "brothers."

Common Misunderstandings:

1. *MISUNDERSTANDING*: The Indians at some point sold their land — and all rights to it.

WRONG. Even when a tribe gave up lands, it often kept specific rights to use the land which was "ceded." (In a treaty, "ceded" means "sold".) This allowed members of that tribe to hunt, fish, gather foods, or make other use of the ceded land. Such "treaty rights" were not "given" to the Indians by the treaty; they were older rights that the Indians kept; the treaty recognized this in writing.

Also, in negotiations, the U.S. government often acted improperly — like giving Indian representatives enormous quantities of alcohol and getting them to sign while drunk. Or giving them documents to sign in a language they could not read — and lying about what was really in the papers being signed. Or getting people to sign who were not authorized to do so by their tribe. Lands taken in that fashion were taken illegally.

2. *MISUNDERSTANDING*: Treaty rights are "special" rights — so Indians are getting special treatment.

WRONG. These are basic rights recognized in U.S. property law. When someone sells land, they can sell "all rights" or just certain rights. For instance, you can sell a piece of land to a neighbor, but in the deed, specifically keep the right to travel through the neighbor's land to get to your own. This then is binding. The neighbor cannot one day say, "Your right to cross my land is outdated, or too inconvenient for me, and now you can't do this." Retained rights are common in U.S. property law and are not special to Indian claims.

3. *MISUNDERSTANDING*: Indian treaty rights are too sweeping and will do terrible damage if they are recognized.

WRONG. Indian tribes are very sensitive and sensible in exercising their rights. For instance, Wisconsin Chippewa (Ojibwa) tribes have rights to hunt and fish in areas outside of their reservations, but they themselves place reasonable limits on this, so as not to over-fish or over-hunt those areas. The tribes wish to protect natural resources, and are thoughtful planners about this.

Likewise, Indian nations generally do not insist that land taken illegally be returned to them unconditionally, if there are non-Natives now living on it. Instead, if land was taken illegally by the U.S. government, the Indian tribes would like their ownership acknowledged, but then wish to work out a reasonable settlement.

Non-Natives will not be kicked off the land they live on. It is the responsibility of the U.S. government to make things right in treaties it signed, not individuals. One common proposal involves turning federal land, like National Forest lands, back to tribal supervision, but not individual property.

4. *MISUNDERSTANDING*: Treaties are old, and therefore out-dated or old-fashioned, and do not apply today.

WRONG. Signed, written agreements between governments (or between people) are not invalidated by age. If agreed to, a new treaty will replace an older one. But age alone does not end a legal agreement. For instance, the U.S. Constitution is an old document that was written into law many year ago — but it is still acknowledged as the highest law of the United States.

5. *MISUNDER-STANDING*: Native/U.S. treaties apply to all Indians.

WRONG. Rights and obligations under any specific treaty apply only to the U.S. government and the tribe that signed the treaty. Each tribe distributes benefits only to members of that tribe, according to an official record of its enrollment. And each tribe decides under its own laws who is a tribal member — just as the U.S. regulates who can hold U.S. citizenship.

Sovereign Nations

A good word to learn is "sovereignty" — to be a "sovereign nation." Many Indians are familiar with this concept, while non-Natives have not thought about it too much.

All of us understand "sovereignty" when applied to a nation outside of the U.S. border — like Canada. The U.S. government cannot make laws to tell Canada what to do. Instead it needs to negotiate a treaty with Canada, with both countries agreeing in writing, to regulate trade or other mutual concerns.

It is the same with the Lakota Nation, with the Navajo Nation, with the Seminole Nation, with the Penobscot Nation, with the Salish Nation, or with any of the 558 Indian tribes recognized by the U.S. government.

Native tribes are "sovereign nations" within U.S. land boundaries. This means they have their own government, their own laws, their own tax systems, their own police. Tribal members actually have dual citizenship: tribal and American.

Although this system of treaties may seem complicated, the U.S. government agreed to it in writing when it wished to acquire a lot of land once held by Native tribes. The U.S. agreed to specific payments, to protect certain rights, and to uphold its end of a lasting relationship.

Tragically, the history of the U.S. government in fulfilling its agreements with Native nations is very poor. The U.S. has never lived up to its end of the bargain.

Still, just because the U.S. did not fulfill its obligation, the treaty itself is not "broken" — it was the promise to do something that was "broken." The treaty is still valid. Legally the U.S. is still bound to do what it promised. And if wrongs were done, the U.S. should try to make compensation that is acceptable to the Native nation which was wronged.

In recent years, Native lawyers have sought justice through the U.S. courts, winning awards for individual tribes — to reclaim certain lands; for hunting, fishing, logging, and water rights; in some cases, for cash settlements — based on treaties still considered valid and the law of the land.

When Indian leaders agreed to treaties, they wanted to preserve a way of life that was decent, that protected their holiest religious sites. They wanted to maintain the health, strong spirit, and well-being of future generations of their people. In signing the treaties, they also wished to live in peace with their American neighbors. They often reminded U.S. negotiators that all living creatures are interrelated and must find a way to live in harmony, without destroying the other.

Native nations are now looking to exercise treaty rights reasonably, in a way which will allow Native nations to survive. In their councils, they often ask their leaders to consider what is good for the seventh generation of their people to come.

Maybe what they are asking for is something we should all hope to share with each other.

Additional information:

Nabokov, Peter, ed. Native American Testimony. *New York: Viking, 1991.*

Contact HONOR (Honor Our Neighbors' Origins and Rights) — see listing in Resources, p. 182.

A MODERN HERO

Rigoberta Menchú

BY DEBORAH MENKART

"We have been fighting for our land for 500 years," says Rigoberta Menchú, a Guatemalan Quiché Indian woman. In Guatemala, as in most of the Americas, the inequities created by the European conquest continue today.

The new conquerors are multinational corporations, and government and military elites. Modern-day conquistadores travel by jet instead of by sailboat, but control of cheap labor and resources are still the paths to gold. Ads in the *Wall Street Journal* encourage businessmen to "Come Discover" the low wages of Puerto Rico or Mexico.

Indians and poor *ladino* peasants (of mixed Indian and European descent) continue to fight for the right to grow enough food for families and to protect cultural traditions.

This division reflects fundamentally different beliefs about society and its relationships to the environment. Mayan Indians hold that the "land is sacred, the corn is sacred, the rain is sacred. The land is alive and gives us life." The multinationals look at land in terms of potential profits. If carnations are more profitable than corn on the international market, then that's what they'll plant, even if as a result children in the local community die of hunger.

U.S.-financed Coup

In Guatemala, native people have consistently resisted the abuse of their land and communities. In 1944, a coalition of Indians and middle-class *ladinos* toppled the government. They instituted land reform, wrote a new constitution, and held elections.

The wealthy landowners and foreign corporations were angry at the new government. In 1954, at the urging of large U.S. corporations such as the United Fruit Company (Chiquita bananas), the Eisenhower administration financed a military coup. The military seized the peasants' new lands and returned them to large landowners.

With the military in power, the landowners and multinationals began an aggressive campaign to expand their holdings. The U.S. Agency for International Development (AID) began massive funding for exports such as beef, with devastating repercussions. To graze cattle, growers took land away from peasants and deforested vast expanses of rainforest. Cattle-ranching produced few jobs and deprived families of farm land.

Though tremendously profitable for a few, this agricultural "boom" resulted in increasing poverty for much of the population, widescale destruction of the rain forest, and intense pesticide contamination of the people and the environment.

Grassroots groups organized to take back their land and resources. But their demands were frequently met with violence. In 1980, Indians marched to Guatemala City to petition the government. Their pleas were ignored and, to call attention to their plight, they occupied the Spanish Embassy. The Guatemalan army attacked and burned the building, killing nearly everyone inside.

Massacres like this marked a turning point that resulted in an upsurge of resistance, as entire Indian communities joined the popular movement or the armed opposition. To try to repress this growing opposition, the army systematically murdered over 150,000 people, mostly Indian, razed hundreds of villages, destroyed vast areas of forests and fields, and displaced more than a million people.

In 1996, peace accords were signed, with an ambitious plan to reform every aspect of society, including giving the Mayan peoples a greater voice in the government. The accords offer hope on paper, but have yet to bring real democracy, peace, or security.

Winner of the Nobel Peace Prize

Rigoberta Menchú provides an example of the spirit of resistance found throughout the Americas. In 1992, she was awared the Nobel Peace Prize.

Her commitment to her ancestors, to her family, and to the future are shared in her book, *I...Rigoberta Menchú*, where she documents not only her life, "but the story of all poor Guatemalans." She describes her work as a child on the coffee plantations, her family and community traditions, and the repression. Below she tells the story of why her family decided to organize.

Rigoberta Menchú's Story

"My father fought for 22 years, waging a heroic struggle against the landlords who wanted to take our land and our neighbors' land. After many years of hard work, when our small bit of land began yielding harvests and our people had a large area under cultivation, the big landlords appeared. They told us we could either stay and work for them or leave the land.

"The first time they threw us out of our houses was in 1967. They turned us out of our houses, and out of the village. The man who worked for the landlords went into the houses without permission and got all the people out. Then they went in and threw out all our things. I remember that my mother had some silver necklaces, precious keepsakes from my grandmother, but we never saw them again; they stole them all.

"They threw out our cooking utensils, and the pottery cooking pots that we had made ourselves. They hurled them up in the air; and, Oh, God! they hit the ground and broke into pieces. All our plates, cups, pots. They threw them out and they all broke. That was the revenge of the landlord on us peasants because we wouldn't give up our land.

"Then they threw out all the corn that we had stored up for the year. I remember it was pouring rain, and we had nothing to protect ourselves from the rain. It took us two days to make a roughly built hut out of leaves. We had only plastic sheets to cover ourselves from the rain. The first night we spent in the fields with streams of water running along the ground....

"We loved our land very much. Since those people tried to take our land away, we have grieved very much. My grandfather used to cry bitterly and say: 'In the past, no one person owned the land. The land belonged to everyone. There were no boundaries.' We were sadder still when we saw our animals going hungry. If our animals went near our crops, they were killed by the men who worked for the landlords....

"We didn't know if it was better to leave and go to work on the coffee plantations, or agree to work for the landlord. We couldn't decide. We discussed it with all our neighbors, among the whole community. During all this time we couldn't celebrate our culture; none of our ceremonies. That's when my father took his stand. he said, 'If they kill me for trying to defend the land that belongs to us, well they'll have to kill me.'

"We began to organize. Our organization had no name. We began by each of us trying to remember the tricks our ancestors used. They used to set traps in their houses, in the path of the conquistadores, the Spaniards. Our ancestors were good fighters, they were real men. It's not true what white people say, that our ancestors didn't defend themselves. They used ambushes.

"Our grandparents used to tell us about it, especially my grandfather when he saw that we were beginning to talk about defending ourselves against the landowners, and wondering if we had to rid ourselves of the landowners before we'd be left in peace. We said: 'If they threaten us, why don't we threaten

Rick Reinhard

Rigoberta Menchú, winner of the Nobel Peace Prize in 1992.

the landowner?' My grandfather gave us a lot of support. My grandfather said, 'Yes you have to defend yourselves. Our ancestors defended themselves. The white men are telling lies when they say we are passive. They fought too. And we, why don't we fight with the same arms the landowners use?' If an elderly person tells us this, then it must be true."

Deborah Menkart is Director of Teaching for Change in Washington, D.C.

Additional reading:

Burgos-Debray, Elizabeth (ed.). I, Rigoberta Menchú: An Indian Woman in Guatemala. *NY: Verso, 1984. Also available in Spanish.*

Carey-Webb, Allen and Benz, Stephen. Rigoberta Menchú and the North American Classroom. *Albany: State University of New York Press, 1996. Teachers' stories of using Menchú's writings in their classrooms.*

Menchú, Rigoberta, Crossing the Borders: An Autobiography. *NY: Verso, 1998.*

For Young Readers:

Brill, Marlene Targ. Journey for Peace: The Story of Rigoberta Menchú. *NY: Dutton, 1996. An accessible, illustrated biography for ages 9-12.*

RESISTANCE AT OKA

BY PETER BLUE CLOUD

In 1990, a confrontation made widespread news as tribal members of the Mohawk Nation protested a plan by the town of Oka, in Quebec province, to expand a nine-hole golf course onto land which had once belonged to the Mohawk people, but had been taken from them illegally, then sold in the 1800s for timber and farmland. The land included a Mohawk cemetery.

The Mohawks lost their legal battle to stop the golf-course expansion, but in March, a sizable contingent of Mohawks, some of them armed, occupied the land and set up barricades. A long stand-off began, with increasing friction between natives and townspeople. In July, hundreds of provincial police were sent to the site, and the tribal clan mothers ordered the Mohawk warriors to blockade all highways through their nearby reservation to restrict police movements. Then, the police were replaced with 2,500 heavily-armed troops of the Canadian Army, with tanks, armored personnel carriers, and helicopters. The warriors waited for the assault.

Day 70. September 18, 1990

A light ground frost shimmers the grass. Bright stars poke in and out of white clouds. I sit in darkness, sipping coffee and thinking of the coming winter. It is time to pick the remaining foods in the garden. As on other mornings in the past few weeks, I try to think of things unrelated to the presence of the Canadian Army surrounding our lands. I am very tired of being a hostage to Canada. I want it to end soon. Why doesn't the government negotiate as they promised?

I am sitting on my porch above the very beach where I learned to swim and to fish as a child, remembering when violence and death were dreamlike happenings in a World War far away — the only visible evidence, back then, in the many uniformed men walking our roads to visit relatives for that final good-bye.

This image of yesteryear ended abruptly with the sudden whacking, roaring sounds of a huge helicopter directly over my house. I was thinking in terms of a rescue mission, or some other such act of humanity, as it crossed the small stretch of water, to hover close to ground and disgorge a fully armed assault team.

Quickly, other choppers appeared and spewed out their loads of troops. At a crouching run, the troops headed for the small bridge which connects the island to the mainland. Other choppers dropped rolls of razor concertina wire, and other equipment to accompany whatever demonic drama was unfolding before my eyes.

The reality of this bizarre scene became evident with the immediate arrival of honking cars from all over town. Mohawks — men, women, and young people — poured onto the bridge, in outrage and anger that our sacred territory was being invaded by an armed force of the military.

The people of Kahnawake, unarmed, crossed the bridge and confronted automatic-weapons-carrying troops. There was no fear on the faces of our Mohawk people, only anger. The army quickly grouped, weapons at the ready, and ready, too, to say, "We were only following orders."

"Get off our land!" was the main cry of the people, nose to nose with those apprehensive-looking soldiers. As the crowd grew and pushed into the line of soldiers, the first barrage of tear gas and concussion grenades was hurled. Little panic ensued as the people returned the canisters of gas accompanied by stones and fists.

Another barrage of tear gas, and the people were forced to retreat. The Army moved quickly to cross and take the bridgehead. They didn't make it, the people regrouped, and by sheer force of bodies pushed the soldiers back to the other side. This began a long, drawn-out retreat by the Canadian army.

I stood at the center of the bridge when the third barrage of tear gas fell. I stood at the center of myself and my people. When I heard the unbelievable chatter of automatic fire I wondered, can it be that they would kill?

Tear gas fell. Screams of outrage echoed across the waters. Rifle butts smashed into bodies to be answered by fists and feet. At least eight helicopters circled and roared overhead, unheard by those creating their own fury of sound. People jumped to water to relieve the burning tear gas. I saw soldiers thrown

> When I heard the unbelievable chatter of automatic fire I wondered, can it be that they would kill?

to ground. There were injured people on the rocks beneath the bridge. I heard fists striking flesh.

The single roll of razor wire the Army managed to unroll was tossed to the side of the bridge. The crowd never let up pressing the Army into retreat, taking their rolls of razor wire with them. The soldiers formed a right-angle wedge, with soldiers behind them. Then, at a command, they stepped back four paces. Then again and again. And again. This went on for a very long time — they were retreating!

We formed our own line thirty feet from the Army. Soldiers in small groups left the wedge and ran to waiting helicopters for evacuation. As it grew dark, we built fires. Spotlights from choppers made the scene glaringly real.

When the last of the soldiers finally left in darkness, a great cheer went up from the crowd. Later, Army Lieutenant Colonel Greg Mitchell, in charge of the invasion of Kahnawake, said, "The strong resistance surprised us. It was amazing the way they reacted, especially since we weren't at the Longhouse or a sacred place."

Dear Mr. Mitchell and Dear Canadians: Will you ever begin to understand the meaning of the soil beneath your very feet? From a grain of sand to a great mountain, all is sacred. Yesterday and tomorrow exist eternally upon this continent. We natives are the guardians of this sacred place.

This excerpt is from the writings of Peter Blue Cloud, Mohawk, who was present at the Oka stand-off. It was included in Native American Testimony, *ed. by Peter Nabokov (Viking, 1991).*

Jim West/Impact Visuals

Mohawk activists face off with Canadian soldiers to prevent sacred lands from becoming a golf course.

THE UNITY OF NATIVE PEOPLES

AN INTERVIEW WITH BILLY REDWING TAYAC

I have learned an important lesson over the years about the use of terminology. When the Nazis occupied France during World War II, those who opposed them were called "freedom fighters." When Indian people have fought back against the taking of our land, we have been called "hostiles" or "communists."

Likewise, when Sioux warriors defeated United States warriors at Little Big Horn in 1876, the popular press called it a "massacre." However, when the United States cavalry machine-gunned unarmed men, women and children at Wounded Knee in 1890, it was called a "battle" by the popular press. More Congressional Medals of Honor were given there than in any previous battle. It took over 70 years for the record to be set straight and for the events to be referred to by the names they deserve: the Battle of Little Big Horn and the Massacre at Wounded Knee.

The rise of the American Indian Movement in the late 1960s helped to restore a sense of pride. People were no longer ashamed to be Indian. They demanded that treaties be upheld. They demanded to be treated as human beings.

When someone committed a murder of an Indian person anywhere around the country, AIM people went there to ask why that murder resulted in only a manslaughter charge if the defendant was European American and the dead man was an Indian. When Indian people were tried by all-white juries, they were more often than not found guilty. Despite being only half of one percent of the United States population, we have the highest rate of imprisonment of any group.

I would like it if every American would take a history book and look at the picture of Chief Big Foot frozen in his grave at Wounded Knee. These people were only seeking food to exist, and the United States exerted military might against them. Today, this military might still exists on the Indian reservations. They use their "legal bullets," the FBI and BIA (Bureau of Indian Affairs) to come onto reservations and investigate and imprison the Indian people. We stood up and exposed the BIA's corruption in our occupation of BIA headquarters in 1972, and stood up and showed the world that Indian people were still alive in our stand at Wounded Knee in 1973.

I had the fortune in the early 1970s of meeting a survivor of the 1890 Wounded Knee massacre. It seemed so impossible that it could have occurred, until you think about the My Lai massacre and the other horrible incidents in Vietnam. Many Indians, like AIM leader Bill Means, served in Vietnam, and recognized that, as soldiers, they were oppressors. Then at Wounded Knee in 1973, he was being shot at by the same soldiers he had served with. The important lesson is that the Indians serving in Vietnam felt a kinship with the Vietnamese.

Indian Wars Continue

The Indian Wars will never be over until the Indian people get their land back. Would the Jews accept money for the Wailing Wall? The Pope accept money for the Vatican? Would a Moslem accept money for the sale of Mecca? No, we can never accept the loss, the theft of ancestral lands. And because Indian people are all one people, we can never forget Wounded Knee, just like the Japanese American people can never forget the internment their people suffered during World War II.

Even today in the United States, there are Native American political prisoners such as Leonard Peltier, who has served over 20 years of two consecutive lifetime sentences for murders he did not commit. After a shoot-out at Wounded Knee in 1975, the FBI used fear tactics and trumped-up charges to get Peltier arrested, tried, and jailed. Peltier is well known to many in Europe and is a modern-day hero, on the scale of Crazy Horse, to Indian people.

We all need to band together today to save Mother Earth. We should be making food so that no one is hungry. Every person should have shelter and health care. There should be no dominant class based on color of skin or gender. There should be no dominant country because of the amount of money they have or the power they wield. All human beings should come together for the good of the earth.

The elders once told me that the Indian people were spared so that we can be the driving force to save Mother Earth. The ashes of our ancestors have been intermingled with the earth on this continent for millennia. It is a good time to remember this.

Billy Redwing Tayac is a leader of the Piscataway people, an eastern tribe now based in Port Tobacco, Maryland. This is an excerpt from a longer interview conducted by Phil Tajitsu Nash in 1992.

LEONARD PELTIER
An American Political Prisoner

BY PHILIP MARTIN

What do Desmond Tutu, Rigoberta Menchú, Jesse Jackson, Nelson Mandela, the late Mother Theresa, and the Canadian and European Parliaments all have in common?

They urge that Leonard Peltier be set free.

Many people around the world understand that Leonard Peltier is a political prisoner, imprisoned by the U.S. government for his presence at the 1973 occupation of Wounded Knee and a later shoot-out in 1975 between the FBI and members of the American Indian Movement (AIM) on South Dakota's Pine Ridge Reservation.

In the several years after Wounded Knee, violence had escalated on the Pine Ridge reservation, targeting those who opposed the federally-supported, corrupt tribal government. In just over two years, 60 murders had taken place, homes had been shot up, and many people assaulted. In 1975, traditional elders requested that AIM send men to Pine Ridge to protect them.

That summer, on June 26, 1975, the FBI arrived in two unmarked cars at the AIM encampment at the home of Harry Jumping Bull, and a shoot-out ensued. The crossfire resulted in the deaths of one Indian man, Joe Stuntz, and FBI agents Ron Williams and Jack Coler. No one was ever charged with the murder of Stuntz.

Leonard Peltier, present in the Jumping Bull home with others, escaped to Canada. Two other AIM members were caught and tried, but were found innocent, having acted in self-defense in the shoot-out.

The U.S. government now focused on Peltier. He had been arrested in Canada, and in 1976 was extradited to the United States to stand trial. Determined not to lose this second trial, the federal prosecution used every means in its power to ensure that Peltier was convicted of murder for the deaths of the two FBI agents.

Nearly 10 years later, in 1986, a U.S. Circuit Court reviewed the case and found that witnesses had been coerced, evidence fabricated, favorable evidence suppressed. The U.S. government admitted it used fraudulent documents to illegally extradite Peltier from Canada. A federal prosecutor admitted that they did not actually know who shot the two agents

Leonard Peltier.

Leonard Peltier Defense Committee

— there was no direct evidence that one individual or another one pulled the trigger.

Yet despite the known false testimony and faked evidence, Peltier has not been allowed an appeal, and has remained in federal prison for over 20 years, steadfastly maintaining his innocence of the crime. All requests for a retrial or parole have been refused. And support for his release has steadily grown around the world.

Former Attorney General, Ramsey Clark, calls the "evidence" against Peltier "fabricated, circumstantial ... mis-used, concealed, and perverted." He is part of a large coalition working to achieve Peltier's freedom.

Messages asking for a presidential pardon for Peltier can be sent to the White House by calling (202) 456-1111, writing to the President at The White House, Washington, DC 20500, or by e-mailing at president@whitehouse.gov.

For more information:

Leonard Peltier Defense Committee (www.leonardpeltier. net), 2626 N. Mesa, #132, El Paso, TX 79902.

News From Indian Country (www.indiancountrynews. com).

LOO-WIT

BY WENDY ROSE

The way they do
this old woman
no longer cares
what we think
but spits
her black tobacco
any which way
stretching
full length
from her bumpy bed.
Finally up
she sprinkles
ashes on the snow,
cold buttes
promise nothing
but the walk
of winter.
Centuries of cedar
have bound her
to earth,
huckleberry ropes
lay prickly
on her neck.
Around her
machinery growls,

snarls and ploughs
great patches of her skin.
She crouches
in the north,
her trembling
the source
of dawn.

Light appears
with the shudder
of her slopes,
the movement
of her arm.
Blackberries unravel,

stones dislodge;
it's not as if
they weren't warned.

She was sleeping
but she heard the boot scrape,
the creaking floor,
felt the pull of the blanket
from her thin shoulder.
With one hand free
she finds her
weapons
and raises them high;
clearing the
twigs from her throat
she sings, she sings,
shaking the sky
like a blanket about her
Loo-wit sings and sings and
sings!

Loo-wit, "Woman of Fire," is the
Cowlitz name for Mount St. Helens,
a volcanic mountain in the state of
Washington that erupted dramatically
in 1980.

Wendy Rose is a poet and writer of Hopi
and Miwok descent.

THE THEFT OF THE BLACK HILLS

BY PHILIP MARTIN

In the early 1800s, the United States paid France for the "Louisiana Purchase," thereby acquiring jurisdiction to a vast territory. However, the U.S. understood it was not exactly "buying" all that land outright, because native peoples lived on it. What the U.S. was really getting was precedence (over other European nations) to enter into trade and other relationships with the sovereign native nations living in that region.

In 1851, now negotiating directly with the Lakota and other nations of the north-central plains, the U.S. government signed the first Fort Laramie Treaty. In this agreement, the U.S. agreed that the Lakota held sovereign rights to a huge area, centering on the sacred Black Hills (called Paha Sapa) in what is today's South Dakota.

Gold is Discovered Farther West

Soon, however, gold and silver were discovered farther west, and the government began to violate the 1851 treaty, constructing a series of forts to secure the "Bozeman Trail" through Lakota lands. Under the great leader Red Cloud, the Lakota joined with Cheyenne and Arapaho to fight back. By early 1868, the U.S. troops were defeated, pinned down helplessly in the new forts. To safely pull out their troops, the U.S. signed the second Fort Laramie Treaty. Again, they signed binding documents to recognize Lakota sovereignty over the territory including the Black Hills, and promised to use U.S. troops to keep non-Indians from trespassing.

The 1868 treaty also clearly said that no future treaty dealing with Lakota lands would "be of any validity or force against said Indians, unless executed and signed by at least three-fourths of all adult male Indians, occupying or interested in the same."

Gold in the Black Hills

Again, however, gold was discovered — this time right in the sacred Black Hills — by a Catholic priest who illegally entered the area. Excited, the U.S. sent its elite 7th Cavalry, led by Lt. Colonel George Armstrong Custer, into the Black Hills on a "fact-finding" mission. Sure enough, gold was confirmed by Custer in his 1874 report.

Quickly, the U.S. government sent a delegation to meet with the Lakota leaders to request to purchase the Black Hills. The Lakota refused to sell. In response, the U.S. ordered the Indians to move to central locations within their territory; those who did not were declared "hostile."

Meanwhile, President Ulysses S. Grant secretly ordered his army commanders to ignore miners who were already illegally moving in to establish gold mines in the hills.

The Lakotas gathered their military forces, and the U.S. army forces attacked. In the most famous battle, on June 25, 1876, Custer's 7th Cavalry charged a vast encampment of Lakotas and their allies, led by the famous military leader Crazy Horse, and was obliterated by them.

In the following winter, however, the native forces scattered into their traditional smaller bands. One by one, Lakota family groups were tracked down and slaughtered — including women and children — by U.S. forces. By the next spring, to protect their families, the Lakota laid down their arms. Crazy Horse was assassinated by a U.S. soldier at Fort Robinson, near the Black Hills, where he had gone to meet with military authorities.

Congress Takes the Black Hills

Now, after cutting off promised subsistence food rations to the Indians, in an attempt to pressure them until they "gave up their claim over the Black Hills," the U.S. Congress sent in another delegation to ask the Indians to sell the coveted, gold-rich hills.

Although the 1868 Fort Laramie Treaty required that 75 percent of all Lakota males must sign for a sale to be valid, the treaty commission came back with only 10 percent signing.

Congress decided this was good enough and passed a law saying the U.S. now "lawfully" owned the Black Hills.

"Mis-Appropriation" or Theft?

Realizing this was really not legal, the U.S. in the 1920s offered to pay in cash for "misappropriations," like the taking of the Black Hills. However, the Lakotas refused to take money; instead, they demanded their sacred lands back. After legal battles, a U.S. judge in 1942 dismissed the demand as just a "moral issue."

In 1946, however, the U.S. reopened the native lands claims. Indigenous-rights author Ward Churchill notes that this was right at the time when the U.S. was planning to put Nazi and imperial Japanese leaders on trial for war crimes like "aggressive war," forced relocations, and attempted genocide, in part on moral grounds. The U.S. realized it had some similar problems at home, and wanted to look like it was "settling" these domestic injustices fairly.

The Lakota promptly re-filed their case. The U.S. offered only cash, naming $17.5 million (supposedly the "value" of the sacred land at the time of its "misappropriation" in the 1800s). The Lakota refused. The U.S. upped the offer to $122.5 million, adding 5% simple interest accrued since the 1877 theft. Again, the Lakota refused, and in 1980 filed for their land back, plus 11 billion dollars in damages. The U.S. courts said the matter was settled (because they said so!); the Lakota could take the money or nothing. Critics noted the offer (about $2,000 per Lakota), was the equivalent of an old used car apiece, in exchange for the sacred land.

The Lakotas also pointed out that, in comparison to this miserly offer for the entire territory, the Hearst Corporation had already extracted more than a billion dollars in gold — from one single Black Hills mine! Other reports cite additional billions of dollars in known uranium deposits and other minerals.

No Agreement Reached

In the mid-1980s, U.S. Senator Bill Bradley introduced a compromise bill to return to the Indians 750,000 acres held by the federal government (avoiding dealing with lands held privately), along with some sites of great spiritual value to the Lakotas. The bill also would have returned water and mineral rights, would pay the $122.5 million (now $200 million with interest), yet would allow the Indians to press further claims in court. However, the bill died.

To date, the Lakotas have refused to accept the only offer on the table, the several hundred million dollars. The U.S. wants to consider the case closed — but why should it get to decide that, when it was the party that took the lands illegally? The Black Hills case is still unsettled.

Philip Martin is a folklorist.

Additional Reading:

Churchill, Ward. Struggle for the Land. *Monroe, Maine: Common Courage Press, 1993. Includes details of this case and many others.*

Native leaders march for respect for treaty rights in Washington, D.C.

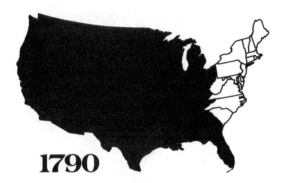

1492

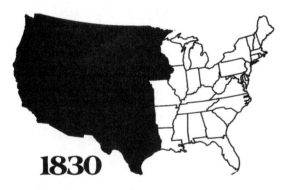

1790

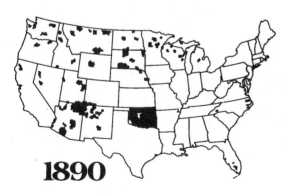

1830

1890

To order a large, detailed wall map showing the location of Native nations today, contact Russell Publications at www.nativedata.com.

SHRINKING INDIAN LANDS

"The utmost good faith shall always be observed toward the Indians; their land and property shall never be taken from them without their consent; and in their property, rights and liberty, they shall never be invaded or disturbed..."
—United States Congress,
Northwest Ordinance of 1787

These maps are rough approximations, but they give a general sense of U.S. policy towards Native peoples. The trend is clear: Native peoples were pushed from their lands by war, theft, and legislation.

By the mid-1800s, British colonists had siezed most land east of the Appalachian Mountains. The British Proclamation of 1763 stated that settlers were not to cross west of the Appalachians. But the colonists were not happy with this; they wanted to push west and claim more Indian lands. This was one cause of the Revolutionary War of 1776 (see p. 56).

In 1829, President Andrew Jackson publicly refused to honor federal treaties. In 1830, he signed the Indian Removal Act, which planned to "remove" selected Indian tribes by sending them west of the Mississippi. Through the 1830s, many tribes were relocated in tragic events like the 1838 Cherokee "Trail of Tears."

In 1887, the U.S. Congress passed the Indian Allotment Act (Dawes Act), which broke up many reservations, forcing each Indian family to accept title to a small parcel of land. Many "landowners" were soon tricked out of their small holdings, and Native lands shrunk rapidly.

For more information:

Nabokov, Peter. Native American Testimony. *New York: Viking, 1991.*

Russell, George. American Indian: Facts of Life *Phoenix, AZ: Russell Publications, 1997.*

THE EARTH IS A SATELLITE OF THE MOON
by Leonel Rugama

Apollo 2 cost more than Apollo 1

Apollo 1 cost plenty.

Apollo 3 cost more than Apollo 2

Apollo 2 cost more than Apollo 1

Apollo 1 cost plenty.

Apollo 4 cost more than Apollo 3

Apollo 3 cost more than Apollo 2

Apollo 2 cost more than Apollo 1

Apollo 1 cost plenty.

Apollo 8 cost a fortune, but no one minded

because the astronauts were Protestant

they read the bible from the moon

astounding and delighting every Christian

and on their return Pope Paul VI

    gave them his blessing.

Apollo 9 cost more than all these put together

including Apollo 1 which cost plenty.

The great-grandparents of the people

    of Acahualinca

    were less hungry than the grandparents.

The great-grandparents died of hunger.

The grandparents of the people of Acahualinca

    were less hungry than the parents.

The grandparents died of hunger.

The parents of the people of Acahualinca were less

    hungry than the children of the people there.

The parents died of hunger.

The people of Acahualinca are less hungry

    than the children of the people there.

The children of the people of Acahualinca,

    because of hunger, are not born

they hunger to be born, only to die of hunger.

Blessed are the poor for they shall inherit the moon.

— from The Earth Is a Satellite of the Moon, *Curbstone Press (bilingual edition). Translations by Sara Miles, Richard Schaaf, and Nancy Weisberg.*

The poet Leonel Rugama died in 1970 while fighting with the Sandinista National Liberation Front.

CONTEMPORARY STRUGGLES

Treaty Rights
Article by Philip Martin (p. 144)

Before students read "Treaty Rights," brainstorm on the question, What is a treaty? Turn the "misunderstandings" from the reading into questions—e.g., If a treaty is really old — made in the 1800s or even the late 1700s — is it still valid?

In an effort to tack on a veneer of legality to their acquisition of Native American land, government officials at times signed treaties with individuals who they claimed were chiefs or could somehow speak on behalf of whole Indian nations. To simulate this process, draw up a treaty between "Teacherland" and your class. Here's a sample:

Be it hereby proclaimed that this is a legal and binding treaty between Teacherland and all the people of History-firstperiod, as represented by _____, chief of the Historyfirstperiod people. In exchange for the payment of one dollar, this treaty grants Teacherland exclusive rights to anything on the desks of Historyfirstperiod. Should Teacherland need any of the territory of any of the provinces of Historyfirstperiod, it shall be relinquished on demand. I understand that once this treaty is signed, it may not be re-negotiated or violated. Should it be violated or resisted in any way whatsoever, the armies of Teacherland are free to attack and subdue any person of Historyfirstperiod.

Choose a student and offer him or her a dollar in exchange for signing your "treaty." Continue the process until you find someone to accept the offer. Don't show the treaty to the whole class until it's signed. Then go after students' desks and property.

Leonard Peltier
Article by Philip Martin (p. 151)

Watch Michael Apted's documentary film, *Incident at Oglala*, widely available for rent in video stores. Encourage students to write letters about the Peltier case — to Congressional representatives or the President. Students might want to write an article for the school paper on the Peltier case. Contact local Native rights organizations for additional ideas. They can find more information by contacting the Peltier Defense Committee at the address on page 151. They can write directly to Leonard Peltier at Leavenworth Federal Prison, P.O. Box 1000, Leavenworth, KS 66048.

Another fine film (unfortunately tagged with an 'R' rating for violence and language) is Michael Apted's *Thunderheart*. Although the film is fictional, it captures the conflicts on the Pine Ridge Reservation in the 1970s. The theme of corporate/government collusion to exploit Native lands for profit is still relevant today. High school students find this film engrossing.

Loo-Wit
Poem by Wendy Rose (p. 152)

Note: As background for understanding the poem, it is important to know that the forests on Mt. St. Helens and throughout the Cascade Range are heavily logged by timber companies.

Write a poem from the perspective of a stream where salmon no longer run, that is no longer fished by Native Americans; of a river that has been dammed; of a meadow that has been turned into a park, had a road cut through it, or is now a city dump. Talk with students about the way Wendy Rose portrays Loo-Wit's consciousness and personality.

An Ojibwe woman stands up for treaty rights.

The Theft of the Black Hills

Article by Philip Martin (p. 153)

Have students research the lives of the great political leader Sitting Bull and military leader Crazy Horse to provide background for understanding the current struggle in the Black Hills.

According to the book, *Labor's Untold Story*, by Richard Boyer and Herbert Morais, during the 1877 railroad strike, U.S. troops under General Phil Sheridan were recalled from fighting the Sioux in the Black Hills and thrown against the workers of Chicago. Why would the U.S. government use the same troops against the Sioux and Chicago workers?

Break your class into two groups or several groups and have them hold a debate: Should the Lakota people be granted their land back, or how much compensation should they be paid? Have students write to officials in Washington DC to find out the current status of negotiations between the U.S. government and the Lakota Nation. Once they find out the current situation, encourage them to voice their opinion to officials and to educate others.

Shrinking Indian Lands

Map Series (p. 155)

Make an overhead of the map and project it onto large poster paper, so students can trace the shrinking lands. Using additional resources, have the students date and mark locations of battles and massacres. Ask students to write about what the map sequence shows them. Have students research the Indian Removal Act of 1830, which ordered all Native Americans across the Mississippi. Have them research the Trail of Tears, to understand the human impact of that law.

Other Teaching Ideas

Compare the conditions of children in the Americas now with conditions when Columbus arrived. You might begin with an overview of the situation in Haiti and the Dominican Republic or Jamaica. (See the *Caribbean Connections* series, available through Teaching for Change, listed in the Resources section, p. 182.)

How did early observers describe living conditions of Taínos, Caribs and others? How do observers describe conditions today? Students might complete a timeline from 1492 to today listing key events that transformed life for Caribbean peoples.

Get United Nations documents on the rights of children. Are these rights being maintained? Who is working to make conditions better?

Members of the Dancing Horse Drum Group rally support to block encroaching development surrounding the Petroglyph National Monument near Albuquerque, New Mexico.

ENVIRONMENTAL ISSUES

The frog
does not drink up
the pond
in which it lives.

— Native proverb

TO THE WOMEN OF THE WORLD
Our Future, Our Responsibility

BY WINONA LADUKE

One hundred years ago, one of our Great Leaders, Chief Seattle, stated: "What befalls the Earth, befalls the People of the Earth."

I am from one nation of Indigenous peoples. There are millions of Indigenous people worldwide, an estimated 500 million in the world today. We are in the Cordillera, we are the Maori of New Zealand, we are in East Timor, we are the Wara Wara of Australia, the Lakota, the Tibetans, the peoples of Hawaii, New Caledonia, and many other nations.

Indigenous peoples. We are not "populations," not "minority groups." We are peoples. We are nations of peoples. Under international law, we meet the criteria of nation states, having common economic system, language, territory, history, culture and governing institutions. Despite this fact, Indigenous Nations are not allowed to participate at the United Nations.

At the United Nations, most decisions today are made by the 180 or so member states. Those states, by and large, have been in existence for only 200 years or less, while most Nations of Indigenous peoples, with few exceptions, have been in existence for thousands of years. Ironically, most decisions made in the world today are actually made by some of the 47 transnational corporations and their international financiers, whose annual income is larger than the gross national product for many countries of the world.

This is a centerpiece of the problem. Decision-making is not made by those affected by the decisions — the people who live on the land — but by corporations. What gives these corporations like Conoco, Shell, Exxon, Daishawa, ITT, and Rio Tinto Zinc, along with the World Bank, a right which supersedes or is superior to my human right to live on my land? Or the rights of my family, my community, my nation, our nations, and to us as women?

What law gives that right to them? Not any law of the Creator, or of Mother Earth. Is that right contained within their wealth — which was acquired immorally, unethically, through colonialism and imperialism, and paid for with the lives of millions of people, or species of plants and entire ecosystems? They should have no such right.

Today, on a worldwide scale, a million Indigenous peoples are slated for relocation by dam projects in the next decade (thanks to the World Bank) — from the Narmada Project in India, to the Three Gorges Dam Project in China, to the James Bay Hydroelectric Project in northern Canada.

Almost all atomic weapons which have been detonated in the world have been detonated on the lands or waters of Indigenous peoples.

In North America, today, over 50% of our remaining lands are forested, but both Canada and the United States continue aggressive clearcutting policies on our land.

And we have the dubious honor of being the most highly bombed nation in the world — the Western Shoshone Nation — on which over 650 atomic weapons have been detonated. We also have two separate accelerated proposals to dump nuclear waste in our reservation lands, and over 100 separate proposals to dump toxic waste on our lands.

The rate of deforestation in the Brazilian Amazon is one acre every nine seconds. Incidentally, the rate of extinction of Indigenous peoples in the Amazon is one nation of Indigenous peoples per year. The rate of deforestation of the boreal forest of Canada is one acre every twelve seconds. Siberia, thanks to American corporations like Weyerhauser, is not far behind. In all cases, Indigenous peoples are endangered.

Uranium mining has devastated a number of Indigenous communities in North America. Uranium mining in northern Canada has left over 120 million tons of radioactive waste. This amount represents enough material to cover the Trans-Canada Highway two meters deep across the country. Present production of uranium waste from Saskatchewan alone occurs at the rate of over 1 million tons annually. Since 1975, hospitalization for cancer, birth defects, and circulatory illnesses in that area have increased dramatically — between 123 and 600 percent.

In other areas impacted by uranium mining, cancers and birth defects have increased to, in some cases, eight times the national average. The subsequent increases in radiation exposure to the larger North American population are also evidenced in broader incidences of cancer, such as breast cancer in North American women, which is significantly on the rise. There is not a distinction in this problem whether it is in the Dene of northern Canada, the Laguna Pueblo people of New Mexico, or the people of Namibia.

The rapid increase in dioxin, organic chlorides, and PCBs in the world, as a result of industrialization, has a devastating impact. Each year, the world's paper industry discharges from 600 to 3200 grams of dioxin equivalents. This quantity is equal the amount which would cause 58,000 to 294,000 cases of cancer every year, based on the Environmental Protection Agency's estimate of dioxin's toxic nature. According to a number of recent studies, this has increased significantly the risk of breast cancer in women.

Similarly, heavy metals and PCB contamination of Inuit women of the Hudson Bay region of the Arctic indicates they have the highest levels of breast milk contamination in the world. In a 1988 study, Inuit women were found to have contamination levels up to 28 times higher than the average of women in Quebec, and ten times higher than that considered "safe" by the government.

It is also of great concern that polar bears in that region of the Arctic have such a high level of contamination from PCBs that they may be facing total sterility, and forced into extinction by early in the next century. As indigenous peoples who consider the Bears to be our relatives, we are concerned about this inability to reproduce, as a consequence of this level of bio-accumulation of toxins. We find that our human communities, like those of our relatives, the Bears, are also in danger of extinction.

These are very common issues for women, not only for Indigenous women, but for all women. What befalls our mother Earth, befalls her daughters — the women who are the mothers of our nations. Simply stated, if we can no longer nurse our children, if we can no longer bear children, and if our bodies themselves are wracked with poisons, we will have accomplished little in the way of determining our destiny, or improving our conditions.

These problems, reflected in our health and well being, are the result of a long set of historical processes which we, as women, will need to challenge if we will ultimately be in charge of our own destinies, our own self-determination, and the future of the Earth, our Mother.

I ask you to look into the charter of the United Nations (Part One, Article 3) which provides that "All peoples have right to self-determination. By virtue of that right they may freely determine their political status and freely pursue their economic, social, and political development."

Consider the following. The U.S. is the largest

Ixil girl, Guatemala.

Patricia Goudvis

energy market in the world. The average American consumes seven times as many wood products per capita as anywhere else in the industrialized world, and overall consumes one third of the world's natural resources. Canada's per-capita energy consumption is the highest in the world. Levels of consumption in the industrial world drive destruction of the world's rainforests and boreal forests, drive production of nuclear wastes, PCBs, dioxin, and other lethal chemicals which devastate the body of our Mother earth, and our own bodies.

Unless we speak and take meaningful action to address the levels of consumption, and the export of technologies and levels of consumption to other countries (like the international market for nuclear reactors), we will never have any security for our individual human rights, or for our security as women.

It is essential to collectively struggle to recover our status as Daughters of the Earth. In that is our strength.

In that, we can ensure our security as the Mothers of our Nations.

Winona LaDuke (Anishinabe) is co-chair of the Indigenous Womens Network and directs the Environmental Program at the Seventh Generation Fund. She was a candidate for Vice-President of the United States in 1996, on a ticket with Ralph Nader (Green Party).

This address is condensed from a 1995 speech given at the United Nations Fourth World Conference on Women in Beijing, China.

PEOPLE VS. NATURE IN 15TH-CENTURY EUROPE

BY KIRKPATRICK SALE

As to Europe's ecological heritage [in the year 1492], it can be seen written across the face of the land. With some significant exceptions, it is a record of deforestation, erosion, siltation, exhaustion, pollution, extermination, cruelty, destruction, and despoliation, all done in the name of utility and improvement or, as often, in ignorance of natural systems and the human connections to them.

The legacy was straight-forward: it was right and "natural" for human societies to fell trees, clear brush, "recover" fens and marshes, till soils, plant crops, graze herds, harness beasts, kill predators and "vermin," dig canals and ditches, and in general make use of the bounty of nature that a benevolent Lord had provided for them.

The costs were naturally great. Cultivated lands were harvested over and over, often with four and five crops a year. Yields were perennially inadequate, harvest failures frequent, and crop efficiencies low. Lands set aside for livestock grazing became progressively barren, with the soils compacted and groundcover deleted. Spain in particular was devastated by great herds of Merino sheep, nearly 3 million in all.

But no alteration of the landscape was so profound or purposeful as the erasure of the European forests. Europe was a civilization made of wood: houses, ships, mills, machinery, plows, furniture, plates, pipes, tools, carriages, clocks. Wood and charcoal provided fuel for heating and cooking in homes and shops, castles and cottages, and in all industries. For example, a 14th-century terra-cotta factory near Dijon employed 423 woodcutters to cut down the forest, and 334 drovers to transport the timber to the ovens. By one estimate, the great forest of Orleans south of Paris was reduced by half — from 120,000 to 60,000 acres — in the single century after 1520.

King James I of England was forced to say, in some despair, "If woods be suffered to be felled, as daily they are, there will be none left."

It had long been assumed that animals, too, were "made for man," in the words of an English churchman. It has even been said that it was primarily to the ox and the horse as domestic animals that Europe owes the very fact of its civilization. It was not so much in its exploitation of animals, however, as in its treatment of them that the medieval world truly revealed itself in bullfights, bear-baiting, cock-fights; in hunting for sport; and in efforts to eradicate wild species like wolves, bears, and foxes. The Mediterranean, once an abundant source of fish, was badly depleted by the 15th century. The Baltic had been overfished since the 11th century, and the right whale, in which the eastern Atlantic once abounded, was depleted by the 16th century and extinct by the 19th.

Is there something about the attitudes and practices of Europe that make it so different? It seems that its fundamental regard for nature was more hostile and antagonistic than was true of any other developed civilization. Nowhere else was the essential reverence for nature seriously challenged, nowhere else did there emerge the idea that human achievement and material betterment were to be won by opposing nature.

Europe's technophilia, its unchecked affection for the machine, also distinguished it among world cultures. Only Europeans, once learning of firearms from the Chinese, went on to perfect them with such ferocious skill. Only the Europeans, too, borrowing again from many other cultures, refined the technology of ocean navigation so as to become the supreme naval power in the world by the middle of the 16th century.

Finally, there was Europe's special emphasis on material acquisition and resource accumulation. The chief reason for this was the power of the still young but increasingly vigorous capitalist system, moving into vacuums left by medieval institutions — more expansionistic, more volatile and energetic, more linked to growth and progress, and almost everywhere without the kinds of moral inhibitions found in the world's other high cultures.

So it was a very special civilization that was about to set foot on the sands of that small Edenic island in the Caribbean, a most proficient civilization in material terms, but one not quite grounded in the living earth.

Excerpted from The Conquest of Paradise: Christopher Columbus and the Columbian Legacy, *by Kirkpatrick Sale (New York: Knopf, 1990).*

RADIOACTIVE MINING
Good Economics or Genocide?

BY WARD CHURCHILL

When Indian nations were confined to reservations, they were typically assigned land that was remote and barren (at least for farming). Ironically, under this land was later discovered rich deposits of valuable minerals. For instance, 1/2 of all uranium in the United States lies under Indian reservations, as does 1/3 of its western low-sulfur coal, 20% of known reserves of oil and natural gas, and much gold, silver, bauxite, and copper.

Why then, are so many reservation communities still poverty-ridden? Because the federal government controls the leasing process. It wields great influence over tribal councils and has close ties with powerful corporations. It also, of course, runs the court system. The result is a legacy of cheap leases, environmental disasters, scarred landscapes, and tribal populations injured by dangerous work, sickened by toxic-waste dumps, and economically reeling from the boom-and-bust cycle of mining operations — a sudden rush of jobs, followed by high unemployment when mines close when resources are exhausted.

> Land-linked peoples cannot simply pick up and leave whenever a given piece of real estate is "used up."

On Diné [Navajo] Lands

In 1952, the U.S. Interior Department's Bureau of Indian Affairs (BIA) awarded the Kerr-McGee Corporation the first contract—duly rubber-stamped by the federally-created and supported Navajo Tribal Council—to mine uranium on Diné land, employing about 100 Indian miners at 2/3 the off-reservation pay scale. By 1959, radiation levels in the Shiprock mine were estimated as being 90 to 100 times the maximums permissible for worker safety. Nothing was done about the situation before the uranium deposit played out and the Shiprock operation was closed in 1970.

At that point, Kerr-McGee simply abandoned the site, leaving the local community to contend with 70 acres of uranium tailings. The huge mounds of waste begin less than 60 feet from the only significant surface water in the Shiprock area, the San Juan River. It was shortly discovered that the BIA had "overlooked" inclusion of a clause requiring

the corporation to engage in any sort of post-operational clean-up.

The Bureau had also neglected to include much in the way of follow-up health care. Of the 150-odd Navajo miners who worked underground at the Shiprock facility over the years, 18 had died of radiation-induced lung cancer by 1975. By 1980, an additional 20 were dead of the same disease, while 95 more had contracted serious respiratory ailments and cancers. The incidence of cleft palate and other birth defects linked to radiation exposure had also risen dramatically, both at Shiprock and at downstream communities that had drinking water contaminated by the uranium tailings. The same could be said for Downs Syndrome, previously unknown among the Diné.

At the Churchrock Site

On July 16, 1979, the United Nuclear uranium mine at Church Rock, New Mexico, was the site of the largest radioactive spill in U.S. history. A millpond dam broke under pressure and released more than 100 million gallons of highly contaminated water into the Rio Puerco.

About 1,700 Navajo people were immediately affected, their single source of water irradiated beyond any conceivable limit. Sheep and other livestock were also found to be heavily contaminated from drinking water in the aftermath, yet United Nuclear refused to supply adequate emergency water and food supplies; a corporate official was quoted as saying, in response to local Diné requests for assistance, "This is not a free lunch."

Elsewhere on Diné Lands

A 1983 study by the federal Environmental Protection Agency (EPA) concluded there were nearly 1,000 additional "significant" nuclear waste sites, large and small, scattered about Diné territory. Cleanup of these locations was/is not required by any law, and they were designated by the EPA as "too remote" to be of "sufficient national concern" to warrant the expense of attempting their rehabilitation.

And so they remain, from White Mesa to the east to Tuba City in the west , hundreds upon hundreds of radioactive "sandpiles," still played on by Diné youngsters and swept by the wind across the land.

At Laguna Pueblo

At the neighboring Laguna Pueblo in New Mexico, the situation is perhaps worse. In 1952, the Anaconda Copper Company, a subsidiary of the Atlantic-Richfield Corporation, was issued a lease by the BIA to 7,500 acres of Laguna land for open pit uranium mining and an adjoining milling operation. By 1980, the resulting Jackpile-Paguate Mine was the largest in the world. By the time the facility closed in 1982, Anaconda had realized $600 million from its operation at Laguna.

In the process, the corporation, in collaboration with federal "development officers," virtually wrecked the traditional Laguna economy, recruiting hundreds of the small community's young people into wage jobs [which prevented them from learning and practicing traditional skills that had sustained the Lagunas for centuries] even as their environment was being gobbled up and contaminated.

The EPA informed the Lagunas in 1973, and again in 1977, that their only substantial source of surface water, the Rio Paguate, was seriously contaminated with Radium-226 and other heavy metals. In 1979, it was also revealed that the groundwater underlying the whole region was also highly irradiated.

By then, it had become known that Anaconda had used low-grade uranium ore, well-pulverized, as the gravel with which it had "improved" and expanded the Laguna road network. Soon, it was discovered that comparable material had been used in the building of the tribal council building, community center, and newly-constructed housing complex, all supposed "benefits" of the uranium boom.

As at Navajo, however, it was quickly discovered that the BIA had failed to make post-operational clean-up a part of the contract.

Development or Genocide?

As American Indian Movement (AIM) leader Russell Means has pointed out, given the land-linked nature of indigenous societies, the sacrifice of any geographical region means the sacrifice of all native peoples residing within it. Unlike the transient, extractive corporations doing business on their land, land-linked peoples cannot simply pick up and leave whenever a given piece of real estate is "used up." To do so would be to engage in an act of utter self-destruction in terms of their identity and sociocultural integrity.

On the other hand, staying put in the face of the sort of "development" previewed at Laguna and Navajo could lead to their rapid physical eradication. This led Means to conclude that U.S. energy policy, especially as regards uranium mining and milling, amounts to "genocide ... no more, no less."

Ward Churchill, of Creek, Cherokee, and Métis heritage, is a coordinator of the Colorado chapter of the American Indian Movement and author of numerous books. This is excerpted from Struggle for the Land *(Common Courage Press, 1993).*

In recent years, there has been a slowdown of building new nuclear power plants and mining uranium. Instead, U.S. government and industrial interests are now pushing to establish toxic nuclear-waste dumps on reservations, from the Nez Perce reservation in northern Idaho to the Mescalero Apache Reservation in New Mexico.

ALL PIGS ON DECK?
The Columbus Myth and the Environment

BY BILL BIGELOW

In all the traditional grade school stories, Columbus plants a flag and takes possession of the land, implicitly telling children that land is property, a thing to be owned and controlled by humans. Indeed, the children's tales imply that its possession is the first order of business, and is required for all subsequent progress. Columbus soon builds a fort on the land, a symbol of that progress.

The presentation of the Columbus story to children as the birth of "our" civilization marginalizes other cultural patterns that children could also come to recognize as "ours," such as those of the Taíno people on Guanahaní and Hayti. As discussed elsewhere in *Rethinking Columbus*, the Taínos lived for hundreds, perhaps thousands of years on these islands in what today we'd call an ecologically sustainable relationship. How did they do it? How did they view their connections to the earth? What myths and traditions carried this alternative worldview?

By 1493, on Hayti, Spaniards were cutting down entire forests to plant sugar cane. The assorted animals the Spaniards brought (sheep, goats, horses, chickens, cattle, pigs, etc.), when mentioned at all to children, are presented as further symbols of Columbus's initiative and creativity, leading inexorably to today's thing-rich society.

In just a few years, the eight pigs Columbus brought with him in 1493 had multiplied such that "all the mountains swarmed with them." They ran amok, eating everything in sight and dramatically disrupting the ecological balance in Hayti. But where in the curriculum are children urged to consider the ecological consequences of the human "progress" Columbus initiated? The Discovery myth promotes an active *not-asking* about environmental concerns.

One publisher searching for a market niche during the Columbus Quincentennial in 1992 published an illustrated children's book, *All Pigs on Deck*. In it, Columbus allows "a little man" to bring his pigs on the second voyage. Illustrations show delighted Indians petting and feeding the smiling pigs. With utter disregard for the ecological history

Letizia Galli/Delacorte Press

of the Caribbean, the book concludes: "So at least one thing Columbus brought from the Old World was suitable for the New. Now, in America today, when we eat juicy sausages and pork chops, barbecued ribs and Virginia hams, we can thank that little man and, of course, Christopher Columbus!" (*Barbeque* is a Taíno word, but Columbus even gets the credit for that.)

Like the stories of later "explorers" that children will encounter, the Columbus tale is the narrative of a rootless, community-less man, doggedly seeking individual knowledge, wealth, and glory. The natural world figures into the story only as so many "things" to be used in one individual's quest for riches and happiness. As but the first chapter in a longer curricular journey that picks up and extends these themes, the metaphors wandering through the Discovery myth are hostile to long-term ecological sustainability. They support a narrow self-centered ideology that neglects more responsible visions.

Bill Bigelow teaches in Portland, Oregon, and is an editor of Rethinking Schools.

Additional Reading:

Bowers, C.A., The Culture of Denial: Why the Environmental Movement Needs a Strategy for Reforming Universities and Public Schools, *Albany, NY: SUNY Press, 1998.*

Sale, Kirkpatrick, The Conquest of Paradise: Christopher Columbus and the Columbian Legacy, *New York: Knopf: 1990.*

THE LAND OF THE SPOTTED EAGLE

BY LUTHER STANDING BEAR

The Indian was a natural conservationist. He destroyed nothing, great or small. Destruction was not a part of Indian thought and action; if it had been, and had the man been the ruthless savage he has been credited with being, he would have long ago preceded the European in the labor of destroying the natural life of this continent.

The Indian was frugal in the midst of plenty. When the buffalo roamed the plains in multitudes he slaughtered only what he could eat and these he used to the hair and bones.

I know of no species of plant, bird, or animal that were exterminated until the coming of the white man. For some years after the buffalo disappeared there still remained huge herds of antelope, but the hunter's work was no sooner done in the destruction of the buffalo than his attention was attracted toward the deer. They are plentiful now only where protected.

The white man considered natural animal life just as he did the natural man life upon this continent, as "pests." Plants which the Indian found beneficial were also "pests." There is no word in the Lakota vocabulary with the English meaning of this word.

There was a great difference in the attitude taken by the Indian and the Caucasian toward nature, and this difference made of one a conservationist and of the other a non-conservationist of life. The Indian, as well as all other creatures that were given birth and grew, were sustained by the common mother — earth. He was therefore kin to all living things and he gave to all creatures equal rights with himself. Everything of earth was loved and reverenced.

The philosophy of the Caucasian was, "Things of the earth, earthy" — to be belittled and despised. Bestowing upon himself the position and title of a superior creature, others in the scheme were, in the natural order of things, of inferior position and title; and this attitude dominated his actions toward all things. The worth and right to live were his, thus he heartlessly destroyed. Forests were mowed down, the buffalo exterminated, the beaver driven to extinction and his wonderfully constructed dams dynamited, allowing flood waters to wreak further havoc, and the very birds of the air silenced. Great grass plains that sweetened the air have been upturned; springs, streams, and lakes that lived no longer ago than my boyhood have dried, and a whole people harassed to degradation and death.

The white man has come to be the symbol of extinction for all things natural to this continent. Between him and the animal there is no rapport and they have learned to flee from his approach, for they cannot live on the same ground....

Excerpted from Land of the Spotted Eagle *(Houghton-Mifflin Co., 1933), the autobiography of Luther Standing Bear (1868-1939), a hereditary chief of the Oglala Sioux.*

THE EARTH AND THE AMERICAN DREAM
Selected Quotes

These quotes are from an extraordinary 77-minute video, Earth and the American Dream, *by Bill Couturie (Direct Cinema Limited, 1993). Beginning with Columbus, the film blends contrasting quotes from Native Americans and European "settlers" with images of the environmental effects of these ideas.*

"There is little in common between us. You wander far from the graves of your ancestors and seemingly without regret. Every part of this soil is sacred in the estimation of my people — every hillside, every valley, every plain and grove has been hallowed by some sad or happy event in days long vanished. When the memory of my tribe shall have become a myth, these shores will swarm with the invisible dead that once filled them and still love this beautiful land."

— Chief Seattle

"My God, a hideous and desolate wilderness, full of wild beasts and wild men. And what multitudes there might be of them we know not."
— Gov. William Bradford, Plymouth Colony

"You shall have dominion over the fish of the sea, dominion over the birds of the heavens, over all the earth, over every creeping thing that creepeth upon the earth. Go forth children, multiply, fill the earth and subdue it."
— The Book of Genesis,
The Bible

"As for the natives, they're near all dead of the smallpox. So the Lord has cleared our title to what we possess. And we shall be the place where the Lord shall create a new heaven and a new earth."
— Gov. John Winthrop,
Massachusetts Bay Colony

"The untransacted destiny of the American people is to subdue the continent. To rush over this vast field to the Pacific Ocean. To confirm the destiny

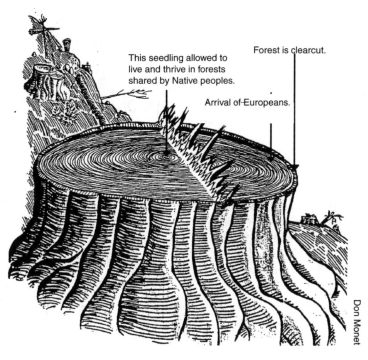

This seedling allowed to live and thrive in forests shared by Native peoples.

Forest is clearcut.

Arrival of Europeans.

Don Monet

of the human race."
— William Gilpin, Territorial Governor

"How beautiful would this natural Eden look if parted off with fences into farms, dotted with cities, villages and farmhouses."
— Miriam Colt, homesteader

"Indians are too lazy and too much like mere animals to cultivate the fertile soil.... What should be done with these Indian dogs in our manger?"
— The Yankton Press & Dakotan

"From the standpoint of humanity at large the extermination of the buffalo has been a blessing."
— President Theodore Roosevelt

"I love the land and the buffalo and will not part with it. I don't want to settle. I love to roam the prairies.... [White settlers and U.S. Cavalry] cut down our timber, they killed my buffalo. When I see that, it feels as if my heart will bust with sorrow."
— Satanta, Chief of the Kiowas

"It is a glorious history our God has bestowed upon his chosen people. A history of statesmen who flung the boundaries of the republic out into unexplored lands and savage wildernesses — a history of a multiplying people who overran a continent in half a century."

— **Senator Albert Beveridge**

"Machinery, science and intelligence ... are man's forces and will be used to hasten his dominion over nature, and each gain upon nature adds to the quantity of goods to be consumed by society."

— **Simon Patten, political economist**

"Industry as a whole can plan and execute towards advancement secure in its belief that there are no limits to the total productive capacity of the country and the resulting purchasing power — because there are no limits to the needs and desires of American consumers.... Human desires seem to have no limits."

— **Paul Mazur, banker**

"To stop our forward progress even if we could, would hardly lead elsewhere than to a complete wreck. Whether we like it or not, we are on our way."

— **Clifford Furnas, chemical engineer**

"In the first one half of the 20th century, people consumed more non-renewable resources than in all of humankind's previous time on earth."

— *narration from the video,*
Earth and the American Dream

"The population explosion is a grand thing for business. Think of all the machines we can sell to more people. The consumer is a great big gaping jaw we're all trying to fill up with whatever we can cram down there. And the great hope is that the jaw will keep getting wider and wider. ... And we can make a lot of money on it."

— **Charlie Landesfahr, advertising executive**

> "In the first one half of the 20th century, people consumed more non-renewable resources than in all of humankind's previous time on earth."
>
> — narration from the video "Earth and the American Dream"

"More people means more markets."

— **Vance Packard**

"Our enormously productive economy demands that we make consumption our way of life ... that we seek our spiritual satisfaction, our ego satisfaction, in consumption."

— **Victor Lebow, marketing consultant**

"The atom will give us all the power we need and more, power seemingly without end, power to do everything man is destined to do. We have found what might be called perpetual youth."

— **Westinghouse Electric**

"We still talk in terms of conquest. We still haven't become mature enough to think of ourselves as only a tiny part of a vast and incredible universe. Man's attitude today toward nature is critically important simply because we have now acquired a fateful power to alter and destroy nature. But man is a part of nature and his war against nature is inevitably a war against himself."

— **Rachel Carson, marine biologist**

"Compare the six days of the Book of Genesis to the four billion years of geologic time. On this scale, one day equals about 666 million years. All day Monday until Tuesday noon, creation was busy getting the earth going. Life began on Tuesday noon, and the beautiful organic wholeness of it developed over the next four days. At 4 p.m. Saturday, the big reptiles; 5 hours later, when the redwoods appeared, there were no more big reptiles. At three minutes before midnight, man appeared. One fourth of a second before midnight, Christ arrived. At 1/40 of a second before midnight, the Industrial Revolution began. We are surrounded by people who think that what we have been doing for 1/40 of a second can go on indefinitely. They are considered normal. But they are stark raving mad."

— **David Brower, conservationist**

Earth and the American Dream *is available in DVD format through Amazon.com or DVD and video format from Direct Cinema Limited (www.directcinema.com).*

THE EARTH AND THE AMERICAN DREAM
Questions

Write a reaction to the video Earth and the American Dream.

You might describe how it made you feel — or what you think ought to be done. You might react to one or more of the quotes — or to the images in the video.

Some questions to think about:

1. How might the North American continent be different today if Columbus and Europeans had never arrived?

2. What patterns do you notice in some Europeans' attitudes toward the earth from 1492 to the present?

3. What attitudes do the Europeans quoted in the video have toward the "wilderness"?

4. Why is there such hostility and contempt directed at Native Americans by some Europeans? What is the relationship between racism and contempt for the earth?

5. What is the "good life" for Native Americans? What is the "good life" for Europeans?

6. Clifford Furnas says, "Whether we like it or not, we are on our way." But *where* are we on our way to? And who is the "we" he refers to?

7. Which of the attitudes expressed in the video do you think "live" in you? How did they get there?

8. If the earth could speak, what would it say to any of the people quoted in the video? What would it say needs to be done to deal with the problems described?

9. "Talk back" to any of the individuals quoted in the video. If they were here in our classroom, what would you ask them; what would you tell them?

10. How would our attitudes, our economic system, our whole society have to change in order to address the environmental problems described in the video?

11. The video suggests that there is something fundamentally wrong with the "American dream." Do you agree? And if so, what should be the new American dream?

To be used with the video Earth and the American Dream, *by Bill Couturie (Direct Cinema Limited, 1993).*

RED RIBBONS FOR EMMA

BY DEB PREUSCH, TOM BARRY, BETH WOOD

This is a true story, set in the early 1980s.

It is about a Navajo woman named Emma Yazzie, who lives in a hogan (a traditional Navajo round house) and herds sheep. Her hogan has no electricity, but nearby is a big power plant that feeds electricity to Los Angeles, Phoenix, and other cities.

All around her are energy companies on reservation land, with coal trucks, gas pipelines, and high-power lines. Near Emma's hogan is the largest coal mine in the United States.

Sometimes it seems there are no more heroes. Every place, even the moon, has been discovered by explorers. All the fun and brave and exciting things to do, like flying alone across the ocean in an airplane or inventing the light bulb, have already been done. Sometimes it seems we were all born too late to be heroes.

But that's not true. We still have plenty of chances to become heroes. We just need to think about becoming a different kind of hero.

Emma Yazzie is a hero. She is a hero in our modern age — the time we all live in.

Indian people have a different way of thinking about the land than the companies do. Emma says the companies only want to make money. They want to take the coal out of the ground, and when the coal is gone they leave the land full of holes. Their big shovels nose their way into the ground to take the minerals out and they tear up the grass roots. Once the grass is gone, the land just blows away in the wind. Then they go to another place to find more coal.

Indian people believe that if you treat the land badly, the land will die. Then the animals will die and soon the people will die, too. The energy companies can find someplace else to go, but the Navajos have no place to go when their land dies.

Inside her hogan, Emma has red ribbons hanging on her wall. They are not the fancy kind people win at state fairs, and nobody gave them to her. She took them! She took them off the wooden stakes the company stuck into the land. Emma knows very well that the stakes are survey markers to show where the company plans to build more power lines and more mines. Every time she or Jeanne Joe, her daughter, see a stake with a ribbon, they pull it out!

One morning, after they had come back from herding sheep, Emma and Jeanne Joe saw a line of trucks coming up the dirt road to Emma's hogan. They were company trucks, and both women knew that trouble was coming.

After herding sheep, Emma and Jeanne Joe are very thirsty and hungry. They were cooking breakfast. They were heating up Navajo fry bread and green chile over the potbelly stove and listening to a Navajo radio program on their transistor radio.

Emma took the food off the stove and went outside to greet the men. At first, the men wearing hard hats tried to treat Emma the way most adults treat children. They began talking to her as if she wasn't as smart as they were and they could tell her what to do whenever they wanted.

The company men had come to tell Emma to stop pulling up the survey markers—the ones with the red ribbons. They told her: we need to build a new power line to carry electricity from the plant. You are slowing our work down. We put the stakes on the land to tell us where to put the power line, which will be on company land.

It is not company land, it is Navajo land, Emma said back to the company men. It is the land where my mother and my grandmother herded sheep. It is not your land. I never gave it to you. The company boss tried to scare Emma. If you don't stop pulling up the stakes, he said, we'll call the police.

Emma is a small woman, but she looked at the boss with mean and angry eyes. I don't care what you do, she said bravely. I don't want this land to be destroyed anymore. I don't care if you hang me up and kill me. I'm ready to die for my land.

Emma is not really mean, but with the companies she acts real mean. The mine would like her to move because she is in their way. She is always causing them trouble.

And Emma will keep up her fight against the power plant and the mine until the day she dies.

The grassroots people like Emma are finding that they can outsmart the monster. When they all get together, they are bigger and more powerful than it is.

When I die, Emma says, I want to be lying right here on the land I love and where I was born.

Excerpted from Red Ribbons for Emma *(Stanford: New Seed Press, 1981; currently out of print).*

Emma Yazzie fights the power companies by pulling up their survey marker stakes.

Deborah Preusch

ENVIRONMENTAL ISSUES

The articles in this section are so rich in content a teacher could develop dozens of lessons from them. Below we have listed a few ideas:

To the Women of the World

Speech by Winona LaDuke (p. 160)

LaDuke describes the "centerpiece of the problem" as the fact that "decision-making is not made by those affected by decisions." Most people believe that Americans live in a democracy (and define democracy to include decision-making being made by those affected by decisions). Have students, individually or in pairs, read the speech and list the evidence LaDuke provides for her assertion that corporations — not people who are affected by decisions — have power. Have students think of developments in their community, state, and country, and examine who made the decisions in each case.

People vs. Nature in 15th-Century Europe

Article by Kirkpatrick Sale (p. 162)

Have students describe the European view of nature back in the 15th century. Have them give examples from Sale's article. Probe with your students: What were the forces that led Europeans to hold this view of nature? Have them contrast that with a Native American view of nature. In whose interest were these viewpoints? How have these viewpoints changed in the last 500 years?

Land of the Spotted Eagle

Article by Luther Standing Bear (p. 166)

Have students read this essay in small groups. Have each group make a chart, listing characteristics of a conservationist and a non-conservationist way of life. Remind students that this was written in 1933. Ask them which way of life our society has been following since then. Ask them to write why they think the way they do, and what they would like our society to value. Students can share their thoughts through writing or by making drawings which depict the two ways of life described in the essay.

Radioactive Mining

Article by Ward Churchill (p. 163)

After reading the article with your students, pose these questions: Who do you think should have the right to determine how land on Indian reservations is used? Why do you think the federal government has played the role it has in regard to radioactive mining? How does the treatment of native peoples on this issue compare to their treatment throughout history? What can we do about this situation?

All Pigs on Deck?

Article by Bill Bigelow (p. 165)

Collect several children's biographies of Columbus or other "explorers" from a school library. Put students in small groups and ask them to read their respective books with one another and to answer questions such as these:

In your story, what do you learn about the new land — including plants and animals — where Columbus "explored"? How did the original people, the Taínos, treat the land? How did Columbus treat the land? What, if anything, did he do to change the land? According to your book, what plants and animals did Columbus bring to the Americas?

Students may find this a challenging exercise, since in most children's books or textbook entries, the earth is little more than a "stage" for Columbus, his men, and the people he encounters. Ask students why the books tell them so little about the environment and how Columbus affected it. What did Columbus want from the land? What did the Taínos want from the land?

Red Ribbons for Emma

Story by Deborah Preusch, et al. (p. 170)

Distribute copies of the story to your students. Read it together and discuss it. In small groups, have students plan how they might dramatically reenact the story. When the groups perform for the whole class, have them end by explaining whether they believe Emma is a "modern-day hero." As an extension, the children could list the attributes of Emma and compare them to other heroes in their own community and to other Native American leaders who have fought for the rights of their people and for the earth.

FINAL WORDS

It's high time America discovered itself.

This necessary discovery,
a revelation of the face hidden
behind the masks,
rests on the redemption of our
most ancient traditions.

It's out of hope, not nostalgia,
that we must recover a
community-based mode of production
and way of life,
founded not on greed but on solidarity,
age-old freedoms, and identity
between human beings
and nature.

— Eduardo Galeano

REMEMBER
BY JOY HARJO

Remember the sky that you were born under,
know each of the star's stories.
Remember the moon, know who she is. I met her
in a bar once in Iowa City.
Remember the sun's birth at dawn, that is the
strongest point of time. Remember sundown
and the giving away to night.
Remember your birth, how your mother struggled
to give you form and breath. You are evidence of
her life, and her mother's, and hers.
Remember your father, his hands cradling
your mother's flesh, and maybe her heart, too
and maybe not.
He is your life, also.
Remember the earth whose skin you are.
Red earth yellow earth white earth brown earth
black earth we are earth.
Remember the plants, trees, animal life who all have their
tribes, their families, their histories, too. Talk to them,
listen to them. They are alive poems.
Remember the wind. Remember her voice. She knows the
origin of this universe. I heard her singing Kiowa war
dance songs at the corner of Fourth and Central once.
Remember that you are all people and that all people
are you.
Remember that you are this universe and that this
universe is you.
Remember that all is in motion, is growing, is you.
Remember that language comes from this.
Remember the dance that language is, that life is.
Remember
to remember.

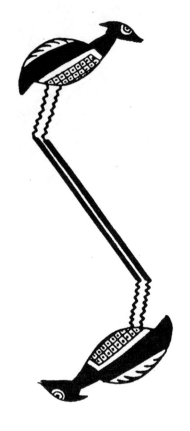

— *from* That's What She Said: Contemporary Poetry and Fiction by Native American Women, *edited by Rayna Green (Bloomington: Indiana University Press, 1984)*

Joy Harjo (Muscogee and Creek) is a poet and musician. Her books include The Woman Who Fell from the Sky.

FOR SOME,
A TIME OF MOURNING

BY WENDY ROSE

As I walk upon my Mother Earth, I listen for the voices. All of my relations whisper to me: the pines and buckeyes, the finches and hawks, the delicate down of spring mountain grass, the tiny spiders and red ants, the enormous vermillion evening sun, Hopi and Me-wuk ancestors whose songs are not finished. My flesh is in contact with the granite bones of my Mother, and Her strong pulse moves softly beneath my feet.

These are not the only voices. There, too, is Joseph, who joined the colonial army in Canada after losing his Irish estate (that his ancestors had stolen five hundred years earlier), and Henrietta, his wife, descended from the native Picts and mystic Celts of the Scottish highlands, my great-grandmother who followed her husband to the California goldfields. But there is a difference.

Is it the pitch of the voices? the volume? the clarity? In all of the voices, I find my life. This is especially true on mornings like this one, cool and deeply dramatic with impending rain and swirling wind. My morning commute takes me from my home in Coarsegold (not far from the place where Joseph and Henrietta settled) to the foggy floor of the Great Central Valley where the native people of the Sierra Nevada were imprisoned when miners wanted their land and treaties were signed in disappearing ink.

I am a modern consumer, a new voice with little substance. I wonder if the generations to come will hear mine among the many, will hear any human voice within the increasing wail of the injured earth. Every blow to the flesh of my Mother drives

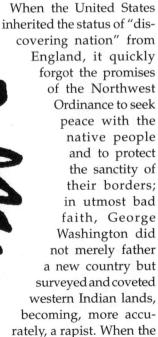

the colonial knife in deeper; this indigenous world, the real world, is crying.

I must remember that all of this death was for money. The very beginning of this episode, five hundred years ago, was the legacy of losing to a stronger market, a sharper sword. Within one generation, the "discoverer's" son had destroyed all native human life on the island his father had claimed. I do not believe that the physical shape of my Mother was ever the question; even then it must have been obvious that, like me, She was round, asymmetrical, large.

I must remember that exploration and genocide have always been just business as usual. Neither scientific nor strictly political, those brave trekkers whose names frost the pages of every American child's schoolbooks carried their banners not for kings, but for companies, for traders, for miners, for every kind of coinage, for the freedom, not to worship or walk or speak or elect, but the freedom to profit beyond the reach of the king. Was there even a single explorer whose concern was the fresh-fallen snow of new knowledge or friendly contact with the citizens of previously unknown (to him) nations?

When the United States inherited the status of "discovering nation" from England, it quickly forgot the promises of the Northwest Ordinance to seek peace with the native people and to protect the sanctity of their borders; in utmost bad faith, George Washington did not merely father a new country but surveyed and coveted western Indian lands, becoming, more accurately, a rapist. When the colonists revolted against the king, I must remember that the king had wanted to protect Indian land from men like Washington. Every American schoolchild learns of George's hatchet and cherry tree as if it were true, but when are they told the truth of his punitive raids into Iroquois country to burn crops and houses, slaughter innocent people?

The voices remind me that there are other things I must remember. The natural people of the earth have survived with their aboriginal wisdom intact. Even if they have lost individuals, the Center has survived. Much more so than the vast destruction, I am in awe of my Elders' strength. As long as they live, there is a place for me, and if they do not live, all of us will go with them.

The voices live in my bones and shiver in them with rage and with prayer. I hear many voices, but of them all, the most enduring ones, the ones with the strongest and sweetest songs, are native. More than that I am irrevocably linked to the two-legged, four-legged, flying and swimming of earth, to the vanished Taíno who first felt the heavy hand of colonialization, to the frozen huddled walkers on the Trail of Tears, to the buffalo skull mountains piled high near prairie railroad tracks, to Bikini Islanders left with invisible brooms for cleaning their devastated sacred land, to the napalmed and betrayed people of Vietnam/Laos/Cambodia, to the misled boys who carried corporate rifles into clouds of Agent Orange, to the shadows of evaporated men on the sidewalks of Nagasaki, to the weeping elders who pray on Big Mountain and keep safe the graves of their grandparents, to the brave new poet-diplomats of Nicaragua, to all who wait for Purification and stand ready within our Mother's heart, to all who remember their origin and have traveled the great circle to return home, to the choice that we made and the promise that we gave to be thankful for each new sunrise, each drop of rain.

> You know, nothing of the past five hundred years was inevitable. Every raised fist and brandished weapon was a choice someone made.

You know, nothing of the past five hundred years was inevitable. Every raised fist and brandished weapon was a choice someone made. The decision to become a nation of thieves and liars was a choice. The decision to censor the native truth was a choice. The decision to manipulate the knowledge of American history was a choice.

My immediate choice is to celebrate or to mourn. With my relations around me, I go into mourning — but I go angry, alive, listening, learning, remembering. I do not go quietly. I do not vanish. I do not forget.

I will not let you forget.

Wendy Rose is a poet, writer, and anthropologist of Hopi and Miwok heritage. This is excerpted from an article in Without Discovery: A Native Response to Columbus, *ed. Ray Gonzalez (Seattle: Broken Moon Press).*

Rock pillars and hogan, Monument Valley, Arizona.

FINAL WORDS

THE BLUE TIGER

BY EDUARDO GALEANO

It seems strikingly clear to me that America wasn't discovered in 1492, just as Spain was not discovered when the Roman legions invaded it in 218 B.C.

And it also seems clear as can be that it's high time America discovered itself.

This necessary discovery, a revelation of the face hidden behind the masks, rests on the redemption of some of our most ancient traditions. It's out of hope, not nostalgia, that we must recover a community-based mode of production and way of life, founded not on greed but on solidarity, age-old freedoms, and identity between human beings and nature. I believe there is no better way to honor the Indians, the first Americans, who from the Arctic to Tierra del Fuego have kept their identity and message alive through successive campaigns of extermination. Today they still hold out vital keys to memory and prophecy for all of America.

Yanomami **shapono,** *a communal home.*

I am not one to believe in traditions simply because they are traditions. I believe in the legacies that multiply human freedom, and not in those that cage it. It should be obvious; when I refer to remote voices from the past that can help us find answers to the challenges of the present, I am not proposing a return to the sacrificial rites that offered up human hearts to the gods, nor am I praising the despotism of the Inca or Aztec monarchs.

On the contrary, I am applauding the fact that America can find its most youthful energies in its most ancient sources. The past tells us things that are important to the future. A system lethal to the world and its inhabitants, that putrefies the water, annihilates the land, and poisons the air and the soil, is in violent contradiction with cultures that hold the earth to be sacred because we, its children, are sacred. Those cultures, scorned and denied, treat the earth as their mother, and not as a raw material

and source of income. Against the capitalist law of profit, they propose the life of sharing, reciprocity, and mutual aid.

To justify usurping the lands of the Sioux Indians at the end of the last century, the United States Congress declared that "community property is dangerous to the development of the free enterprise system." And in March of 1979, a law was promulgated in Chile requiring the Mapuche Indians to divide up their lands and turn themselves into small land owners with no links between them; the dictator Pinochet explained that the communities were incompatible with the nation's economic progress. From capitalism's point of view, communal cultures that do not separate human beings from one another or from nature are enemy cultures. But the capitalist point of view is not the only one.

In our time, the conquest continues. Under the banner of Progress, onward march the legions of modern pirates, with hooked hand, eye patches, or wooden legs, the multi-nationals that swoop down on the uranium, petroleum, nickel, manganese, and tungsten.

"The conquest isn't over," gaily proclaimed the advertisements published in Europe [in 1980], offering Bolivia to foreigners. The military dictatorship held out to the highest bidder the richest land in the country, while treating the Indians as in the 16th century. In the first phase of the conquest, Indians were compelled to describe themselves in public documents as, "I, wretched Indian...." Now the Indians only have the right to exist as servile labor or tourist attractions.

"Land is not sold. Land is our mother. You don't sell your mother. Why don't they offer 100 million dollars to the Pope for the Vatican?" a Sioux [Lakota] leader asked recently. A century earlier, the Seventh Calvary had ravaged the Black Hills, sacred territory to the Sioux, because they held gold. Now multi-national corporations mine its uranium, although the Sioux refuse to sell. The uranium is poisoning the rivers.

A few years ago, the Colombian government told the Indians of Cauca valley, "The subsoil does not belong to you, but to the Colombian nation," and immediately turned it over to the Celanese Corporation. After a time, part of the Cauca had been turned into a lunar landscape.

Throughout America, from north to south, the dominant culture acknowledges Indians as objects of study, but denies them as subjects of history: The Indians have folklore, not culture; they practice superstitions not religions; they speak dialects not languages; they make handicrafts not art.

Perhaps [examining the legacy of Columbus] could help turn things around, so topsy-turvy are they now. Not to confirm the world but to denounce and change it. For that, we will have to celebrate the vanquished — not the victors.

And perhaps in this way we could get a bit closer to the day of justice that the Guaraní, pursuers of Paradise, have always been awaiting. The Guaraní believe that the world wants to be different, that it wants to be born again. And so the world entreats the First Father to unleash the blue tiger that sleeps beneath his hammock.

The Guaraní believe that someday that righteous tiger will shatter this world so that another world, with neither evil nor death, guilt nor prohibitions, can be born from its ashes.

The Guaraní believe, and I do too, that life truly deserves that festival.

Eduardo Galeano is a novelist and writer from Uruguay, author of the trilogy, Memory of Fire. *This is excerpted from "The Blue Tiger and the Promised Land,"* NACLA's Report on the Americas, *Vol. XXIV, No. 5, Feb. 1991.*

Indian Law Resource Center

"Maya Dancer" portrayed in needle-point by the Mukanel Women's Maya Craft Cooperative of Golden Stream in Belize.

Colibrí
FOR KATHERINE, ONE YEAR LATER
BY MARTÍN ESPADA

In Jayuya,
the lizards scatter
like a fleet of green canoes
before the invader.
The Spanish conquered
with iron and words:
"Indio Taíno" for the people
who took life
from the rain
that rushed through trees
like evaporating arrows,
who left the rock carvings
of eyes and mouths
in perfect circles of amazement.

So the hummingbird
was christened "colibrí."
Now the colibrí
darts and bangs
between the white walls
of the hacienda,
a racing Taíno heart
frantic as if hearing
the bellowing god of gunpowder
for the first time.

The colibrí
becomes pure stillness,
seized in the paralysis
of the prey,
when your hands
cup the bird
and lift him
through the red shutters
of the window,
where he disappears
into a paradise of sky,
a nightfall of singing frogs.

If only history
were like your hands.

Colibrí
PARA KATHERINE, UN AÑO DESPUÉS
BY MARTÍN ESPADA

En Jayuya,
los lagartijos se dispersan
como una flota de canoas verdes
ante el invasor.
Los españoles conquistaron
con hierro y palabras:
"indio taíno" para el pueblo
que tomaba la vida
de la lluvia
arrojada entre los árboles
como flechas evaporándose,
ellos que dejaron huellas en la roca
de ojos y bocas
en círculos perfectos de espanto.

Y el zumbador
fue bautizado "colibrí."
Ahora el colibrí
se precipita y se estrella
entre los muros blancos
de la hacienda,
un corazón taíno agitado,
frenético como si oyera
el bramido del dios de la pólvora
por primera vez.

El colibrí,
presa paralizada,
cae en la más pura quietud,
cuando tus manos
lo acopan
y lo alzan
por las celosías rojas
de la ventana,
donde se desaparece
en un paraíso celeste,
un anochecer de coquíes.

Si la historia
sólo fuera como tus manos.

—*from* Rebellion Is the Circle of a Lover's Hand
*(Willimantic, CT: Curbstone Press, 1990). Martín Espada
is an award-winning poet who teaches at the University of
Massachusetts.*

RESOURCES

Knowledge
is like
the wind...

once obtaining it,
you can go
anywhere.

— Yellow Horse

RESOURCES

Please note that, in this book, a few key resources are often listed at the end of each article. The materials listed below are only a beginning for further research and learning. Books listed for a particular age group might be appropriate for other ages so please look over the entire list.

General Catalogs of Books and Videos

Africa World Press, P.O. Box 1892, Trenton NJ 08607; 609-695-3200. www.africaworldpressbooks. com. Publishes and distributes excellent books on Africa and the Americas.

Children's Book Press, 2211 Mission St., San Francisco, CA 94110; 415-821-3080. www. childrensbookpress.org. An important publisher of anti-racist, multicultural books for children featuring stories from indigenous and third-world nations.

Curbstone Press, 321 Jackson St., Williman-tic, CT 06226; 860-423-5110. www.curbstone.org. "Books That Make a Difference" is Curbstone's catalog of high-quality poetry, fiction, and nonfic-tion books, with a focus on Latin America, political struggle, and U.S. writers of color.

Maryknoll Videos & Posters. P.O. Box 308, Maryknoll, NY 10545-0308; 800-227-8523. www. maryknollsocietymall.org. Catalog includes low-priced videos with study guides on Guatemalan and Brazilian indigenous peoples, and issues of global inequity.

National Museum of the American Indian, Resource Center. 1 Bowling Green, New York, NY 10004-1415; 212-514-3799. www.nmai.si.edu. This Smithsonian museum offers free, 1-2 page bibliog-raphies on American Indian topics, including *Books for Teachers*, *Books for Children*, and *Books on Religion and Spirituality*.

Oyate, 2702 Mathews St., Berkeley, CA 94702; 510-848-6700. www.oyate.org. Oyate carefully evalu-ates books and other media on Native Americans and offers a thoughtful catalog of resources for all ages, also curriculum guides for educators.

Shenandoah Film Productions. 538 "G" St., Arcata CA 95521; 707- 822-1030. www. shenandoahfilms.com. Offers a catalog of videos on native issues, including Leonard Peltier's case, Wounded Knee, Black Hills land rights, broken treaties, and other indigenous struggles.

Teaching for Change, P.O. Box 73038, Wash-ington, DC 20056-3038; 800-763-9131. www. teachingforchange.org. Maintains a webstore with some of the best curricular resources for multicul-tural teaching for all grade levels and subjects, as well as for teacher education and staff development. Carries many key resources mentioned in *Rethinking Columbus*.

Elementary Books

Columbus Day, by Vicki Liestman; illustrated by Rick Hanson. Minneapolis: Carolrhoda Books, 1991. Tells in simple language the story of Columbus's earliest encounters with Native Americans and raises questions about how Columbus Day should be ob-served to more accurately reflect the consequences of his voyages. However, it does share some of the Eurocentric biases of other Columbus biographies.

Encounter, by Jane Yolen, illus. by David Shan-non. New York: Harcourt, Brace, Jovanovitch, 1992. The Columbus story as seen through the eyes of a Taíno boy. An important resource to encourage stu-dents to think about the perspectives missing from the traditional "discovery" tale. (See review, p. 64.)

The Invisible Hunters/Los Cazadores Invisibles, by Harriet Rohmer, Octavio Chow, and Morris Vi-daure; illus. by Joe Sam. San Francisco: Children's Book Press, 1987. A trio of Miskito Indian hunters falls prey to greed and carelessness as a result of contact with foreigners. A beautiful bilingual book, illustrated with collage art, with the powerful mes-sage that the people will survive only by staying true to their communal cultural values, while adapting to change.

The People Shall Continue, by Simon Ortiz; illus. by Sharol Graves. San Francisco: Children's Book Press, 1988 (rev. ed.). A simple, eloquent outline of the history of Native American peoples, from creation to the present, emphasizing their endur-ance. A useful starting point for discussions about cultural survival.

This Land Is My Land, by George Littlechild. San Francisco: Children's Book Press, 1993. The stunning colors of Littlechild's (Cree) paintings make this book irresistible, but it is the simple, forthright text that gives this book its educational value. Littlechild touches on sensitive issues, opening doors to conversations about Columbus, boarding school, honoring ancestors, the slaughter of the buffalo, women's roles in Native America, and other subjects.

Who Belongs Here? An American Story, by Margy Burns Knight; illus. by Anne Sibley O'Brien. Gardiner, ME: Tillbury House, 1993. A thought-provoking, intelligent introduction to the complex question, "Who is an American?" Tells the story of Nary, a Cambodian boy who fled his war-ravaged homeland with his grandparents. In looking at his life and the prejudice encountered in school, the book explores how other groups — Irish immigrants, Latino farmworkers, Haitian refugees, and the Iroquois — have struggled to fit into the "American" definition.

Upper Elementary/ Middle School Books

Morning Girl, by Michael Dorris. New York: Hyperion, 1992. In this delightful novella about Morning Girl and her brother, Star Boy, it's the summer before the arrival of Columbus on the Taíno island of Guanahaní. This is the only book for young readers we know of that attempts to imagine the world of the Taínos in story form. (See review, p. 65.)

Sparrow Hawk, by Meridel Le Sueur. Stevens Point, WI: Holy Cow! Press, 1987. This fiction book about an interracial friendship during the Black Hawk War, originally published 1950, was one of the "radical" works for which Le Sueur was blacklisted during the McCarthy era.

Secondary Books

500 Años del Pueblo Chicano/500 Years of Chicano History, by Elizabeth Martínez. Albuquerque, NM: Southwest Organizing Project, 1992. A bilingual pictorial history of the Chicano people.

Black Indians: A Hidden Heritage, by William Katz. Riverside, NJ: Macmillan, 1986. Inspiring stories of the historic links between African-American and Native American peoples and their common fight against oppression.

Columbus and the World Around Him, by Milton Meltzer. New York: Franklin Watts, 1990. Describes Columbus's voyages, the impact of the Spanish, and the ultimate cultural influence of Native Americans on the European invaders.

Hear My Voice: A Multicultural Anthology of Literature from the United States, ed. by Laurie King. Addison-Wesley, 1994. A 398-page volume with fiction, poetry, essays, and speeches from many different groups that make up America. Each selection is followed by discussion questions. A companion annotated bibliography is available.

A People's History of the United States, by Howard Zinn. NY: HarperCollins, 1980. The best single-volume history of the United States. Zinn's groundbreaking book covers 1492 to the present, emphasizing perspectives of working people, people of color, and other groups neglected in most American history books. Essential reading. (Available from Teaching for Change.)

Wounded Knee: An Indian History of the American West, by Dee Brown, adapted by Amy Ehrlich. New York: Henry Holt, 1974. An abridged version of Dee Brown's classic, *Bury My Heart at Wounded Knee* (1970), adapted for younger readers. Like the original, this is a readable history of the "Indian Wars" of the 1800s, covering battles, massacres, and treaty negotiations. This history from a Native American perspective focuses on the thoughtful leadership, courage, and adaptability Indian nations showed during this difficult period.

Books for Adults
(key Columbus resources)

Columbus: His Enterprise, by Hans Koning. New York: Monthly Review Press, 1991. Valuable resource for teachers trying to overcome the myths about Columbus. May also be used with high school students.

The Conquest of Paradise: Christopher Columbus and the Columbian Legacy, by Kirkpatrick Sale. New York: Plume, 1991. Very detailed, with extensive quotes from far-ranging original sources. Links Columbus's legacy to environmental degradation. Highly recommended.

A Short Account of the Destruction of the Indies, by Bartolomé de las Casas, edited and translated by Nigel Griffin. New York: Penguin, 1992. Read it. Las Casas is the most qualified and compassionate of all the 16th-century chroniclers.

The Journal of Christopher Columbus, edited by Cecil Jane. New York: Bramhall House, 1960.

Books for Adults
(related topics)

The Conquest of America: How the Indian Nations Lost Their Continent, Hans Koning. New York: Monthly Review, 1993. A useful summary, from Columbus to the present, of the war against Native Americans. A narrative both personal and political, like Koning's classic, *Columbus: His Enterprise*.

Custer Died for Your Sins: An Indian Manifesto, by Vine Deloria, Jr. Norman, OK: U of Oklahoma Press, 1988. A powerful and influential work first published 1969.

Europe and the People Without History, by Eric Wolf. Berkeley: University of California Press, 1982. An economic and political survey of Europe and Europe's victims ("people without history") at the time of the Conquest.

Facing West: The Metaphysics of Indian-hating and Empire-building, by Richard Drinnon. New York: Schocken, 1990. Connects the suppression of native nations and liberation movements throughout the world.

Fulcrums of Change, by Jan Carew. Trenton, NJ: Africa World Press, 1988. Essays on Columbus and the origins of racism in the Americas.

Indian Givers: How the Indians of the Americas Transformed the World, by Jack Weatherford. New York: Crown, 1988. Weatherford documents Native American contributions to medicine, government, food production and processing, and the post-encounter European economic boom. A popularly written book with intriguing facts and stories.

Lies My Teacher Told Me: Everything Your American History Textbook Got Wrong, by James Loewen. New York: New Press, 1995. A highly readable critique of some of the major high-school U.S. history texts still in use. Entertaining and astute, with worthwhile chapters on Columbus and Thanksgiving. (Available from Teaching for Change.)

Memory of Fire, by Eduardo Galeano. New York: Pantheon Books. A three-volume documentary history (*Genesis*, 1987; *Faces and Masks*, 1988; *Century of the Wind*, 1988) of the Americas from the first human inhabitants to 1984. Highly recommended.

Native American Voices: A Reader, ed. by Susan Lobo and Steve Talbot. New York: Longman, 1998. A 494-page, wide-ranging Native American studies reader. Articles on the image of the Indian in popular culture, Native activism for cultural survival and environmental protection, Indian education and health problems, and indigenous spirituality. Each section includes discussion questions, key terms, and a suggested reading list. Although some selections are scholarly, many can be used at the high-school level.

Native Roots: How the Indians Enriched America, by Jack Weatherford. New York: Fawcett Columbine, 1991. Another valuable resource detailing Native contributions to America.

Open Veins of Latin America: Five Centuries of the Pillage of a Continent, by Eduardo Galeano. New York: Monthly Review, 1998. A new edition of this classic book whose argument firmly roots the present economic status of Latin America to the European conquest of the 15th and 16th centuries. Highly recommended.

The State of Native America: Genocide, Colonization, and Resistance, ed. by M. Annette Jaimes. Boston: South End Press, 1991. Essays by Native American authors and activists on contemporary Native issues including land rights and sovereignty.

Struggle for the Land, by Ward Churchill. Monroe, ME: Common Courage, 1993. Prolific Native author and AIM leader offers a 472-page collection of his essays on land rights and ongoing indigenous struggles against "genocide, ecocide, and expropriation in contemporary North America."

View from the Shore: American Indian Perspectives on the Quincentenary, ed. by José Barreiro. Ithaca, NY: Akwe:kon Press, 1990. Explores the effects of Columbus's arrival on indigenous peoples. Also by Barreiro: *Indian Roots of American Democracy* (1992), documenting the contributions of the Haudenosaunee (Iroquois) to American government and the women's suffrage movement.

Wasi'chu: The Continuing Indian Wars, by Bruce Johansen and Roberto Maestas. New York: Monthly Review, 1980. How past conquests inform the suppression of modern Native struggles.

Additional Primary Sources

From the Heart: Voices of the American Indian, Lee Miller, ed. New York: Knopf, 1995. Well-documented book of quotes from Native Americans (and selected colonists and invaders), arranged by geographical region and by struggles (such as battles, government campaigns, and epidemics).

Native Heritage: Personal Accounts by American Indians, 1790 to the Present, Hirschfelder, Arlene, editor. New York: Macmillan, 1995. A collection of brief excerpts by Native Americans from varied background on topics such as Family, Land and Its Resources, Language, Native Education, Traditional Storytelling, Traditions, Worship, and Discrimination.

Guaman Pomo: Writing and Resistance in Colonial Peru, by Rolena Adorno. University of Texas Press, 1986. A Peruvian chief's account of life under the Incas and under Spanish rule.

The Broken Spears: The Aztec Account of the Conquest of Mexico, by Miguel León-Protilla. Beacon Press , 25 Beacon St., Boston, MA 02108. 800- 631- 8571. www.beacon.org. 1962. ISBN 0-8070-5499-2. $11.95. The Aztec left a particularly rich written record which Leon-Portilla uses to provide a Native perspective on the "discovery."

Indian Oratory: Famous Speeches by Noted Indian Chieftains, compiled by W.C. Vanderwerth. Univ. of Oklahoma Press, www.oupress.com. 1971. Inspiration from Tatanka Iotanka (Sitting Bull), Geronimo, Chief Joseph, others.

Curricular Guides

Anti-Bias Curriculum: Tools for Empowering Young Children, by Louise Derman-Sparks and the ABC Task Force. Washington, DC: National Assn. for the Education of Young Children, 1313 L St., NW, Suite 500, Washington, DC 20005; 800-424-2460. www.naeyc.org. 1989. A pioneering book for early childhood and elementary levels on teaching children about all forms of bias and how to counter it.

A Peoples History for the Classroom, by Bill Bigelow. Milwaukee, WI: Rethinking Schools, 2008. Collection of teaching ideas and lesson plans that emphasize the role of working people, women, people of color, and social movements in shaping history.

Beyond Heroes and Holidays: A Practical Guide to K-12 Anti-Racist, Multicultural Education and Staff Development, edited by Enid Lee, Deborah Menkart, and Margo Okazawa-Rey. Washington, DC: Teaching for Change, 2006. An outstanding K-12 and teacher education interdisciplinary resource, packed with lesson plans, background readings, personal reflections, and additional resource ideas for creating anti-racist classrooms and schools. (Available from Teaching for Change.)

Caribbean Connections, edited by Catherine Sunshine. Washington, DC: Teaching for Change/ EPICA, 1991. Stories, interviews, songs, drama, and oral histories, accompanied by lesson plans for secondary language arts and social studies. Separate volumes on Puerto Rico, Jamaica, the Dominican Republic, Regional Overview, and Moving North. (Available from Teaching for Change.)

Keepers of the Earth: Native American Stories and Environmental Activities for Children, Michael J. Caduto and Joseph Bruchac. Golden, CO: Fulcrum, 1988. A beautiful book featuring North American Indian stories and related hands-on activities, for an interdisciplinary approach to teaching about the earth and Native American cultures. Also in the series are *Keepers of the Animals* (1991) and *Keepers of Life* (1994), both by Caduto and Bruchac. Teacher Guides are available.

Learning Together Through Inquiry: From Columbus to Integrated Curriculum, Kathy Short, et al. York, ME: Stenhouse, www.stenhouse.com. 1996. A 214-page book by six elementary school teachers who used the broad idea of "discovery" to develop year-long integrated curriculums for their classrooms.

The Line Between Us: Teaching About the Border and Mexican Immigration, by Bill Bigelow. Milwaukee, WI: Rethinking Schools, 2006. Curriculum materials that explore the roots and human consequences of Mexican migration to the United States. Includes simulations, role plays, short stories, poetry, background articles, and extensive resources.

Open Minds to Equality: A Sourcebook of Learning Activities to Promote Race, Sex, Class, and Age Equity, by Nancy Schniedewind and Ellen Davidson. Milwaukee, WI: Rethinking Schools, 2006, 3rd ed. An activity-packed guide for grades 3-12 that does an excellent job addressing controversial topics and teaching how to effect change. Emphasizes cooperative learning and community-building activities.

Rigoberta Menchú: The Prize that Broke the Silence, Resource Center of The Americas, 3019 Minnehaha Ave., Suite 20, Minneapolis, MN 55406; 612-276-0788. An activity booklet for grades 7 and up on the relationship between Guatemala and the United States that led to the violent suppression of indigenous liberation movements in that country.

Rethinking Columbus: The Next 500 Years, edited by Bill Bigelow and Bob Peterson. Milwaukee, WI: Rethinking Schools, 1998, 2nd ed. A resource guide for teachers and community activists which includes 90 essays, poems, short stories, interviews, historical vignettes, and lesson plans that re-evaluate the legacy of Columbus.

Rethinking Our Classrooms: Teaching for Equity and Justice, Volume 1, edited by Wayne Au, Bill Bigelow, and Stan Karp. Milwaukee, WI: Rethinking Schools, 2007, 2nd ed. This 240-page book includes creative teaching ideas, compelling narratives, and hands-on examples of ways teachers can promote values of community, justice, and equality—and build academic skills.

Rethinking Our Classrooms: Teaching for Equity and Justice, Volume 2, edited by Bill Bigelow, Brenda Harvey, Stan Karp, and Larry Miller. Milwaukee, WI: Rethinking Schools, 2001. Extends and deepens many of the themes introduced in *Rethinking Our Classrooms, Volume 1*, which has sold almost 200,000 copies. Practical from-the-classroom stories from teachers about how they teach for social justice.

Rethinking Globalization: Teaching for Justice in an Unjust World, edited by Bill Bigelow and Bob Peterson, Milwaukee, WI: Rethinking Schools, 2002. The most comprehensive volume of background readings, from-the-classroom articles, role plays, lesson plans, poetry, interviews, and resources, on teaching about globalization.

Through Indian Eyes: The Native Experience in Books for Children, Beverly Slapin and Doris Seale. Los Angeles: UCLA American Indian Studies Center, 1998, 4th edition. An excellent resource for elementary teachers and librarians. Articles, stories, poetry, and in-depth reviews of books dealing with Native Americans. Includes one of the best bibliographies of books for children on Native Americans. (Available from Oyate catalog.)

Slide Programs/Audio Tapes/CDs

Native Realities, by Thunderchief (Francis Steindorf) a member of the Hochungra (Wisconsin Winnebago) Nation. Eleven songs available on cassette/CD on topics ranging from Protecting Mother Earth, Sovereignty, Mascots, Honoring the Treaties. Teaching guide is available. Contact: Thunderchief, P.O. Box 5273, Madison, WI 53705 (715-664-6464).

Rethinking Columbus: Christopher Columbus in Children's Literature (slide show), by Bill Bigelow, 1992. This presentation (54 slides with 10-page script) based on the article, "Once Upon a Genocide" (see. p. 47), offers a visual critique of the traditional tale of the "discovery of America." It focuses on how Columbus biographies teach children contempt for Native Americans and to view the European takeover of native lands as just and necessary. (Available from Teaching for Change.)

Videos

The Columbus Controversy: Challenging How History Is Written, American School Publishers, 1992. A 25-minute video offers an overview of the real consequences of the Columbus invasion, including the destruction of Native populations, establishment of the trans-Atlantic slave trade, and the encomienda system. Historical information and interviews with historians John Mohawk and William McNeil are interspersed with scenes from Bill Bigelow's high-school classroom in which he and students talk about what they learned about Columbus in elementary school and what they think should be taught now. A great video for beginning a discussion about Columbus.

In the White Man's Image, 1991, PBS Video, 1320 Braddock Pl., Alexandria, VA 22314-1698; 800-424-7963. This hour-long video from PBS's "The American Experience" series tells of the efforts of Capt. Richard Pratt to create schools for Native Americans which would "kill the Indian to save the man" by teaching them white ways. Considered a socially progressive endeavor at the time, the infamous boarding schools spearheaded governmental attempts to assimilate the American Indians.

In Whose Honor? 1997, New Day Films, P.O. Box 1084, Harriman, NY 10926. 888-367-9154. www. newday.com. This 46-minute, deeply-moving video follows the work of Spokane activist Charlene Teters, fighting the use of Native American mascots by sports teams, including at the University of Illinois, where the fictitious "Chief Illiniwek" has represented the school for over 70 years. Discusses issues of appropriation of Indian culture and symbols for sports teams, and is an effective teaching tool about why their use is so offensive to Native Americans.

Surviving Columbus: The Story of the Pueblo People, 1995. PBS Video, 1320 Braddock Pl., Alexandria, VA 22314-1698; 800-424-7963. A beautifully composed two-hour program on the Pueblos, with a major focus on Pueblo/Spanish interactions, from first encounters in 1539 to the Pueblo Revolt of 1680. Excellent discussion of the Church's role in subjugating native people. An inspiring account of one indigenous group's successful struggle for physical and cultural survival.

Videoforum: Native American Issue, Winter 1993. Available from National Video Resources, 73 Spring St., Ste. 403, New York, NY 10012; 212-274-8080. Videoforum is a videography series for librarians.

The Native American issue (vol. 1) includes detailed descriptions of over 40 videos on Native American themes for children and adults, and essays on Native Americans and filmmaking.

El Norte, Gregory Nava, Director, 1983. Approx. 130 minutes. The fictional story of a brother and sister who flee the repression of Indians by the Guatemalan military. Follows their travels through Mexico into the United States. Painful, funny, and poignant. A valuable high-school resource.

Thunderheart, by Michael Apted, Director, 1992 (118 minutes). Although fictional, *Thunderheart* effectively captures some of the conflicts on the Pine Ridge Reservation in the 1970s. Its theme of corporate/government collusion to exploit Native lands for profit is still relevant today. High school students find this film engrossing. An unfortunate 'R' rating for violence and language.

Incident at Oglala, by Michael Apted, Director, 1992, (approx. 90 min). This dramatic documentary exposes the U.S. government's desperate attempts to convict Leonard Peltier of the murder of two FBI agents on the Pine Ridge Reservation in South Dakota. Highly recommended for high-school classes. Available at many commercial video outlets.

500 Nations (Episode 3: *Clash of Cultures: The Peoples Who Met Columbus*), by Jack Leustig, producer, hosted by Kevin Costner, 1994. One segment of this episode covers the rebellion of the Taíno leader, Enrique, described on p. 111. A gripping story and a useful rejoinder to the one-dimensional portrayals of the Taínos as a "simple, gentle people."

Viva La Causa, by Elizabeth Martinez and Doug Norberg (60 min.). Available in Spanish or English. A valuable introduction to Mexican American history for grades 5-12 and higher ed.

Internet Resources

(Also see p. 143 for internet resources on contemporary struggles in the hemisphere.)

Cradleboard Teaching Project. Website is at: www.cradleboard.org. This website is created by Nihewan Foundation for American Indian Education, founded by Cree singer Buffy Sainte-Marie. The site has many links to official home pages of various tribes, Indian political and social welfare groups, and Native American media, arts, and cultural groups.

Native American Home Pages. www.nativeculturelinks.com. A well-maintained collection of links to Native Nations and other websites.

Native Web. www.nativeweb.org. Many valuable links to sites and bulletin boards on contemporary native issues, also to literature and cultural databases.

Organizations

Amnesty International, Human Rights USA, 310 4th Ave. S, Ste. 1000, Minneapolis, MN 55415-1012; 612-341-8084 or 888-HREDUC8. www.amnesty.org. Their Human Rights Educators' Network offers a Resource Notebook on rights of indigenous peoples, including many teaching activities and an examination of the Universal Declaration of Human Rights.

HONOR (Honor Our Neighbors' Origins and Rights), Main Office, Rte. 1, P.O. Box 79A, Bayfield, WI 54814 (715-779-9595). Resource Center, 6435 Wiesner Rd., Omro, WI 54963; (920-582-4619). A national coalition of more than 175 organizations working to affirm Indian treaties, promote tribal sovereignty, and counter anti-Indian bias. Offers a catalog of books, videos (for rental or purchase), pamphlets, maps, and other items for children and adults.

Indigenous Women's Network, P.O. Box 2967, Rapid City, SD 57709-2967 (605-399-0867). www.indigenouswomen.org. Publishes *Indigenous Woman* magazine. This native women's organization is active in social-justice, environmental, and health concerns.

North American Congress on Latin America, 475 Riverside Dr., Ste. 454, New York, NY 10115 (212-870-3146). www.nacla.org. A research organization which publishes *NACLA Report on the Americas*, a bimonthly magazine on economic, political, and social trends in Latin America and the Caribbean.

Resource Center of the Americas, 3019 Minnehaha Ave., Suite 20, Minneapolis, MN 55406 (612-276-0788). www.americas.org. Publishes monthly *Connection to the Americas*, and offers curricular materials on economic rights, history, and contemporary struggles of Latin America.

Posters and Maps

Native American Women of Hope, by Bread and Roses Cultural Project. This set of twelve 18" x 24" color posters features Native American and Native Hawai'ian activists, leaders, scientists, and artists, with a 48-page study guide.

Peters' Projection World Map. ODT Maps, P.O. Box 134, Amherst, MA 01004. 800-736-1293. www.odtmaps.com. A more accurate projection of the continents, showing their true size. Traditional Mercator maps distort size, making Europe seem much larger than South America, for example.

Russell Publications. www.nativedata.com. Offers maps of Indian Nations, along with several publications, such as *American Indian: Facts of Life*, with an overview of native history and statistics of populations by state and by tribe.

The Truth About Columbus: A Subversively True Poster Book for a Dubiously Celebratory Occasion, by James Loewen. New York: New Press, www.newpress.com. 1992. This brief (38 pp.) but ambitious critique takes 15 common American history textbooks to task for perpetuating myths about Columbus as an American hero. Loewen counters each myth with primary source documentation, including Columbus's own journals.

Contemporary Native Americans. Knowledge Unlimited, 800-356-2303. www.thekustore.com. Six 17" x 22" posters of prominent Native Americans today, with teacher's guide.

Newspapers and Periodicals

Aboriginal Voices, 116 Spadina Ave., Ste. 201, Toronto, Ontario, Canada M5V 2K6; 416-703-4577. www.lights.ca/sifc/abvoices.htm. A bi-monthly magazine devoted to contemporary indigenous topics. A recent issue included articles on Native Canadian and American artists, youth suicide, fund-raising, and sports.

Cultural Survival Quarterly, 46 Brattle St., Cambridge, MA 02138 (617-441-5400). www.cs.org. Highlights indigenous issues around the world.

Indian Country Today, Native American Publishing, Inc., 1920 Lombardy Dr., Rapid City, SD 57701 (605-341-0011). www.indiancountrytoday.com. A Native American weekly newspaper with activist updates, reservations news, and economic and cultural reporting, and special sections on Northern Plains and Southwest news.

Native Peoples Magazine. www.nativepeoples.com. *Native Peoples Magazine* is a glossy magazine of feature articles on contemporary Indian life and arts. Its website carries study guides for elementary, middle, and high school classrooms on Native American topics.

News From Indian Country, Rt. 2 Box 2900-A, Hayward, WI 54843. www.indiancountrynews.com. A Native American bi-weekly that covers national news about Native issues. $2 for a sample copy.

Rethinking Schools, 1001 E. Keefe Ave., Milwaukee, WI 53212. 800-669-4192. www.rethinkingschools.org. A quarterly news and analysis magazine devoted to school reform in public schools with an emphasis on equity and social justice.

Winds of Change, AISES, 5661 Airport Blvd., Boulder, CO 80301-2339 (303-444-9099). www.wocmag.org. This quarterly journal highlights Native American education issues and opportunities, and seeks to bridge Indian traditional ways and modern schools and employment.

Resources from RETHINKING SCHOOLS

RETHINKING SCHOOLS MAGAZINE

Rethinking Schools is a quarterly magazine written by teachers, parents, and education activists—people who understand the daily realities of reforming our schools. No other publication so successfully combines theory and practice while linking classroom issues to broader social policy concerns.

Three years: $39.95 (Save $19.45!)
Two years: $29.95 (Save $9.65!)
One year: $17.95

Subscriptions to Canada and Mexico add $5 per year.
Other international subscriptions add $10 per year.

RETHINKING GLOBALIZATION
Teaching for Justice in an Unjust World

Edited by Bill Bigelow and Bob Peterson
"A treasury of ideas and information," according to historian Howard Zinn. Includes role plays, interviews, poetry, stories, background readings, and hands-on teaching tools.

Paperback • 400 pages • ISBN: 978-0-942961-28-7

ONLY $18.95!*

RETHINKING COLUMBUS
The Next 500 Years

Edited by Bill Bigelow and Bob Peterson
Includes more than 80 essays, poems, historical vignettes, and lesson plans that re-evaluate the legacy of Columbus. Packed with useful teaching ideas for kindergarten through college.

Paperback • 192 pages • ISBN: 978-0-942961-20-1

ONLY $16.95!*

UNLEARNING "INDIAN" STEREOTYPES

Narrated by Native American children, the DVD *Unlearning "Indian" Stereotypes* teaches about racial stereotypes and provides an introduction to Native American history through the eyes of children. Includes teaching ideas, lessons, and resources. Elementary through adult education.

DVD • 12 minutes, plus teaching guide • ISBN: 978-0-942961-40-9

ONLY $19.95!*

ORDER ONLINE: **www.rethinkingschools.org**
CALL TOLL-FREE: **1-800-669-4192** FAX TO: **802-864-7626**
OR USE ORDER FORM IN BACK

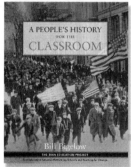
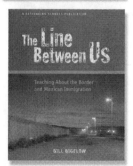
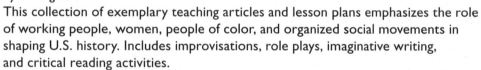

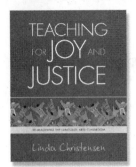

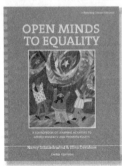

RETHINKING SCHOOLS

FOUR EASY WAYS TO ORDER

❶ **CALL TOLL-FREE:** 1-800-669-4192 8am-9pm (ET) M-F
❷ **SECURE ONLINE ORDERING:** www.rethinkingschools.org
❸ **FAX ORDER FORM TO:** 802-864-7626
❹ **MAIL ORDER FORM TO:** Rethinking Schools, PO Box 2222, Williston, VT 05495

MASTERCARD, VISA AND PURCHASE ORDERS ACCEPTED

Name _____

Organization _____

Address _____

City/State/Zip _____

Phone _____

E-mail _____

METHOD OF PAYMENT

❏ Check or money order made payable to Rethinking Schools
❏ Purchase order   ❏ MasterCard   ❏ Visa

Credit Card No. _____

Exp. Date _____

Authorized Signature _____

QUANTITY	TITLE/ITEM	UNIT PRICE	TOTAL

Subtotal	$
Shipping	$
Donation	$
TOTAL	$

MAIL TO: Rethinking Schools, P.O. Box 2222, Williston, VT 05495
FAX TO: 802-864-7626
CALL 1-800-669-4192 FOR A FREE CATALOG OF ALL OUR MATERIALS

* U.S. shipping and handling costs are 15% of the total (minimum charge of $4.00). Canadian shipping and handling costs are 25% of the total (minimum charge of $5.00). Subscriptions already include shipping costs. Payment in U.S. dollars.

2BRC

**If you liked *Rethinking Columbus*,
then *Rethinking Schools* magazine is for you!**

Take advantage of this special discount coupon to receive the country's leading magazine for school reform.

"Rethinking Schools is a teacher's close friend — insightful, intelligent, and compassionate. I have read, used, and loved this publication for over a decade. I'm a better teacher because of it."

—MICHELE FORMAN, 2001 National Teacher of the Year

INTRODUCTORY OFFER!
Subscribe today and save!

❏ **$22** Two-year subscription (*Save $17.60 off the cover price!*)
❏ **$14** One-year subscription (*Save $5.80 off the cover price!*)

❏ Please send me a free catalog of all your materials
❏ Bill me
❏ Enclosed is my check payable to Rethinking Schools

Name _____

Organization _____

Address _____

City/State/Zip _____

Phone _____

E-mail _____

RETHINKING SCHOOLS

P.O. Box 2222, Williston, VT 05495 • toll-free: 800-669-4192 • fax: 802-864-7626

2BRC

BUSINESS REPLY MAIL
FIRST-CLASS MAIL   PERMIT NO.2222   WILLISTON VT

POSTAGE WILL BE PAID BY ADDRESSEE

RETHINKING SCHOOLS
PO BOX 2222
WILLISTON VT 05495-9940